I have a deep appreciation for how Brian Rosner addresses the theme of the kno
it practical and relational, as it is meant to be. This work is an exegetical treasure
along the way. Its message invites us, even ushers us, into the very intimacy wi

Craig S. Keener, F. M. and Ada Thompson Chair
Asbury Theological Seminary

Amidst the ceaseless clamor to "know thyself" and the constant barrage of identity politics, Rosner offers a needed corrective by looking at identity through a biblical lens. *Known by God* is a beautifully written exploration into the biblical story of identity. Rosner demonstrates that identity is both personal and social; it is about knowing God and, even more importantly, being known by God. Woven throughout the book is his own journey from shattered identity to redemptive wholeness. Identity is not ours to make but ours to receive from the One who knows and loves us and calls us into the family of God.

Lynn H. Cohick, Chair, Biblical and Theological Studies Department,
and Professor of New Testament, Wheaton College

From the very first page, Brian Rosner succeeds beautifully in doing what few today dare to attempt. He seamlessly integrates raw personal experience with depth of biblical insight and sophisticated cultural analysis. *Known by God* is like nothing else you'll read. It deftly explores the weighty theme of human identity, with one eye firmly on the Word of God in all its clarity and another on the world in all its confusion about the self. Rosner is an expert guide through beautiful and largely unmarked territories, in the end opening up for the reader a marvellous vista of the human being from the divine perspective. To know oneself fully, Rosner shows, is really to understand and accept how one is viewed by the Creator and Redeemer.

John Dickson, author, historian, and founding director
of the Centre for Public Christianity

The question of human identity is complex, interesting, and perplexing all at the same time! What is it that makes us who we are, and what sustains us in our identity when many of our earthly markers of identity are taken from us? Much of the thinking within this area has emerged from philosophy or ethics. Brian Rosner draws the debate into the world of the Bible. In this deep but accessible book Rosner carefully lays out a biblical foundation for human identity and in so doing offers clarity and practical wisdom to a profound, personal, and intensely important set of questions. The book is deeply grounded in the practices of the church and in Rosner's own narrative. The combination of scholarly biblical exegesis and meaningful, sometimes moving personal narrative makes this book a wonderful resource for church and academy. In the end, we are who we are because God knows us. Our identity is gifted to us by a God who knows us and desires that we come to know God. There is beauty, hope, and safety in such knowledge. Brian Rosner has given us a vital gift.

John Swinton, Professor in Practical Theology and Pastoral Care,
University of Aberdeen

Who am I? The only truthful answer is "God knows!" Leavened by autobiographical touches, Rosner's book teaches us that God knows us when our struggles with our own identity feel hidden from everyone else. *Known by God* is the most balanced and down-to-earth book about personal identity that I have read. It profoundly illuminates the Bible's teaching that God fathers, owns, and remembers each of his human children.

Francesca Aran Murphy, Professor of Theology, University of Notre Dame

Every last page of Brian Rosner's *Known by God* is filled with careful, convincing exegesis of both testaments of the Christian Bible. But even more striking is how this exegesis is interwoven with the author's disarming self-disclosure, keen pastoral insight, charitable engagement with contemporary literature and culture, and infectious zeal for gospel proclamation. It is that combination that marks this book as a wonderful example of the best of distinctively evangelical biblical theology.

Wesley Hill, Assistant Professor of Biblical Studies, Trinity School for Ministry, Ambridge, Pennsylvania

I heard a theologian say in a public meeting that he knew who Jesus was but he did not know who he was. He needed this book by Brian Rosner. Drawing expertly on the biblical witness in conversation with modern angst about human identity, Rosner finds in Scripture the key to answering the identity question. Of particular value in Rosner's argument is his exploration of the idea of being known by God, which is a neglected theme in biblical theology as he rightly points out. Resources found in Dietrich Bonhoeffer and C. S. Lewis also figure helpfully in his account. A book to savor.

Graham A. Cole, Dean and Vice President of Education and Professor of Biblical and Systematic Theology, Trinity Evangelical Divinity School

In this timely and thoughtful book, Dr. Rosner provides a biblical, practical guide to understanding ourselves as God understands us. He makes the persuasive case that society's call to "find yourself," "be true to yourself," and "be authentic" can only lead to human flourishing when these efforts are grounded in one's union with Christ and God's prior knowledge of us. This is an ideal book to place into the hands of any believer experiencing the disorientation of life's big changes, especially when those changes involve suffering and loss. With both theological precision and pastoral experience, Dr. Rosner describes how in times of difficulty we can rest in the identity that we have as members of God's family.

Frank Thielman, Professor of Divinity, Beeson Divinity School

It's been some time since I read a book this important. Rosner's *Known by God* achieves what the subtitle claims: a truly biblical theology of personal identity. In an age of "identity angst," exacerbated by social media and inauthenticity, people are asking the crucial question, "Who am I?" Rosner explains the question, then walks us through Scripture where we listen to the voice of God answer. Clearly written and cogently presented, this is no self-help, how-to, waste-of-your-time piece. Rosner plumbs the depths, biblically and otherwise, and surfaces with treasure. Spoiler alert! Personal identity centers on knowing that I am known by God. Don't miss this gem!

David L. Allen, Dean, School of Preaching, and Distinguished Professor of Preaching, George W. Truett Chair of Pastoral Ministry, Southwestern Baptist Theological Seminary, Fort Worth, Texas

What makes me the person I am? Who am I? These are surely fundamental existential questions with which we all wrestle. In his new book, Brian Rosner takes up the task of addressing these concerns in a biblically focused way. He maintains that personal identity in Scripture has to do with being made in the image of God, being known by God, and being in Christ—reframing how we think about who we are from a God's-eye view. The result is a clear and compelling account of human personal identity that sheds new light on some of the most important and contested issues in theological anthropology.

Oliver D. Crisp, Professor of Systematic Theology, Fuller Theological Seminary

BIBLICAL THEOLOGY FOR LIFE

KNOWN BY GOD

A Biblical Theology of Personal Identity

BRIAN S. ROSNER

general editor JONATHAN LUNDE

ZONDERVAN®

ZONDERVAN

Known by God

This title is also available as a Zondervan ebook.

Requests for information should be addressed to:
Zondervan, *3900 Sparks Dr. SE, Grand Rapids, Michigan 49546*

ISBN 978-0-310-49982-4

All emphases in Scripture quotations, unless otherwise noted, are the author's.

Cover design: Ron Huizinga
Cover photo: Marko Milovanovic / Stocksy
Interior design: Matthew VanZomeren and Kait Lamphere

Printed in the United States of America

HB 11.26.2024

For Frank Szanto, Martin Riley, Peter and Sheana Brown, and in memory of Soullis Tavrou, all of whom rate an honourable mention

CONTENTS

QUEUING THE QUESTIONS

ARRIVING AT ANSWERS

REFLECTING ON RELEVANCE

DETAILED TABLE OF CONTENTS

REFLECTING ON RELEVANCE

ABBREVIATIONS

ASV	American Standard Version
BDAG	Bauer, W., F. W. Danker, W. Arndt, and F. W. Gingrich. *A Greek-English Lexicon of the New Testament and Other Early Christian Literature*. 3rd ed. Chicago: University of Chicago Press, 2000.
BDB	Brown, Francis, S. R. Driver, and Charles A. Briggs. *A Hebrew and English Lexicon of the Old Testament.*
BNTC	Black's New Testament Commentaries
CEV	Contemporary English Version
ESV	English Standard Version
GNT	Good News Translation
HCSB	Holman Christian Standard Bible
ICC	International Critical Commentary
LXX	The Greek Old Testament (the Septuagint)
NAB	New American Bible
NAC	New American Commentary
NASB	New American Standard Bible
NET	New English Translation
NIGTC	New International Greek Testament Commentary
NIV	New International Version
NJB	New Jerusalem Bible
NLT	New Living Translation
NRSV	New Revised Standard Version
NSBT	New Studies in Biblical Theology
PNTC	Pillar New Testament Commentary
TNTC	Tyndale New Testament Commentaries
WUNT	Wissenschaftliche Untersuchungen zum Neuen Testament

SERIES PREFACE

The question "What does the Bible have to say about that?" is, in essence, what the Biblical Theology for Life series is all about. Not unlike other biblical explorations of various topics, the volumes in this series articulate various themes in biblical theology, but they always do so with the "So what?" question rumbling about and demanding to be answered. Too often, books on biblical theology have focused mainly on *description*—simply discerning the teachings of the biblical literature on a particular topic. But contributors to this series seek to straddle both the world of the text and the world in which we live.

This means that their descriptions of biblical theology will always be understood as the important *first* step in their task, which will not be completed until they draw out that theology's practical implications for the contemporary context. Contributors therefore engage both in the *description* of biblical theology and in its contemporary *contextualization*, accosting the reader's perspective and fostering application, transformation, and growth. It is our hope that these informed insights of evangelical biblical scholarship will increasingly become enfleshed in the sermons and discussions that transpire each week in places of worship, in living rooms where Bible studies gather, and in classrooms around the world. We hope that this series will lead to personal transformation and practical application in real life.

Every volume in this series has the same basic structure. In the first section, entitled "Queuing the Questions," authors introduce the main questions they seek to address in their books. Raising these questions enables you to see clearly from the outset what each book will be pursuing, inviting you to participate in the process of discovery along the way. In the second section, "Arriving at Answers," authors develop the biblical theology of the topic they address, focusing their attention on specific biblical texts and constructing answers to the questions introduced in section one. In the concluding "Reflecting on Relevance" section, authors contextualize their biblical-theological insights, discussing specific ways in which the theology presented in their books addresses contemporary situations and issues, giving you opportunities to consider how you might live out that theology in the world today.

Long before you make it to the "Reflecting on Relevance" section, however, we encourage you to wrestle with the implications of the biblical theology being described by considering the "Relevant Questions" that conclude each chapter. Frequent sidebars spice up your experience, supplementing the main discussion with significant quotations, illustrative historical or contemporary data, and fuller explanations of the content.

In sum, the goal of the Biblical Theology for Life series is communicated by its title. On the one hand, its books mine the Bible for theology that addresses a wide range of topics, so that you may know "the only true God, and Jesus Christ, whom [he] sent" (John 17:3). On the other hand, contributing authors contextualize this theology in ways that allow the *life*-giving Word (John 1:4; 20:31) to speak into and transform contemporary *life*.

Series Editor
Jonathan Lunde

AUTHOR'S PREFACE

Some subjects in the study of the Bible can be treated at "arm's length." Personal identity is not one of them. You can't write a book about personal identity without saying something about yourself. At least that's what people kept telling me; impersonal won't do when it comes to a book answering the most personal of questions. In writing the book, this was quite a struggle for a biblical scholar still shaking off the modernist ruse of dispassionate neutrality towards the text. But I am convinced that the book is far more engaging for my having done so.

While this book can hardly be described as autobiographical—it is a book of biblical exegesis and theology—at one level it does tell the story of my own crisis of identity and the comfort I found in being known by God. And as Paul insists in 2 Corinthians 1:3–4, those who have received comfort from God are obliged to comfort those in trouble with the comfort they themselves have received. This book is my attempt to do just that.

The book seeks to show how profoundly helpful the Bible is in addressing the identity angst and confusion that is so rife in our day, drawing deeply on the neglected theme of being known by God. In writing the book I have, of course, used a wide range of secondary sources. Five authors stand out for addressing issues pertinent to questions of personal identity with considerable insight and are regularly cited: John Calvin, Marilynne Robinson, Tim Keller, Tom Wright, and Richard Bauckham.

Known by God has a long backstory. In 2005 I explored the theme in two giants of Christian literature in an *Evangelical Quarterly* article: "Known by God: C. S. Lewis and Dietrich Bonhoeffer."[1] In 2007 I gave the Tyndale Biblical Theology Lecture in Cambridge on the relevant biblical and Jewish material, which was later published in *Tyndale Bulletin* as "Known by God: The Meaning and Value of a Neglected Biblical Concept."[2] Parts of that article are adapted and used here with permission from the journal. Third, I had the privilege of coauthoring a chapter for an interdisciplinary book exploring the theme's practical significance with academic psychiatrist Loyola McLean: "Theology and Human Flourishing: The Benefits of Being Known by God."[3]

I owe a debt of gratitude to many other people who have contributed in various ways. In 2010 I worked for ten weeks at the Centre for Public Christianity in Sydney.

1. Brian S. Rosner, "Known by God: C. S. Lewis and Dietrich Bonhoeffer," *Evangelical Quarterly* 77.4 (2005): 343–52.

2. Brian S. Rosner, "Known by God: The Meaning and Value of a Neglected Biblical Concept," *Tyndale Bulletin* 59.2 (2008): 207–30.

3. Brian Rosner and Loyola McLean, "Theology and Human Flourishing: The Benefits of Being Known by God," in *Beyond Well-Being: Spirituality and Human Flourishing*, ed. Maureen Miner, Martin Dowson, and Stuart Devenish (Charlotte, NC: Information Age, 2012), 65–83.

My task was to work on the topic of personal identity, and it was during this time that the main lines of my thinking on the subject took shape. I am grateful to Vanda and Debbie Gould, generous Christian benefactors, whose support made that time of research and writing possible. I am also grateful to my friends at the Centre for Public Christianity for the opportunity to learn from their sterling example of Christian public engagement. Whilst that research was never published, it laid the foundation for the book you are about to read. Early in 2015 Ridley College ran a conference in partnership with Gordon-Conwell Theological Seminary on being known by God, a rich and stimulating event from which I learned a great deal. I wrote most of *Known by God* on study leave from Ridley College in the second half of 2015. I thank the Ridley Board for granting me leave and colleagues for their encouragement along the way.

I am particularly grateful to a number of people for their assistance. Michele Smart and Rebecca Hanlon read the entire manuscript, told me exactly what they thought, made invaluable suggestions, and helped with the questions that conclude each chapter. My personal assistant, Annabelle Crane, helped in many ways, as calmly and competently as ever. Natalie, my wife, who is my partner in every sense, supported me in ways too numerous to list.

I could not have asked for better editors. Jonathan Lunde provided critical advice at just the right moments and went the extra mile with the manuscript. Over at Zondervan, Katya Covrett was a pleasure to work with and acted with consummate professionalism at every stage. I am grateful to Christopher Beetham and Nathan Kroeze for their excellent work on final edits and marketing, respectively. Thanks also to John Schoer for preparing the indexes.

The book is dedicated to five good friends. There is indeed something reassuring and beautiful about someone really knowing you.

Writing this book and, more importantly, living it have been an enormous blessing to me personally. If knowing God is life's greatest challenge, being known by God is life's greatest comfort. My hope and prayer to God is that you will find this to be the case in your own life.

PART 1

QUEUING THE QUESTIONS

CHAPTER 1

IDENTITY ANGST

It was a typical early afternoon for a northeastern Scotland winter's day in 1998. The sun was setting, the wind was howling, black ice was forming on the roads, and condensation had fogged up my car both inside and outside. Sitting there waiting for the engine to warm up sufficiently to demist the windscreen, I reached up to adjust the rearview mirror and stared for a few moments at someone I didn't recognize. Seeing I was alone, it was a tad unnerving. After a few moments of confusion, and upon further reflection, the stranger I had seen turned out to be me!

It wasn't that I was losing my mind. A psychologist might describe such an event in terms of a dissociative disorder, the state of being disconnected from your sense of identity. My experience, however, was more symptomatic of an emotional state than a mental illness.

Certain events had changed my life dramatically. I'm sure I'm not the first person to have my marriage end unexpectedly. But for my wife of thirteen years to disown me and renounce our life together left me shattered. Cherished memories seemed like they belonged to someone else. Half of the photos in my mind's album went missing, and the rest were spoiled with coffee stains. My hopes and aspirations evaporated. Looking forward became a luxury I couldn't afford.

With damaged memories, an uncertain destiny, and a troubled present, I had lost my sense of self and was forced to revisit the question that you're supposed to settle for good in your childhood and adolescence. That most personal question of all: *Who am I?*

It's a big question with many layers. How important is self-knowledge? How do your circumstances affect your sense of self? What role do your relationships play in knowing who you are? How about your possessions, your job, and so on? What makes you, you? What is a human being, anyway?

> *"Nothing is more unfathomable than ourselves, individually and collectively, at any given moment and from the earliest beginning of human time."*
>
> *Marilynne Robinson*[1]

Being a Christian, I turned to God and the Bible for answers. What I found has made an enormous difference to me personally. It doused a destructive pessimism that threatened to engulf me, instilled in me a sense of value when I felt worthless, and steadied my course when I went close to coming off the rails.

1. Marilynne Robinson, *The Givenness of Things: Essays* (New York: Farrar, Straus and Giroux, 2015), 199.

Twenty years on, it continues to supply me with a stable and satisfying sense of self, along with the blessings of significance, comfort, humility, and direction for living.

I believe that I am far from alone in wrestling with questions of personal identity. Over the years I've had countless conversations with people of all ages in a myriad of circumstances who are wondering who they really are: people who've lost their job; people whose parents have died; people whose online identity leaves them feeling like a phony; people who feel deflated by their aspirations for life not coming to fruition; people who feel diminished by consuming responsibilities for children or parents; and people who feel at sea in our rapidly changing world. There are in fact good reasons to think that "identity angst," to coin a phrase, is on the rise in the twenty-first century. And it is not just those who are suffering a crisis who are not sure who they really are.

In our day and age the question of personal identity is subject to two powerful but opposing forces. On the one hand, nothing is more important than knowing who you are and acting accordingly. But the problem is that it is harder to know who you are today than at any other point in human history.

"BE TRUE TO YOURSELF"

There is one piece of advice that you hear everywhere today in all sorts of contexts. It's a big mantra for the self-help book and seminar industry. It turns up in everything from school captains' speeches, celebrity interviews, and children's books to high-brow literature and philosophical discussions of ethical dilemmas. To disagree with it is almost unthinkable. And most people think it's about the best advice you can give. It is this: "Be true to yourself."

> "We live in an age of self-obsession. Everywhere we look, we encounter a preoccupation with self-interest, self-development, self-image, self-satisfaction, self-love, self-expression, self-confidence, self-help, self-acceptance . . . the list goes on."
>
> *Michael Allen Fox*[2]

To be true to yourself means to act in accordance with who you think you are. Its appealing corollaries are to follow your heart, think for yourself, resist external pressures, and be willing to stand out from the crowd. Put another way, to be true to yourself "captures the fullness of our commitment to authenticity as a moral ideal."[3] According to social researcher John Zogby, people today are hungry for authenticity because there is "a deep-felt need to reconnect with the truth of our lives and to disconnect from the illusions that everyone from advertisers to politicians tries to make us believe are real."[4] Many people,

2. Michael Allen Fox, "We're Self-obsessed—But Do We Understand the Nature of the Self?" The Conversation, August 31, 2004, http://theconversation.com/were-self-obsessed-but-do-we-understand-the-nature-of-the-self-30912.

3. Andrew Potter, *The Authenticity Hoax: Why the "Real" Things We Seek Don't Make Us Happy* (New York: Harper Perennial, 2011), 18.

4. John Zogby, *The Way We'll Be: The Zogby Report on the Transformation of the American Dream* (New York: Random House, 2008), as reported in Potter, *The Authenticity Hoax*, 5.

it seems, feel that they are surrounded by a mediated reality, by the shoddy, shallow, and superficial; that is, the inauthentic. The call to authenticity is a broad movement calling for congruity between our inner and outer selves.

Despite its currency and widespread popularity, some dampening of our enthusiasm for being true to yourself might actually be needed. The problem is that the appeal to authenticity can be just an excuse for questionable behavior. If I do something that is inconsiderate of others or even harmful to myself, I can just claim I am being true to myself. Virtues like patience, kindness, and faithfulness can take a back seat to following your heart. What if my self is selfish? After all, the abusive spouse, the dishonest friend, the greedy workaholic, and the malicious gossip can all claim to be true to themselves when they behave in character. The problem with being true to yourself is that too often the self abuses the privilege.

The advice to be true to yourself probably goes back to Shakespeare. In Act I, scene iii of *Hamlet*, the character of Polonius prepares his son Laertes for travel abroad with a speech (ll.55–81) in which he directs the youth to commit a "few precepts to memory." At the top of the list is the dictum: "This above all: to thine own self be true."

However, Shakespeare probably meant something different from what we mean. Whereas we think in terms of self-fulfillment and "keeping it real," Polonius's advice was concerned with avoiding self-indulgent pursuits that might be harmful to his son's image, such as borrowing money, lending money, and carousing with women of dubious character. For Shakespeare, "to thine own self be true" means to keep your reputation intact.

THE ELUSIVE SELF

The biggest problem with the advice to be true to yourself is that in order to do so, you have to know who you are. And while these days more and more people are telling us to be true to ourselves, many of us are unsure of our true identity.

A myriad of factors weighs against having a stable and satisfying sense of self. Living our lives in the separate compartments of home, work, and leisure can produce superficial relationships and problems for genuine self-knowledge. Multiple careers and marital breakdown can lead to confusion about some of the most basic answers to the question of who you are, namely your occupation and marital status. Juggling the competing demands of work and family can make us feel that there is no space left in our lives for ourselves. However, even if living longer in retirement gives more time for yourself, the later years of life can also be plagued by feeling redundant and, if you live long enough, being "deserted" by your peers who know you best.

In the past an individual's identity was more established and predictable than it is today. Many of the big questions in life were basically settled before you

"If you are true to 'yourself,' you will end up a complete mess. The challenge is to take the 'self' you find within, and to choose wisely which impulses and desires to follow, and which ones to resist."

N. T. Wright[5]

5. N. T. Wright, *The Early Christian Letters for Everyone: James, Peter, John, and Judah* (London: SPCK, 2011), 8.

were born: where you'd live, what you'd do, the type of person you'd marry, your basic beliefs, and so on. It's not that there was no choice. Rather, the shape of your life was molded by constraints that limited your choices. Today we are literally spoilt for choice, which can be both a source of joy and anxiety.

Polish sociologist Zygmunt Bauman explains:

> Traditional communities are rivers, while modern societies are oceans. A river has a direction and carries you along with the current, just as traditional societies direct their members in a particular way. In modern societies there is no current; we can choose to go any direction, no direction, or to shift direction with every change of winds.[6]

To extend the metaphor, there is also more chance of getting lost or drowning in an ocean!

Sociologists talk about the phenomenon of "churning" where globalization, consumer culture, and hypermobility leave us giddy with choice. Journalist Brigid Delaney believes that this smorgasbord of options leaves us with a gnawing uncertainty and restlessness. She writes from experience, with a career of some 144 jobs in six countries by the age of thirty-five! Not surprisingly, Delaney complains of a sense of not belonging anywhere. While Delaney is an extreme example, her experience does underline a trend towards living widely rather than deeply: "In the fatigue of living widely with all the spending and experiences this involves, no great collective wisdom has emerged."[7] Modern life, with all its possibilities, can leave us with a feeling of dissatisfaction and something short of a healthy sense of self.

According to Peter Leithart, our world destabilizes the self by uprooting people from the traditional fixity of class and place, custom and community. Today our sense of belonging and identity is not supported by continual contact with the same set of friends, the same family members, or the same coworkers. Leithart paints a picture of a society marked by fragmentation and fluidity, where relationships are temporary and loose. In this context, self-fashioning is the order of the day, and self-knowledge is superficial at best.[8] This is often brought into sharper focus when a crisis hits.

In previous times the question of personal identity was settled for most people in their adolescence when they recognized, revised, or rejected the identity given to them by their parents. An optional additional chapter to this narrative of identity formation was the midlife crisis. Dissatisfied with how their lives were panning out, such people set out to "find themselves," often indulging in out-of-character behavior involving anything from having an affair to buying a red convertible or a Harley-Davidson.

---

6. Cited in Peter J. Leithart, *Solomon Among the Postmoderns* (Grand Rapids: Brazos, 2008), 40–41.

7. Brigid Delaney, *This Restless Life* (Melbourne: Melbourne University Press, 2009), 40.

8. Leithart, *Solomon Among the Postmoderns*, 114, 116, 127.

These days, life-cycle dilemma experts believe that for many people identity transitions occur earlier than midlife and much more often. The age of discontent can happen at any and every age, since the obligation to define or design yourself is always at hand. You don't have to wait for midlife to have doubts about how your life is tracking. The dreaded "thrisis" awaits those turning thirty, who having climbed the ladder of success are disillusioned to discover it's leaning against the wrong wall.[10] Those of us turning forty, fifty, or sixty years of age might experience "cuspiety," the *anxiety* associated with reaching the precipice of so-called *cusp* ages.

"The human race at the dawn of the third millennium, following the demise of the Christian paradigm and the break-up of modernity, is suffering from a collective identity crisis."

Kevin Vanhoozer[9]

The digital age has added a new dimension to the question of personal identity. The web is now the platform on which many of us live our lives. With social media, the internet is the way you tell the world not just what you are up to and what you are thinking, but *who you are*. Regular profile and status updates on sites like Facebook, Instagram, and Snapchat have taken defining yourself to a new level. Many believe that the web has affected our very identity.[11] The jury is still out on whether or not this is a good thing. Some decry the torrent of self-absorbed output; others are more positive about the new possibilities for social connection. Certainly social media offers the temptation to project an inauthentic self. If humans have always worn "masks," as Peter Leithart notes, "with the arrival of postmodern communication technologies the masks have become thicker and more concealing."[12]

WHO AM I REALLY?

The twentieth-century German pastor and spy Dietrich Bonhoeffer was imprisoned by the Nazis during the Second World War for his part in plots to kill Adolf Hitler. Bonhoeffer wrote letters and papers from prison that are still in print. One of his prison poems, "Who Am I?" was written as a kind of self-analysis the year before his execution. It raises poignantly several of the issues that are germane to this book. Many people who read the poem resonate with Dietrich's predicament, albeit usually with less intensity.

The question of the title "Who Am I?" occurs five times in the body of the poem. The "they" in the first third of the poem are the prison guards reporting their view of the prisoner. Remarkably, the guards' view of Bonhoeffer is very positive. Bonhoeffer's view of himself in the following lines is understandably more anguished

9. Kevin Vanhoozer, "Human Being, Individual and Social," in *The Cambridge Companion to Christian Doctrine*, ed. Colin E. Gunton (Cambridge: Cambridge University Press, 1997), 158.

10. See Kasey Edwards, *30 Something and Over It* (Sydney: Random House, 2009).

11. E.g., James Harkin, *Cyburbia: The Dangerous Idea That's Changing How We Live and Who We Are* (London: Little Brown, 2009).

12. Leithart, *Solomon Among the Postmoderns*, 123.

as he struggles under the ghastly circumstances of his imprisonment. The last eight lines wrestle with this dilemma of personal integrity and identity.

Who Am I?[13]

Who am I? They often tell me
I stepped from my cell's confinement
Calmly, cheerfully, firmly,
Like a squire from his country-house.
Who am I? They often tell me
I used to speak to my warders
Freely and friendly and clearly,
As though it were mine to command.
Who am I? They also tell me
I bore the days of misfortune
Equally, smilingly, proudly,
Like one accustomed to win.

Am I then really all that which other men tell of?
Or am I only what I myself know of myself?
Restless and longing and sick, like a bird in a cage,
Struggling for breath, as though hands were
compressing my throat,
Yearning for colors, for flowers, for the voices of birds,
Thirsting for words of kindness, for neighborliness,
Tossing in expectation of great events,
Powerlessly trembling for friends at an infinite distance,
Weary and empty at praying, at thinking, at making,
Faint, and ready to say farewell to all?

Who am I? This or the other?
Am I one person today and tomorrow another?
Am I both at once? A hypocrite before others,
And before myself a contemptibly woebegone weakling?
Or is something within me still like a beaten army,
Fleeing in disorder from victory already achieved?
Who am I? They mock me, these lonely questions of mine.
Who I really am, you know me, I am yours, O God![14]

13. Quoted with permission from Eric Metaxas, *Bonhoeffer: Pastor, Martyr, Prophet, Spy* (Nashville: Thomas Nelson, 2010), seventh page of photo inset found between pages 466–67.

14. The final line in German consists of twelve monosyllables, which climaxes the poem in striking fashion: "Wer ich auch bin, Du kennst mich, Dein bin ich, O Gott!" (Dietrich Bonhoeffer,

Bonhoeffer's poetic reflections raise several uncomfortable questions:

- What part do the impressions of others play in the way I perceive myself?
- What happens when these impressions differ substantially from my own opinion of who I am?
- What would be left of me if the props of my identity (my job, possessions, roles, etc.) were removed?
- What impact would a stolen past and a bleak future have on my sense of who I am now?
- What happens if the goals and aspirations that define me are left unfulfilled?
- What should I do with negative thoughts about myself, whether or not others confirm them?
- Where should we turn for answers when our sense of self is shaken to the core?
- Who am I, really?

The final line of the poem gives a sneak preview of the major thesis of this book. Bonhoeffer points to the critical and comforting notion of belonging to and being known by God: "Who I really am, you know me, I am yours, O God!" I made the same discovery in my own search for a stable and satisfying sense of self in the years following my own crisis of identity. As I wondered who I was, it was a great comfort to be reminded that I am known by God. The goal of this biblical theology of personal identity is to explore that insight in full.

Widerstand und Ergebung: Briefe und Aufzeichnungen aus der Haft, ed. E. Bethge [Muenchen: Christian Kaiser, 1964], 243). The English translation of this final line found in Metaxas reads: "Whoever I am, Thou knowest, O God, I am Thine!" I have replaced this rendering with my own translation to update the archaic language and bring out what I think is the sense.

PART 2

ARRIVING AT ANSWERS

CHAPTER 2

PERSONAL IDENTITY AND THE BIBLE

Marilynne Robinson observes that human beings have "the odd privilege of existence as a coherent self, the ability to speak the word 'I' and mean by it a richly individual history of experience, perception and thought."[1] Kevin Vanhoozer agrees: "What distinguishes humans from all other creatures is the ability to say 'I.'"[2] Personal identity, then, is a mark of humanness.

But is the Bible interested in the subject of personal identity? Does it encourage us to think about ourselves? What should we expect from our investigation, and how should we proceed?

As it turns out, thinking about your *self* is thoroughly biblical. The Bible often takes for granted a measure of self-awareness and self-knowledge and expects believers to think about themselves aright. Paul admonishes the Roman Christians: "Do not *think of yourself* more highly than you ought, but rather *think of yourself* with sober judgment" (Rom 12:3). And he warns the Galatians: "If anyone thinks they are something when they are not, they deceive themselves" (Gal 6:3).

A BIBLICAL THEOLOGY OF PERSONAL IDENTITY

"Christianity and Judaism must be called anthropologies, whatever else."
Marilynne Robinson[3]

Books and articles about the doctrine of humanity often start by investigating the image of God and end with debates about the meaning of what constitutes a human being through the so-called anthropological terms (body, soul, spirit, mind, heart, etc.). But this misses much of the Bible's teaching.

"In sum, theological anthropology is the attempt to think through the meaning of the human story, as it unfolds from Genesis through the Gospels to the Apocalypse and as it is lived out before, with and by God."
Kevin Vanhoozer[4]

Teaching about humanity and personal identity appears everywhere in Scripture, but it is rarely the main focus. Kevin Vanhoozer contends: "Theological anthropology is an implicit and derivative, not explicit and foundational,

1. Marilynne Robinson, *Absence of Mind: The Dispelling of Inwardness from the Modern Myth of the Self*, The Terry Lectures Series (New Haven: Yale University Press, 2011), 110.
2. Kevin Vanhoozer, "Human Being, Individual and Social," in *The Cambridge Companion to Christian Doctrine*, ed. Colin E. Gunton (Cambridge: Cambridge University Press, 1997), 180.
3. Robinson, *Absence of Mind*, 126.
4. Vanhoozer, "Human Being, Individual and Social," 159.

doctrine."[5] As Graham Cole puts it, "Scripture does not theorize about the essence of things." The variety of genres that make up the Bible mean that we must respect "the non-postulational character of Scripture."[6]

To appreciate what the Bible has to say about human beings, we need to cast a wide net. Texts to do with humanity and personal identity appear in every type of literature in the Bible, including wisdom literature, the poetry of the Psalms, narratives, and apocalypses. More often than not these are embedded in passages whose main point is to teach something else.

What is biblical theology? Biblical theology may be defined as theological interpretation of Scripture in and for the church. It proceeds with historical and literary sensitivity and seeks to analyse and synthesize the Bible's teaching about God and his relations to the world on its own terms, maintaining sight of the Bible's overarching narrative and Christocentric focus.[7]

The best biblical theology attempts to read all parts of the Bible on their own terms, taking full account of their literary and theological features. Along with looking for the details in every corner of the Bible, we must pay attention to the big picture across all of Scripture. If our lives are stories, where do our stories fit into the story of God?

A biblical theology of personal identity, like all evangelical theology, should be "gospel-driven theology."[8] In particular, the relevance of the Lord Jesus Christ, the last Adam, to the future of humanity is of vital importance. At Jesus's trial in the Gospel of John, Pilate said more than he realized: "Behold the man!" (John 19:5; RSV). As Martin Luther put it, Jesus is "God's proper man."[9] And the whole course of Jesus's life, death, and resurrection has much to say about what it means to be human.

THREE INTERRELATED QUESTIONS

The simple question of personal identity can only be answered by addressing two other questions. Along with *"Who am I?"* we must ask the prior question, *"What is a human being?"* as well as the subsequent question, *"Who are we?"* Put differently, I cannot know who I am without first considering what I am and then to whom I belong.

We begin our study of personal identity in the Bible by noticing that all three questions are posed in the pages of Scripture. Intriguingly, among the Bible's answers in the first two cases is the affirmation that *we are known by God.*

---

5. Ibid.

6. Graham Cole, *Engaging with the Holy Spirit: Real Questions, Practical Answers* (Wheaton, IL: Crossway, 2008), 79.

7. Brian S. Rosner, "Biblical Theology," in *New Dictionary of Biblical Theology*, ed. T. D. Alexander and B. S. Rosner (Downers Grove, IL: InterVarsity Press, 2000), 10.

8. See Michael F. Bird, *Evangelical Theology: A Biblical and Systematic Introduction* (Grand Rapids: Zondervan, 2013), 80–83.

9. Cited in Philip E. Hughes, *The True Image: The Origin and Destiny of Man in Christ* (Grand Rapids: Eerdmans, 1989), viii.

What Is a Human Being?

This question turns up, in the plural, on three occasions: "What are human beings?" (Ps 8:4a NRSV; Ps 144:3 NIV; Job 7:17 NRSV). The context of all three is the wonder of God singling out humanity for his attention from among all his creation. The two psalms marvel at God's care for something seemingly so insignificant:

> When I look at your heavens, the work of your fingers,
> the moon and the stars that you have established;
> *what are human beings* that you are mindful of them,
> mortals that you care for them? (Ps 8:3–4 NRSV)

> LORD, *what are human beings* that you care for them,
> mere mortals that you think of them? (Ps 144:3)

Job, on the other hand, cannot fathom why God would give so much attention to testing and examining something as inconsequential as human beings:

> *What are human beings*, that you make so much of them,
> that you set your mind on them,
> visit them every morning,
> test them every moment? (Job 7:17–18 NRSV)

Whereas Job does not receive an answer to his question from God (at least not until God's reply to his entire situation in Job 38–41), answers to the question of the identity and status of human beings appear in both psalms in the following verses. In Psalm 8, with a clear allusion to the creation account in Genesis 1, the psalmist recalls the honored status of humanity and our responsibility under God in his world:

> You have made them a little lower than the angels
> and crowned them with glory and honor.
> You made them rulers over the works of your hands;
> you put everything under their feet. (Ps 8:5–6)

The answer in Psalm 144 points in a different direction, reinforcing the status of humanity as "mere mortals" (Ps 144:3b) in their transitory and temporary existence:

> They are like a breath;
> their days are like a fleeting shadow. (Ps 144:4)

However, in both psalms there are in fact two answers to the question, "What is a human being?"—Psalm 144 in the following verses, as we have seen, and Psalm 8 in the way in which the questions themselves are framed. In one sense the answer to the question in Psalm 8 begins in the second half of each line of the verse:

> What are human beings *that you are mindful of them*,
> mortals *that you care for them*? (Ps 8:4 NRSV)

Human beings are those about whom God is "mindful," those whom he "remembers" (HCSB; Hebrew *zakar*) and about whom he cares. The lofty station of humanity described in vv. 5–6 depends on God knowing us in the first place.

The same point is made in Psalm 144, where being known by God is also part of the answer to the question, "What is a human being?" The full question itself indicates something of what it means to be a human being:

> Lord, what are human beings *that you care for them*,
> mere mortals *that you think of them*? (Ps 144:3)

Again, humans are those for whom God "cares" and about whom he "thinks." The verb "to care" is *yadah* in Hebrew, and in other contexts it is usually translated "to know." Here it means that God takes "notice" (GNT) of us. In other words, human beings are those of whom God "take[s] knowledge" (NKJV; NASB), those who are known by God.

Who Am I?

The precise question, "Who am I?" is put to God by both Moses and David at points when they felt overwhelmed by the task God had set them to do. These appear at three pivotal moments in the biblical narrative. In response to his commission to confront the pharaoh, Moses asks, "*Who am I* [to take on such a responsibility]?" (Exod 3:11). David asks the same question for similar reasons at the giving of the Davidic covenant (2 Sam 7:18) and the building of the temple (1 Chr 29:14). A final example occurs when David receives the daunting news that he was to marry Saul's daughter: "*Who am I*, and what is my family or my clan in Israel, that I should become the king's son-in-law?" (1 Sam 18:18).

What answers did they get? Saul does not answer David's question, apparently regarding it as a rhetorical question and a mark of modesty. God likewise takes Moses's question as one of self-doubt and an expression of his sense of inadequacy. God's response is to reassure Moses that he will be with him when Moses meets the pharaoh (Exod 3:12). David's question at the prospect of building the temple is an expression of both his own unworthiness and insufficiency and that of the nation. Reassurance comes from recalling that everything comes from and belongs to God (1 Chr 29:14b, 16).

The most intriguing answer to David's question, "Who am I?" comes in 2 Samuel 7 in response to the news that instead of building God a "house," in the sense of a physical building, God will build David a "house," in the sense of the Davidic dynasty.[10] Once again, the full version of the question is revealing:

10. The two senses of "house" are a play on words in the Hebrew with the word *bayit*.

> Then King David went in and sat before the LORD, and he said: "Who am I, Sovereign LORD, and what is my family, that you have brought me this far? And as if this were not enough in your sight, Sovereign LORD, you have also spoken about the future of the house of your servant—and this decree, Sovereign LORD, is for a mere human!" (2 Sam 7:18–19; see also 1 Chr 17:16–17)

"Reading the Bible can be like walking into a new café desperate for your coffee fix and finding the barista standing there holding your favorite double shot latte with one sugar. This book knows us."

John Dickson[11]

In the next verse David answers the question himself: "What more can David say to you? For *you know your servant*, Sovereign LORD" (2 Sam 7:20). If David wonders who he is, the answer is that he is known by God.

Who Are We?

Are human beings mere individuals? What role do others have in defining you? Kevin Vanhoozer strikes the right balance: "The human creature is neither an autonomous individual nor an anonymous unit that has been assimilated into some collectivity, but rather a particular person who achieves a concrete identity in relation to others. Human being is inherently *social*."[12] This observation goes to the heart of a biblical answer to the question of personal identity.

"The human person is both irreducibly individual and constitutionally interrelated. . . . Whereas individuals are defined in terms of their separation from other individuals, persons are understood in terms of their relations to other persons. . . . I am a child in relation to my parents, a husband in relation to my wife, a father in relation to my children, a neighbor in relation to those who live near me, a teacher in relation to my students, a creature in relation to God and a disciple in relation to Christ."

Kevin Vanhoozer[14]

Although the question, "Who are we?" does not appear in the Bible in as many words,[13] both the Old Testament and New Testament contain an abundance of answers to it in reference to the identity of the people of God. For example, Israel is told: "You [plural] will be for me a kingdom of priests and a holy nation" (Exod 19:6) and so on. And the church is informed that "you" (plural) are the "church of God," "the body of Christ," "God's temple," and so forth (Acts 20:28; Rom 7:4; 1 Cor 3:16).

The Bible has a direct interest in answering the questions of personal identity, including its three forms of the identity of human beings, individuals, and groups of people: What is a human being? Who am I? Who are we?

THE REST OF THIS BOOK

An outline of where we are heading will help you to keep track of the main argument of this book, and hopefully whet your appetite for what is to come and keep you reading!

11. John Dickson, *A Doubter's Guide to the Bible: Inside History's Bestseller for Believers and Skeptics* (Grand Rapids: Zondervan, 2014), 201.

12. Vanhoozer, "Human Being, Individual and Social," 174–75. Emphasis original.

13. The closest approximation is in 1 Chr 29:14 where David asks God, "Who am I, and *who are my people*?"

14. Vanhoozer, "Human Being, Individual and Social," 172, 174.

The rest of part two (chapters three to ten) seeks to answer the questions posed in chapter one. If in our day identity angst is at epidemic proportions, where should we look for a stable and satisfying sense of self?

In *chapter three*, "The Foundations of Personal Identity," we consider the markers most commonly used in our day to establish a person's identity. These include a person's occupation, marital status, and material wealth, as well as race, gender, age, sexual orientation, physical appearance, and so on. The Bible offers a radical perspective on such markers, qualifying their significance in the light of other matters and insisting that, as important as they are, they do not define us. The Bible does not deny their ongoing significance, but has a different way of looking at these markers and warns us against regarding them as having ultimate significance.

In *chapter four*, "Human Beings according to the Bible," we begin to answer the question: What is a human being? The opening chapters of Genesis will be our primary focus in this and the next chapter. However, along with noticing that we are souls, have bodies, and are made from dust, we will also consider the meaning of other constitutional features of humanity such as flesh, mind, heart, and spirit, especially in Paul's letters.

In *chapter five* we look at the critical notion of humanity made in "The Image and Likeness of God." Clearly a fundamental feature of human beings, the concept of being made in the image of God has a long and contested history of interpretation. Does it refer to our endowment with reason or conscience or some other attribute? Or does it focus on our capacity for relationships with God and other humans? Or does the image of God entail the task of being God's representatives on earth? While each of these suggestions has some merit, my view is that being made in God's image means that we are God's offspring, his children, and stand in a familial relation to our Creator. We will also look at the Genesis account of Adam and Eve's transgression of God's word as a crisis of identity.

The heart of this book's investigation of personal identity in the Bible is the notion of being known by God. Sorely neglected in the study of the Bible and theology, being known by God appears throughout the Bible and is a theologically profound and immensely practical truth. And as I noted in chapter one, thinking about it has been of great benefit to me personally.

Two chapters explicitly trace the theme of being known by God in the Bible: *chapter six*, "Known by God in the Old Testament," and *chapter seven*, "Known by God and Christ in the New Testament." To be known by God is related to the themes of being chosen by God and belonging to God. At its heart is the truth that we are known intimately and personally by God as his children.

In *chapter eight*, "Known in Christ, the Son of God," we consider the relevance of Jesus Christ to human identity and, in particular, focus on the notion of union with Christ. Being in Christ, who is God's Son, carries with it the identity of being children of God.

Thus chapters five to eight supply three different answers to the question, who am I?

1. "I am made in the image of God" (ch. five),
2. "I am known by God" (chs. six and seven), and
3. "I am in Christ" (ch. eight).

But this is slightly misleading, since these four central chapters of the book in effect give one answer to the question; each points to our identity as God's children. As God's children we are made in God's image; as his children we are known by him; and as those in Christ, we are children of God.

A Venn diagram is the best way to illustrate and explore the relationships between the three interrelated concepts. It is not that "image of God," being "known by God," and being "in Christ" are simply codes for being a child of God. But together they have a common center. And it is the reality of being a child of God that is the Bible's best answer to the question, who am I?[15]

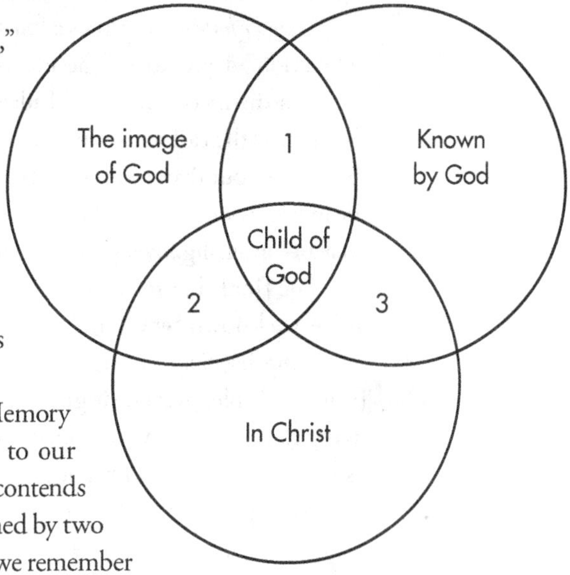

The image of God
1
Known by God
Child of God
2
3
In Christ

Chapter nine, "Child of God and Son of God," considers the idea of adoption into God's family. This doctrine, which J. I. Packer described as the greatest blessing of the gospel, is a key theme in biblical theology as well as in understanding human identity. And imitating God as his children is a vital point in living as those made in the image of God and known by him as his children. As Ephesians 5:1 says: "be imitators of God, as beloved children" (ESV).

Chapter ten looks at the place of our "Shared Memory and Defining Destiny" in helping to give shape to our personal identity as children of God. Bruce Waltke contends that in the Old Testament, personal identity is formed by two factors, namely memory and destiny.[16] We are what we remember of ourselves; and where we think we are heading also impacts our identity in the present. But such memories and future expectations can be corporate as well as individual, and the Bible shapes our personal identity by including us in a larger narrative.

Part three (chapters eleven to fifteen) explores some of the personal benefits that flow from the identity of being known by God. These are blessings that I have experienced personally. And they make being known by God such a powerful and compelling truth. The first is in *chapter eleven*, "Significance," where we see that being known by God gives our lives lasting value. Being known by God fulfills our

15. The diagram is also useful in showing how image of God, being known by God, and being in Christ overlap in other respects (see cells 1, 2, and 3): cell 1 points to the notion of God "seeing," seeing his image in us on the one hand, and seeing (as in knowing) us on the other; cell 2 identifies that the image of God relates to being in union with Christ since Christ the Son "is the image of the invisible God" (Col 1:15); and cell 3 highlights the fact that we are known by God in Christ. These thematic connections are explored at appropriate points in the book.

16. Bruce K. Waltke, *An Old Testament Theology: An Exegetical, Canonical, and Thematic Approach* (Grand Rapids: Zondervan, 2007), 13.

longing for recognition and gives a solid foundation to our identities when all else fails.

Chapter twelve shows how being known by God provokes needed "Humility." The Bible has a lot to say about pride. Pride leads us to seek a name for ourselves and to audacious ambition in defiance of God. Being known by God and having our names written in heaven releases us from such destructive impulses and promotes a healthy modesty before God and other human beings.

Chapter thirteen, "Comfort," acknowledges that to be human is to experience sorrow. Part of the comfort we can expect from God in times of trouble is the reassurance that we are known by him. In the Old Testament when Israel was oppressed and enslaved, wandering in the desert, or in exile longing for home, God reassures his people that he is attentive to their plight. As the prophet Nahum put it: "The Lord is good, a stronghold in the day of trouble; he knows those who take refuge in him" (Nah 1:7 ESV).

Chapter fourteen explores a fourth benefit of being known by God, namely the moral "Direction" it provides. The identity of those known by God as his children carries with it a distinctive lifestyle. Indeed, a frequent strategy for moral transformation in the Bible is the call to live in accordance with our new identity in Christ. The defining moment of our lives took place two thousand years ago when we died and rose to new life in union with Christ. And just as our identity as children of God was forged through an act of amazing love, so too we are to live lives of costly, selfless, other-centered love.

The final chapter, *chapter fifteen*, "Known by God," looks at knowing ourselves as we are known by God. As it turns out, the basic disciplines of the Christian life, including baptism, going to church, reading the Bible and listening to preaching from the Bible, prayer, singing the faith, saying the Creed, taking communion, and living the gospel, serve to confirm our true identity as people who are known by God as his children. Such practices reinforce and confirm our new identity and ensure that we experience its life-transforming blessings.

RELEVANT QUESTIONS

1. In Western society many would argue that a human being is a highly intelligent animal, the end product of a long evolutionary chain. In contrast, this chapter defines human beings as created, known, and cared for by God. What are the implications of these contrasting ideas for us as individuals, and for society as a whole?
2. In an age of social media where "personal branding" and a carefully constructed online "image" of ourselves is increasingly valued, how might the idea of being "known by God" challenge us and/or free us?
3. What do you think about the idea that human beings are inherently social and that our identity is given its final form in relation to others? How do you answer the question, "To whom do I belong?"

CHAPTER 3

THE FOUNDATIONS OF PERSONAL IDENTITY

Who are you? What defines you? What makes you, you? The answers to these questions are the foundations upon which your personal identity is built. Some things about you can be discovered at first sight, such as your gender, race, and approximate age. Others take some self-disclosure. Sometimes we are defined by our relationships. At a certain primary school, I am Toby's father. At church, I am Natalie's husband. In southwest Sydney, I am Valerie's son. In Adelaide, I am Lyn's brother. When you are speaking to a medical professional, the critical thing about you is your physical condition. In some contexts, your job is the most important thing about you. In others it can be the country in which you were born, the color of your skin, your address, the clothes you wear, or even the car you drive.

TRADITIONAL IDENTITY MARKERS

In this section, we examine eleven things that are commonly seen as essential dimensions of a person's identity:

1. Your race, ethnicity, and nationality;
2. Your culture;
3. Your gender and sexuality;
4. Your physical and mental capacity;
5. Your family of origin;
6. Your age;
7. Your relationships;
8. Your occupation;
9. Your possessions;
10. Your religion; and
11. Your personality and character.

How important is each of these to your personal identity?

"It is worth bearing in mind a simple truth: no human being is only a Muslim and no human being is only an American. The people one might call Muslims, or Americans, are also women and men; mothers, fathers, daughters, and sons; lovers and doctors and writers and schoolteachers; poor and wealthy; politically engaged and apathetic; sure in their beliefs and utterly uncertain. They are, in other words, complex, multidimensional, unique, and ever changing."

Mohsin Hamid[1]

1. Mohsin Hamid, *Discontent and Its Civilizations: Dispatches from Lahore, New York and London* (London: Penguin, 2014), 111.

Which of the eleven would you use to describe yourself? In what order would you list them in terms of priority? Which do you regard as essential? Which are important? Which are unimportant to you? Which, if any, is all-important?

All of these markers of identity deserve greater attention than a biblical scholar can offer in a few pages of one chapter in a book. Many have layers of interest to anthropologists, sociologists, biologists, psychologists, and so on. And several are highly controversial in our day. My purpose in addressing them is quite modest and consists of answering a single question: *How important are the standard identity markers to personal identity according to the Bible?*

As it turns out, the Bible confirms the legitimacy of the standard personal identity markers, but denies their ultimacy. Many of them are indispensable, but they are an insufficient foundation upon which to build your identity.

Race, Ethnicity, and Nationality

Who am I? How important to my identity are my race, ethnicity, and nationality? I am a white Australian of Austrian Jewish descent on my father's side and English on my mother's. As an Australian citizen, when I travel overseas I carry an Australian passport. Are these things important to me? The answer is yes, but only to a limited extent. I've lived in several countries for extended periods, but since they've all been Western and predominantly Caucasian, the color of my skin has never made me stand out. For that reason I don't give my race and ethnicity much thought. My father was a Jew who fled Nazi persecution in Vienna with his parents in 1938. So while I am grateful for the stability and freedoms of the nation of Australia, with the evils of nationalism scarring my family history I've never been particularly patriotic.

Who are you? How important to your identity are your race, ethnicity, and nationality?[2] What does the Bible teach concerning race, ethnicity, and nationality? Are they legitimate aspects of the order of creation, or are they the consequences of Adam and Eve's disobedience against God?

The racial, ethnic, and geographical spread of humankind across the world has two beginnings in the Bible. The first is in the account of creation in Genesis 1. It is notable for its insistence that all human beings are made in the image of God (see chapter five). However, the second account—that of the spread of Noah's family after the flood in Genesis 9—is more significant for our purposes:

2. How are race, ethnicity, and nationality related? In my understanding, *race* concerns genetically distinct populations that exhibit different physical appearances, such as variations in skin color and facial features. *Ethnicity* refers to a culture in a particular geographical region and includes language, heritage, and customs. Race and ethnicity can overlap but they can also be distinguished. For example, Chinese-Americans might consider themselves to be Asian by race but not identify with an Asian ethnic group in terms of their behavior and customs. While race is biologically transmitted, ethnicity is about owning a shared cultural heritage. *Nationality*, on the other hand, concerns the country to which someone belongs, the legal relationship between a person and a state. To complicate matters further, it is possible to be mixed race, identify with several ethnic groups, and have more than one nationality! In sum, the three terms refer to the different ways in which we identify ourselves by pointing out our connections to larger groups of people.

> The sons of Noah who came out of the ark were Shem, Ham and Japheth. (Ham was the father of Canaan.) These were the three sons of Noah, and from them came the people who were scattered over the whole earth. (Gen 9:18–19)

Genesis 10–11 fills out the picture of this scattering. In Genesis 10:1–32 we have what is often called "The Table of Nations," a genealogy that details the location of peoples and their relationships to each other. Then, in Genesis 11:1–9 the story of the Tower of Babel explains that it was God's judgment against the hubris of humankind that led to their dispersion: "The LORD confused the language of the whole world. From there the LORD scattered them over the face of the whole earth" (Gen 11:9).

However, it is a mistake to assume that the division of people on earth into different groups and languages is simply a consequence of human disobedience. God had already told Noah and his sons to "be fruitful and increase in number and fill the earth" (Gen 9:1), a command which echoes his words to human beings in Genesis 1:28. There is a tension between divine blessing and punishment in Genesis 9–11, one which sets up God's program for blessing all the families of the earth announced in his call of Abraham in Genesis 12:1–3. Sometimes God works through human disobedience to fulfill what he had in mind all along.

> "Ethnic diversity is the gift and plan of God in creation. It has been spoiled by human sin and pride, resulting in confusion, strife, violence and war among nations. However, ethnic diversity will be preserved in the new creation, when people from every nation, tribe, people and language will gather as the redeemed people of God. We confess that we often fail to take ethnic identity seriously and to value it as the Bible does, in creation and redemption. We fail to respect the ethnic identity of others and ignore the deep wounds that such long-term disrespect causes."
>
> *The Cape Town Commitment*[3]

J. Daniel Hays explains:

> Genesis 10–11, the Table of Nations and the Tower of Babel, stand as the Prologue to Genesis 12:1–13. Recall that Genesis 10 describes the division of the world according to family/tribe/clan, language, land/country/territory, and nation (Gen. 10:5, 20, 31). The call of Abraham picks up on three of these terms: "Go from your *country*" (12:1); "I will make you a great *nation*" (12:2); and "in you all the *families* of the earth will be blessed" (12:3) (NRSV). . . . The promise to Abraham is the answer to the sin and the scattering of Genesis 3–11.[4]

In Genesis 10, the population of the world is described as families/tribes, languages, lands, and nations. Significantly, the theme of the blessing of the nations in the book of Revelation is framed in similar terms. In Revelation 5:9–10, those who have been redeemed sing a new song:

3. *The Cape Town Commitment: A Confession of Faith and a Call to Action* (The Third Lausanne Congress on World Evangelization, Cape Town, 16–25 October 2010), 40.

4. J. Daniel Hays, *From Every People and Nation: A Biblical Theology of Race*, ed. D. A. Carson, NSBT 14 (Downers Grove, IL: InterVarsity Press, 2003), 61. I have introduced the emphases to underscore the links.

You are worthy to take the scroll
 and to open its seals,
because you were slain,
 and with your blood you purchased for God
 persons from every *tribe* and *language* and *people* and *nation*.
You have made them to be a kingdom and priests to serve our God,
 and they will reign on the earth.

The same fourfold formula is picked up in Revelation 7:9:

> After this I looked, and there before me was a great multitude that no one could count, from every *nation*, *tribe*, *people* and *language*, standing before the throne and before the Lamb. They were wearing white robes and were holding palm branches in their hands.

Clearly, the Bible acknowledges the racial, ethnic, and national distinctions that form the foundations for personal identity for all people to a lesser or greater extent in every age. And God's plan of redemption had a global and multi-ethnic intention from the very beginning. As Hays puts it, "the picture of God's people at the climax of history portrays a multi-ethnic congregation from every tribe, language, people, and nation, all gathered together in worship around God's throne."[5]

However, while recognition of racial, ethnic, and national distinctions is present in the Bible, which regards them as genuine identity markers for human beings, there is also an insistence that something overshadows them. As Hays correctly observes,

> The New Testament teaches equality of all believers in regard to status and value, but it also teaches that the believer's *identity* should be based on Christ and not on culturally driven differentiations.[7]

A new belonging defines those who have trusted in Christ.

In the Judaism of Paul's day, the world was seen as comprising just two groups: Jews and gentiles. Paul reflects the same worldview at several points in his letters (see Rom 1:16; 2:9–10; 3:9; 10:12). It is thus highly significant that in 1 Corinthians 10:32, Paul breaks with this view and introduces a third grouping that supersedes

> "Although the concept of 'ethnicity' is difficult to delineate precisely, it is possible to determine distinctions between four major ethnic groups that appear in the Old Testament. The group appearing most frequently, of course, is the Northwest Semitic group, composed of Israel and many of her neighbours (Canaanites, Moabites, Edomites, Ammonites, etc). Also playing a role in the Old Testament are the Cushites (Black Africans), the Egyptians (probably a mix of Asiatic and Black African), and the Indo-Europeans (Philistines and Hittites). Thus the Old Testament world was completely multi-ethnic."
>
> *J. Daniel Hays*[6]

5. Hays, *From Every People and Nation*, 205.
6. Ibid., 45.
7. Ibid., 200. Emphasis original.

the other two. There he mentions Jews, Greeks (another term for gentiles), and "*the church of God*." At root, being a Jew or a gentile is displaced in importance by a more important identity, that of belonging to the new people of God.

For many people their race, ethnicity, and nationality are of vital importance to their personal identity. The Bible nowhere disputes that such factors are legitimate aspects of the identity of human beings. However, the Bible also teaches that ultimately human identity cannot be grounded in such distinctions; such matters are not all-important. You are more than your race, ethnic group, and nationality.[8]

Culture

Who am I? How important to my identity is my cultural background? I am a non-indigenous Australian who also identifies with my family's European roots. Broadly speaking, Australians value mateship, classlessness, and the "fair go." This is in part due to the convict origins of the first settlement in the eighteenth century and to other nation-defining events, such as the heroism of the tragic Gallipoli campaign of 1915 in World War One, which is commemorated on Anzac Day each year on April 25. These events had a leveling effect on the society as the struggles of ordinary people became chiseled into the nation's memory. Such values run deep for me, and, although they are mainly subconscious, I am sure that they have been formative. For example, like many Australians, I barrack for the "underdog" in sporting events. But I am also partial to a game of chess, like my Austrian father. A person's cultural background is rarely straightforward and may contain a number of roots and branches.

Who are you? How important to your identity is your cultural background?

Thinking about your culture is like talking to a fish about water; the fish might wonder: What's water? You only notice your culture when you are not in it.[9] I have been most aware of my cultural identity when living outside of Australia. I studied in Texas and in Cambridge, England, worked for eight years in Scotland, and had one year in Germany on study leave. To give one example, the cultural differences required some major shifts in the way I expressed myself. My volume had to be adjusted (up in the US; down in the UK), along with the way in which I teased my mates (less mercilessly in Texas and more subtly in England).

There is no doubt that the social class of a society to which a person belongs will also shape their personal identity. The various social classes provide the cultural narratives that give people's lives meaning, identity, and security. Tim Foster explains how cultural narratives are transmitted:

8. It should also be recognized that placing too much weight on racial and ethnic identity can lead to racism, just as pride in one's nationality can go from patriotism to a destructive nationalism. Christian faith provides the perspective and resources for effectively countering both excesses.

9. The other way to notice your own cultural context is to read history and to learn about other times and cultures.

> A cultural narrative is found hidden beneath a multiplicity of symbols, myths and rituals. It is told through the myths found in books, magazines, films, advertising, blogs and anecdotes. It is symbolised in fashion, brands, technology, art, music and architecture. It is ritualised in the practices that govern each day, week and year. It is embodied in the values, pronouncements and lifestyles of our heroes and celebrities. In countless ways and from the earliest age our cultural narrative is told, and it is absorbed.[10]

The attitudes of many people to material possessions and aspirations, education, refugees, gender roles, welfare, music and culture, and so on can in large part be explained in terms of their cultural narrative, the story they have been told and to which they have become a part. This is the case for urbanites, suburban dwellers, the working class, and people who live in rural settings. To understand who you are, you need also to know whose you are.

What does the Bible teach about human culture? Does the gospel announce the end of human culture? Does redemption annul cultural differences? A text like Galatians 3:28 certainly seems to suggest that culture is of no consequence for Christians: "There is neither Jew nor Gentile, neither slave nor free, nor is there male and female, for you are all one in Christ Jesus."

A short case study is instructive at this point. Richard Twiss was an American Indian who became a Christian. Soon after his conversion, Twiss pondered how his Native American identity related to following Christ. His Caucasian American pastor gave him this advice on the basis of Galatians 3:28: "So, Richard, don't worry about being Indian anymore—just be like us." Years later Twiss reflected on how he had acted on the pastor's advice, and regretted it:

> Though he was unaware of it, essentially what he as saying was, "Forget your Indian-ness and embrace our white culture as the only Christian culture." Being young and naive as well as deeply grateful for the Creator's love in setting me free from drug and alcohol abuse, and sincerely committed to becoming a wholehearted follower of Jesus, I believed that church leader. I really had no choice, being a new Christian, and he, being in a position of spiritual power/authority, gave an answer from the Bible about cultures. So for the next twelve years I lived the Christian life as it was culturally modeled for me by non-Native friends and Christian brethren—something I later found to be less than I am, and much less than the Lord Jesus wants me to be![11]

10. Tim Foster, *The Suburban Captivity of the Church: Contextualising the Gospel for Post-Christian Australia* (Moreland, Victoria, Australia: Acorn, 2014), 33.

11. Richard Twiss, *Rescuing the Gospel from the Cowboys: A Native American Expression of the Jesus Way* (Downers Grove, IL: InterVarsity Press, 2015), 104.

As it turns out, Galatians 3:28 does not signal the end of cultural differences. Being "all one in Christ Jesus" is a statement about the equal status of all human beings who trust in Christ as members of the body of Christ. It does not render invalid cultural differences.

Paul's reflections on his own missionary practice make this abundantly clear. Far from ignoring cultural differences, Paul is willing to surrender his right to live according to his own culture, context, and preferences and adapt to the realities and ways of those with whom he works and whom he hopes to reach for Christ:

> To the Jews I became like a Jew, to win the Jews. To those under the law I became like one under the law (though I myself am not under the law), so as to win those under the law. To those not having the law I became like one not having the law (though I am not free from God's law but am under Christ's law), so as to win those not having the law. To the weak I became weak, to win the weak. I have become all things to all people so that by all possible means I might save some. (1 Cor 9:20–22)

Many identity markers have to do with shared understandings, practices, and values that shape us. In other words, personal identity is in large part shaped by the cultural group, or groups, with which you identify. The Bible neither disputes nor opposes this. Paul's willingness to forgo behaving according to his own cultural background and to adapt his behavior to the culture of others was driven by a missional motivation—that is, in his own words, to "save some." His example does not imply that culture does not matter for personal identity; Twiss is right (see above). On the contrary, Paul's "all things to all people" strategy was a costly one personally and testifies to his commitment to the task of preaching the gospel effectively.

Of all the world religions, the Christian faith is in fact the most culturally adaptable. Every culture has both its good and unique elements along with failings and blind spots. At its best, Christianity does not impose a culture of its own. Rather, it looks for Christ to redeem our various cultures. As Timothy Keller observes, "Biblical texts such as Isaiah 60 and Revelation 21–22 depict a renewed, perfect, future world in which we retain our cultural differences ('every tongue, tribe, people, nation')."[12]

> "Cultural diversity was built into the Christian faith. . . . in Acts 15 the apostles declared that the new gentile Christians didn't have to enter Jewish culture. . . . The converts had to work out a Hellenistic way of being a Christian. There is no 'Christian culture' the way there is an 'Islamic culture' which you can recognize from Pakistan to Tunisia to Morocco."
>
> *Andrew Walls*[13]

Culture, along with many of the markers of personal identity, is rooted in the Bible's accounts of creation, including the fact that human beings have bodies,

12. Timothy Keller, *The Reason for God: Belief in an Age of Skepticism* (New York: Penguin: 2008), 45.

13. Quoted in Keller, *Reason for God*, 44.

gender, and language; undertake work; have children; live in cities; and so on. These are vital dimensions of what it means to be human in God's world. And neither the destructiveness of the fall nor God's plan of redemption removes them as marks of personal identity. But as important as cultural identity is, there is an identity that goes deeper than a person's cultural background, as Galatians 3:28 asserts.

"Christianity has been more adaptive of diverse cultures than secularism and many other worldviews. The pattern of Christian expansion differs from that of every other world religion. The center and majority of Islam's population is still in the place of its origin—the Middle East. The original lands that have been the demographic centers of Hinduism, Buddhism and Confucianism have remained so. By contrast, Christianity was first dominated by Jews and centered in Jerusalem. Later it was dominated by Hellenists and centered in the Mediterranean. Later the faith was received by the Barbarians of Northern Europe and Christianity came to be dominated by western Europeans and then North Americans. Today most Christians in the world live in Africa, Latin America and Asia. Christianity soon will be centered in the southern and eastern hemispheres."

Timothy Keller[14]

Gender and Sexuality

Who am I? How important to my identity is my gender? I'm sure that my maleness determines much of my behavior, along with affecting the expectations of those around me concerning how I dress and act, the opportunities I have enjoyed, and the roles that I play.

Who are you? How important to your identity is your gender?

Most of us would regard our gender as fundamental to who we are and take our maleness or femaleness for granted. However, for a small minority gender is much more of an issue for their identity, especially those identifying as intersex, transgender, or transsexual. In some circles in our day, gender is thought of as socially constructed and a matter of personal choice. There is no space in this short section to unpack these issues.

What can be said in relation to our subject is that even given the foundational importance of gender for personal identity, the gospel announces an identity that eclipses it; namely, belonging to Christ and being in Christ. The most striking pair of terms that Galatians 3:28 negates concerns gender: "There is neither Jew nor Gentile, neither slave nor free, *nor is there male and female*, for you are all one in Christ Jesus." In short, when it comes to personal identity, being "in Christ" trumps even being male or female, or any other gender. (We will deal with the notion of being in Christ in chapter eight, "Known in Christ, the Son of God.") It is not that being in Christ removes our maleness or femaleness. Rather, how we express being a man or woman, the man or woman we become, will be radically different when we find our identity in Christ.

What about human sexuality? How important is your sexuality to your personal identity? For most people who are attracted to the opposite sex, being heterosexual is unlikely to be one of the first things they would say about themselves. However,

14. Keller, *Reason for God*, 40–41.

for those who identify as being same-sex attracted, their homosexuality is at the top of their mind when thinking about themselves. Indeed, for many gay and lesbian people, their sexuality is of vital importance to their identity.

As it turns out, the idea that your sexuality is an important part of your identity is a modern notion. As Ed Shaw notes: "People only started being labeled as homosexuals back in the nineteenth century; philosopher Michel Foucault traced its first use to an article published in 1870."[15] While homosexual behavior was widely known in the ancient world, it was thought of as a sexual behavior rather than in terms of sexual orientation.[16]

For our purposes, in terms of a biblical theology, while important, your sexuality is not all-important to your personal identity. In Matthew 19:12 Jesus refers to those who do not have sex for one reason or another:

> There are eunuchs who were born that way, and there are eunuchs who have been made eunuchs by others—and there are those who choose to live like eunuchs for the sake of the kingdom of heaven.

This was a radical view in the first century. Indeed, as Philip Johnston notes, "Jesus's own celibacy and his encouragement of celibacy for the sake of the kingdom questioned the traditional view of marriage as necessary for human completeness."[17] Furthermore, Jesus taught that there will be no marriage in the age to come (Matt 22:30; Luke 20:34–35). In the Bible's view, you are not your sexuality. There is something more fundamental to your identity.

On February 14, 2014, Facebook made this announcement: "When you come to Facebook to connect with the people, causes, and organizations you care about, we want you to feel comfortable being your true, authentic self. An important part of this is the expression of gender, especially when it extends beyond the definitions of just 'male' or 'female.' So today, we're proud to offer a new custom gender option to help you better express your own identity on Facebook." There are more than fifty options, including genderqueer, intersex, pangender, gender fluid, and transgender.

"Sexuality is intrinsic to humanity and vital for its continuation on earth. Its very preciousness leaves it vulnerable to abuse. But it is limited to this life, as Jesus indicates in his rebuttal of the Sadducees' disbelief in the resurrection (Mark 12:25). In heaven procreation will be unnecessary and inappropriate, while love will be perfected in all relationships."

Philip Johnston[18]

Physical and Mental Capacity

Who am I? How important to my identity is my physical and mental capacity? It is no doubt quite important. Both affect the opportunities available to me and my

15. Ed Shaw, *The Plausibility Problem: The Church and Same-Sex Attraction* (Nottingham, UK: Inter-Varsity Press, 2015), 38.

16. In our day homosexuality is a highly personal and complex issue that deserves more space than I can devote to it here. For two recent treatments, see Wesley Hill, *Washed and Waiting: Reflections on Christian Faithfulness and Homosexuality* (Grand Rapids: Zondervan, 2010); and Preston Sprinkle, *People to be Loved: Why Homosexuality is Not Just an Issue* (Grand Rapids: Zondervan, 2015). I affirm the historic Christian sexual ethic, summarized by Wes Hill: "Homosexuality was not God's original creative intention for humanity. . . . It is, on the contrary, a tragic sign of human nature and relationships being fractured by sin, and therefore homosexual practice goes against God's express will for human beings, especially those who trust in Christ" (*Washed and Waiting*, 14–15).

17. Philip S. Johnston, "Humanity," in *New Dictionary of Biblical Theology*, ed. T. D. Alexander and B. S. Rosner (Downers Grove, IL: InterVarsity Press, 2000), 565.

18. Ibid.

place in society. But as an able-bodied person, it is not something I think about very often.

Who are you? How important to your personal identity is your physical and mental capacity? People with a disability often regard such matters as a big part of their identity, and for good reason. It is often one of the first things that others notice about them and may be one of the first things they are asked about when introducing themselves. And, sadly, many are reminded of their disability by their lack of acceptance in society.

The Bible deals at length with issues we term disabilities. Numerous passages touch on blindness, deafness, muteness, and lameness as well as congenital disorders and loss of function due to aging. This is too big a subject to tackle in one small section of this chapter. With respect to our purposes, namely the specific question of disability and personal identity, we should note that numerous passages in the Bible push against the world's assessment of the disabled and urge that people should not be defined by their disability.

If in the ancient world disability generally accorded someone a low status in society, Paul's insistence that "God chose the weak things of the world to shame the strong. God chose the lowly things of this world and the despised things—and the things that are not—to nullify the things that are" (1 Cor 1:27–28), should not go unnoticed. The fact that God saves us through the seemingly weak and foolish word of the cross indicates that he takes no notice of what the world counts as wise and powerful.

Further examples of God taking a different view of the place of the disabled in society include King David's welcoming of Mephibosheth, Jonathan's only surviving son, to his table, even though he was "lame in both feet" (2 Sam 9:13); Jesus's insistence that what his followers do for "the least of these" is determinative at the final judgment (Matt 25:40); and Paul's conviction that in the body of Christ, God gives "greater honor to the parts that lacked it" (1 Cor 12:24).

In short, people with disabilities are not defined by their physical or mental limitations in God's sight. Their identity, value, and worth is determined, as we will see in chapter eleven,[19] in a different way than how the world might see them.

Family of Origin

Who am I? How important to my identity is my family of origin? My father was born and spent his first thirteen years in Austria. When I visited Vienna for the first time in 1990, uncannily, I saw my father everywhere: his mannerisms, values, tastes, choices in music and food, and so on. No doubt some of these features have been passed onto me. Parents leave an indelible mark on their children through both nature and nurture.

19. See the section, "A Diminished Life."

How about you? How important is the family in which you grew up to who you are today? Does it define you?

How important is the family to a person's identity? Families certainly play a major role in the formation of someone's identity. Typically, parents name their children and pass on to their children much of their identity, especially in their earliest years. Of course, children grow up and become responsible for who they become. But like it or not, you never completely outgrow your family's formative influence.

Without question, your family will have a big impact on who you are: your appearance, values, and worldview along with the way you talk, walk, eat, play, work, and so on. Who you are is substantially an inheritance from your family. This is the case to a lesser or greater extent whether you feel over-connected or disconnected from your parents, siblings, grandparents, uncles, aunts, and cousins. All of us can credit or blame our families for their part in forming our personal identity.

The common experience of moments when we do or say something that reminds us of our mother or father is captured in colloquial sayings: "A person who is thought to resemble one of their parents in character or behaviour can be described as a 'chip off the old block.' The phrase was originally found in the form 'chip of the same block,' so that the person appeared to be made from the same material."[20]

The Bible recognizes that families are a critical and formative source for personal identity. In both the Old and New Testaments, the extended family, rather than the nuclear family, was the more common family structure. Households tended to include not only parents and children, but also other relatives, servants, and long-stay guests. Jacob's family, for example, comprised three generations (Gen 46:8–26).

In both Testaments, fathers and mothers were expected to teach their children. And as today, parents inevitably model for their children a host of beliefs, attitudes, and behaviors. The notion of a family likeness is assumed at many points in the biblical narratives and in the Wisdom literature. A striking example is Genesis 26 where Isaac passes off his wife as his sister for his own safety, exactly as Abraham his father had done (see 26:7 with 12:13 and 20:11–13). Isaac illustrates the old saying, "like father, like son." Thankfully, Isaac also imitates his father in more positive ways, such as acting on the promises of God as Abraham had done (see Gen 26:2–6).

In the Bible and the ancient world generally, children commonly took on the occupations of their parents. Jesus was the carpenter's son and a carpenter. Indeed, the assumption behind Jesus's words in John 5:17, 19 is that sons follow their father: "My [heavenly] Father is always at his work to this very day, and I too am working. . . . The Son can do nothing by himself; he can do only what he sees his Father doing, because whatever the Father does the Son also does."

The Bible also acknowledges the prevalence of conflicts within families, and

20. *Oxford Dictionary of Word Origins* (Oxford: Oxford University Press, 2002), 84.

it is anything but blindly sentimental about families. To consider just the book of Genesis again, Abraham quarrels with Lot his nephew (13:5–8); Sarah sends Hagar away (21:9–10); Esau hates his brother Jacob (27:41); Joseph is sold by his brothers into slavery (37:12–36); and, not to forget, Cain kills his brother Abel (4:8)! Families can have a dark side.

In the Old Testament, "house" (Hebrew *bayit*) can refer literally to those who live together, and it can also extend to tribes and even nations, as in the phrase, "house of Israel." Likewise, in the New Testament the word "family" (Greek *patria*) can refer to a "people group," as in the quotation of Genesis 12:3 in Acts 3:25: "And in your offspring shall all the *families* [*patriai*] of the earth be blessed" (ESV). However, the "household" (Greek *oikos*) is the more common way of talking about family in the New Testament. Paul, for example, regularly mentions households by name: "You know the *household* of Stephanas" (1 Cor 16:15); "May the Lord show mercy to the *household* of Onesiphorus" (2 Tim 1:16).

In the Old Testament, disloyalty to one's family was a most serious sin. The fifth of the Ten Commandments is to "honor your father and your mother" (Exod 20:12). Deuteronomy 21:18–21 states that "a stubborn and rebellious son who does not obey his father and mother" is deserving of the most severe punishment. The prophet Micah laments the state of the people of God in a time when "a son dishonors his father, a daughter rises up against her mother, a daughter-in-law against her mother-in-law—a man's enemies are the members of his own household" (Micah 7:6). Likewise in the traditional Greek and Roman cultures of the first century, "family ties were paramount."[21]

With this in mind, several sayings of Jesus seem quite radical in their original setting:

> If anyone comes to me and does not *hate father and mother, wife and children, brothers and sisters*—yes, even their own life—such a person cannot be my disciple. (Luke 14:26; see also Matt 10:34–36; 12:46–50).

However, it would be a mistake to take such sayings in an absolute sense. The language of *hating* one's family members (Luke 14:26) can be a bold way of saying that we should love something else more.[22]

In Matthew 10 and 12 and Luke 14, Jesus is saying that a new allegiance and belonging must take precedence even over the closest of ties, namely those of a family. Leon Morris concludes that when Jesus says to hate the members of your family, "Jesus is not saying that earthly familial ties are unimportant, only that they are not all-important."[23] As with race, ethnicity, nationality, and culture, in the Bible

21. Craig S. Keener, *The Gospel of Matthew: A Socio-Rhetorical Commentary* (Grand Rapids: Eerdmans, 2009), 370.

22. This use of the language of love and hate can be seen in Genesis 29 with reference to Jacob's love for Rachel. In Genesis 29:30, it is said that Jacob loved Rachel more than Leah: "His love for Rachel was greater than his love for Leah." The same situation is then described in Genesis 29:31 in terms of Jacob *hating* Leah: "When the LORD saw that Leah was hated" (ESV). Most English versions soften the language and translate: "When the Lord saw that Leah was not loved" (NIV; see also HCSB, NET, NRSV). A NET Bible note describes the use of the verb "to hate" in Genesis 29:31 as the use of "the rhetorical device of overstatement to emphasize that Rachel, as Jacob's true love and the primary object of his affections, had an advantage over Leah." See Robert H. Stein, *Luke: An Exegetical and Theological Exposition of Holy Scripture*, NAC 24 (Nashville: Broadman & Holman, 1992), 397. See also Luke 16:13, where a love-hate, devote-despise dichotomy describes preferring one master over another.

23. Leon Morris, *The Gospel according to Matthew*, PNTC (Grand Rapids: Eerdmans, 1992), 332.

someone's family of origin, while significant, is not ultimately determinative for their personal identity. Another family belonging takes precedence. As we will see in chapter nine, the identity of being a "Son of God and Child of God" introduces a more important belonging and family likeness.

Age

Who am I? How important to my identity is my age? As I write this sentence, I am fifty-six years old with a birthday next month. At my age, you become more aware of your mortality. I have a few minor abiding aches and pains. I still exercise, but whereas I used to be able to grab a basketball rim, it seems to me that someone has raised the rim. A few years ago, I had a chest-pain scare that, thankfully, proved not to be my heart. But the trip to the hospital in an ambulance got me thinking. Some of my peers are now sadly struggling with serious issues of health. I am beginning to think about retirement, not because I want to stop working (or can afford to), but because some of those a little older than I are retiring or moving toward it.

How about you? How important to your identity is your age?

Typically in our day, children, those in midlife, and those in later life seem to refer to their age when thinking about themselves and describing who they are: "I am three and three quarters"; "I am turning forty"; "I am an octogenarian." There are big individual differences, yet there is no doubt that a person's age at any time can be very significant.

The Bible highlights two age brackets as especially significant for personal identity: youth and old age. *Youth* is a time of vigor, strength, and promise, but also of pressure and temptation. On the one hand, Proverbs 20:29 describes "the glory of young men" as "their strength," and Jeremiah 2:2 speaks of the devotion of youth. The Bible holds numerous examples of godly young men (e.g., David defeating Goliath[24]) and women (e.g., Ruth caring for Naomi[25]). On the other hand, the inexperience of youth is acknowledged.[26] Moreover, 2 Timothy 2:22 speaks of "the evil desires of youth," and Titus 2:6 encourages "young men to be self-controlled." And there are plenty of examples of sinful young men in particular (e.g., the sons of Samuel[27]).

Old age, on the other hand, is seen in the Bible as a blessing from God. It can bring wisdom and discernment, but it also leads to physical decline and diminishing strength. Paul observes that, "outwardly we are wasting away" (2 Cor 4:16). But he

24. 1 Sam 17:33: "Saul replied, 'You are not able to go out against this Philistine and fight him; you are only a young man, and he has been a warrior from his youth.'"

25. Ruth 1:15–16a: "'Look,' said Naomi, 'your sister-in-law is going back to her people and her gods. Go back with her.' But Ruth replied, 'Don't urge me to leave you or to turn back from you. Where you go I will go, and where you stay I will stay.'"

26. E.g., 1 Kgs 3:7: "Now, Lord my God, you have made your servant king in place of my father David. But I am only a little child and do not know how to carry out my duties"; and 1 Tim 4:12a: "Don't let anyone look down on you because you are young."

27. 1 Sam 8:1–3: "When Samuel grew old, he appointed his sons as Israel's leaders. The name of his firstborn was Joel and the name of his second was Abijah, and they served at Beersheba. But his sons did not follow his ways. They turned aside after dishonest gain and accepted bribes and perverted justice."

also appeals to his age to add authority to his words,[28] and in both testaments leaders can be described as "elders" (e.g., Exod 3:16; 1 Tim 5:17). However, old age does not necessarily lead to wisdom,[29] and the reality of failing health and reduced capacities is freely acknowledged.[30] Ecclesiastes 12:1 describes old age as "the days of trouble," in which a person will say, "I find no pleasure in them."

There is no doubt that your age will affect who you are. But age does not determine your personal identity in any definitive sense. Every age brings its opportunities and challenges; you can be a foolish old man or woman or an admirable youth. And for believers in Christ, just as we don't grieve like those who have no hope (see 1 Thess 4:13), we don't age as those who grieve despairingly of their lost capacities.

Ecclesiastes 12:1–5 is an unflattering allegory about the diminished capacities of the aged:

> Remember . . . the days of your youth . . .
> before the sun and the light
> and the moon and the stars grow dark,
> and the clouds return after the rain;
> when the keepers of the house tremble,
> and the strong men stoop,
> when the grinders cease because they are few,
> and those looking through the windows
> grow dim;
> when the doors to the street are closed
> and the sound of grinding fades;
> when people rise up at the sound of birds,
> but all their songs grow faint;
> when people are afraid of heights
> and of dangers in the streets;
> when the almond tree blossoms
> and the grasshopper drags itself along
> and desire no longer is stirred.
> Then people go to their eternal home
> and mourners go about the streets.

Here a person's body is compared to a house, with "trembling keepers" referring to arthritic hands, "strong men stoop[ing]" to feeble legs, "grinders cease" to missing teeth, and "those looking through the windows grow dim" to failing vision. Even if some of the rest of the details are unclear, the poem obviously presents images evoking dread and sorrow as old age encroaches and death awaits, when "mourners go about the streets."

Relationships

Who am I? How important is being married to my identity? As I indicated in the opening pages of this book, having my marriage end back in 1998 struck at the heart of who I thought I was. I'd been married for thirteen years and fully expected my marriage to go the distance. To be suddenly single, and a single parent of three children to boot, changed all sorts of things for me, not least the way I thought about myself and how others related to me. Remarrying some six years later similarly changed my identity again. Becoming a father likewise has changed me permanently. No day goes by without thoughts of my four children. And no one knows me well who does not know of my children and how they are getting on.

How about you? Does your marital status

28. Phlm 9: "I prefer to appeal to you on the basis of love. It is as none other than Paul—an old man and now also a prisoner of Christ Jesus." See also Job 12:12: "Is not wisdom found among the aged? Does not long life bring understanding?" The description of God as "the Ancient of Days" (Dan 7:9; also Rev 1:14: "The hair of his head was white like wool"), one advanced in years, suggests that being aged can bring authority and respectability.

29. See Eccl 4:13: "Better a poor but wise youth than an old but foolish king who no longer knows how to heed a warning."

30. Ps 71:9: "Do not cast me away when I am old; do not forsake me when my strength is gone."

define you? Does having children or not having children affect your identity? How important are such things to how you think about yourself?

While the dowry or "glory box" is long gone for most families in the West, the sentiment remains. Some girls still fantasize about their bridal gowns and weddings. Some boys look forward to sharing their lives with the woman of their dreams. And the desire to have a brood of children, being "clucky," is common to both genders.

People understandably attach great significance to becoming a partner or parent. Getting married and having children inevitably make a lasting change to a person's identity, not least legally. And having children means that you end up with "dependents," who are in some sense an extension of your identity. Big social events commonly mark the transitions, with everything from "buck" or "stag" and "hen" nights, weddings, and honeymoons, to baby showers, christenings, and dedications.

But what if such hopes are never realized? What if Mr. or Mrs. Right fails to show up? What if the marriage ends badly? What happens when your partner dies? And what of those couples, as many as one in six, who struggle with infertility? It is no accident that the old-fashioned description of this condition was "barren," which in other contexts means "bleak." Envy of one's peers, so many of whom seem to be achieving the desired changes in their identity, understandably heightens the sense of dejection.

What does the Bible teach about marriage and singleness? At first blush, the Bible seems to be very positive about marriage. In Genesis 2 the first thing that is said to be imperfect in God's creation is the man's singleness: "It is not good for the man to be alone. I will make a helper suitable for him" (Gen 2:18). With no suitable helper to be found, God creates "woman," who is taken out of Adam's flesh (2:22–23), and is then united with Adam in marriage, becoming "one flesh" with him (2:24). In Genesis 1:28, having created a man and a woman, "God blessed them and said to them, 'Be fruitful and increase in number.'" As "People of the Book" in New Testament times, "mainstream Jewish society regarded marriage and childbearing as solemn responsibilities."[31]

In our day, many people desire to be married or to be in a relationship with someone. And being sexually inactive is seen as undesirable and even unhealthy.

However, the Bible's teaching about marriage is less positive than might first appear. Genesis 2:18 does not in fact concern Adam's loneliness but rather his taking on the task of tending the garden on his own. The context of it not being good for Adam to be alone is verse 15: "The Lord God took the man and put him in the Garden of Eden

> "It is a truth universally acknowledged, that a single man in possession of a good fortune must be in want of a wife."
>
> *Jane Austen*[32]

31. Keener, *Gospel of Matthew*, 469–72.

32. Jane Austen, *Pride and Prejudice* (New York: Charles Scribner, 1918), 1.

to work it and take care of it." The job of working and keeping the garden is too big for Adam by himself. Eve may relieve Adam's loneliness, but that is not the point. In Genesis 2:20, the woman is his "helper" or "partner," one who works alongside, not primarily his companion.[33]

When it comes to the New Testament, Jesus himself was not married. And Paul saw advantages in singleness and encouraged the Christians in Corinth to stay single: the one who gets married does right, but the one who does not marry does better (1 Cor 7:38).[34]

Most significant for our purposes is Paul's shocking advice to married men in 1 Corinthians 7:29b: "*Those who have wives should live as if they do not.*" This verse must be read in context to grasp what Paul is saying. It is not an instruction to neglect your marriage or to stop sleeping with your spouse, let alone get divorced. Rather, Paul aims to downgrade the importance of whether you are married or not in the light of the glorious future that awaits all believers in Christ: for "the time is short" (v. 29) and "this world in its present form is passing away" (v. 31). As Jesus pointed out, marriage will play no part in the age to come (Matt 22:30). We will return to 1 Corinthians 7:29–31 in chapter ten with respect to the way in which our "Defining Destiny" affects our identity now. Suffice to say at this point, Paul is urging those who are married, and those who are single for that matter, not to define themselves by their marital status.

Occupation

Who am I? How important to my identity is my work? If you include summer jobs as a student, I have racked up my share of work experience: factory worker, storeman and packer, electrician's offsider, management trainee in the railway, university lecturer, high school teacher, theological college lecturer, and principal/president of a theological college. All of my jobs have had their joys and challenges. And all of them affected how people seemed to think of and respond to me. Work has always been a big part of my life and who I am.

Perhaps more so than at other times in history, what you do is often equated with who you are. An advertisement for a university law degree asked, "*Who* do you want to be?" rather than, "*What* do you want to be?" Indeed, many people define themselves chiefly by their work.

Who are you? How important to your identity is your work? Do you describe who you are to others in terms of your work?

It is true that what someone "does" can tell you something about them. Whether you're a teacher or a mechanic or a hairdresser or an accountant or a lawyer or a retail worker or a doctor might say something about your aptitudes, your diligence, your opportunities, your parents, your income, your

33. See Christopher Ash, *Married for God: Making Your Marriage the Best It Can Be* (Nottingham, UK: Inter-Varsity Press, 2007), 35–36.

34. See also Matt 19:12: "There are those who choose to live like eunuchs for the sake of the kingdom of heaven."

lifestyle, your values, and so on. Certainly, involuntary unemployment can take a toll on how people perceive themselves and how others perceive them.

Some jobs evoke a certain stereotype that may or may not be true. Most are not complimentary: accountants are boring; engineers don't read books; pool cleaners are flirtatious; used-car salesmen are dishonest. And even within an occupation will be those who work sensible hours and maintain a work/life balance and those who overwork to their own cost.[35]

How important is work to a person's identity according to the Bible? In the Bible, work, broadly defined, is closely related to what it means to be a human being. Genesis 1:26 connects humans working to being made in the image of God: "God said, 'Let us make mankind in our image, in our likeness, *so that* they may rule over the fish in the sea and the birds in the sky, over the livestock and all the wild animals, and over all the creatures that move along the ground.'" As the narrative of Genesis 2 proceeds, Adam and Eve engage in the cultivation of the earth (vv. 5, 15) and the classification of the species of wildlife (v. 20). While the fall rendered work more arduous and frustrating (3:17–19; cf. 5:29), work is still generally regarded as part of the normal rhythm of life:

> He made the moon to mark the seasons,
> and the sun knows when to go down.
> You bring darkness, it becomes night,
> and all the beasts of the forest prowl.
> The lions roar for their prey
> and seek their food from God.
> The sun rises, and they steal away;
> they return and lie down in their dens.
> *Then people go out to their work,*
> *to their labor until evening.* (Ps 104:19–23)

Still, layoff and retirement suggest that making work central to your identity is a bad idea. Putting the word "former" before your occupation when describing yourself drains away a good portion of its significance. And death ultimately robs us of the fruits of our labors.

Your job can only tell so much about who you are. If in 1 Corinthians 7 with poetic license Paul advised the married to live as if they were not married (v. 29; see discussion above), he can also say, "[let] those who deal with the world [live] as if

The Bible mentions a wide range of occupations: Along with prophets, priests, and kings and queens, there are builders, soldiers, merchants, engravers, blacksmiths, gem cutters, bodyguards, cooks, butchers, executioners, chariot drivers, hunters, jailers, grape pickers, tentmakers, idol makers, horsemen, musicians, innkeepers, bankers, messengers, stonemasons, landowners, carpenters, embroiderers, scribes, weavers, gardeners, bakers, ambassadors, midwives, athletes, goldsmiths, perfumers, preachers, interpreters, moneylenders, poets, philosophers, sheepshearers, treasurers, water carriers, writers, stewards, spies, prostitutes, launderers, shepherds, farmers, fishermen, doctors, linen workers, servants, lawyers, and tax collectors.

35. See Exod 18:17–18; Ps 127:2; Luke 10:41–42; 12:15–21.

they had no dealings with it" (v. 31 NRSV). There is something more important to your identity than your job.

Possessions

Who am I? How important to my identity are my possessions? I grew up in a working class area. We were not poor, but by Sydney standards most other regions were more affluent. I remember going to university and being somewhat nonplussed by the importance some of my fellow students attached to where they lived, the school they attended, and the car they drove in describing themselves. It wasn't until I got married and our second child was on the way that buying a house became a priority.

I've also had my ups and downs in the area of possessions. When I was in my late forties, the company behind a major investment that I had taken out to help pay off my mortgage went bust; I ended up having to sell my house. Currently I am doing better financially. While enjoying a nice meal and a good holiday when we can afford it, I still have no interest in luxury cars.

"It's not your hair. It's not your income. It's not your music, it's your watch that tells most about *who you are.*"
Seiko Advertisement

How about you? Who are you? How important to your identity are your possessions?

Much of our lives is spent earning money and acquiring our belongings: what we wear, where we live, the car we drive, and so on. Peter Leithart explains how the materialism of our age teaches us to define ourselves by our possessions:

> In a consumer society, the good life is defined by the goods I am able to afford. I am defined by what I'm able to afford. I'm identified by what I buy, and the continuity of my personal identity is a continuity of lifestyle, forged by frequent visits to the mall and to online catalogs.[36]

> In a consumer culture, *people gain their identity and significance through what they purchase and own.*[37]

What does the Bible teach about the place of possessions in relation to personal identity? First of all, the Bible affirms the goodness of creation. It also opposes the dualism whereby material things are considered evil and spiritual things good. In 1 Corinthians 10:26 Paul cites Psalm 24:1 to explain why Christians should feel free to eat any food without having to know whether it had been sacrificed to an idol: "The earth is the Lord's, and everything in it." Material things are not evil; on the contrary, they belong to God! The idea that creation is good and the material things that God provides should be received with thanksgiving is a thoroughly biblical one.

36. Peter J. Leithart, *Solomon Among the Postmoderns* (Grand Rapids: Brazos, 2008), 120.

37. Ibid., 140 (emphasis added).

There is nothing wrong with cars, clothes, and condominiums in and of themselves. Indeed, 1 Timothy 6:17 affirms that God "richly provides us with everything for our enjoyment."

However, the Bible also warns of the dangers of wealth. Jesus famously cautioned against loving, trusting, and serving wealth instead of God: "You cannot serve both God and money" (Matt 6:24). And Paul condemned greed as an insidious form of idolatry (Eph 5:5; Col 3:5).[38] Both also underscored the uncertainty of money and possessions: Jesus warns that moths eat them and rust destroys them, and thieves break in and steal them (Matt 6:19); and Paul warns the rich not "to put their hope in wealth, which is so uncertain" (1 Tim 6:17).

An advertisement for a luxury condominium/apartment complex reads: "Define Yourself."

With reference to the importance of material things for personal identity, Jesus concluded that there are more important things in your life than your possessions: "Is not life more than food, and the body more than clothes?" (Matt 6:25b; cf. Luke 12:15).[39] Rather than running after such things, like those who do not know God are prone to do (Matt 6:32), Jesus says run after (or "seek") first God's kingdom and righteousness (Matt 6:33). Paul similarly counsels "those who are rich in this present world" to be "rich in good deeds" and to "take hold of the life that is truly life" (1 Tim 6:17–19). Returning to 1 Corinthians 7 once more, Paul says with full rhetorical force, "[let] those who buy something, [live] as if it were not theirs to keep" (v. 30).

Belonging to the kingdom of God and possessing eternal life are of much greater importance for your identity than your belongings and possessions.

In the cult science fiction film *The Matrix* (1999; The Wachowskis), the matrix is an elaborate facade created by a malevolent cyber-intelligence that symbolizes the material world. It has everyone in its thrall, except a small band of freedom fighters. Hoping to win over Neo (played by Keanu Reeves) to the cause, a mysterious woman named Trinity (Carrie-Anne Moss) gives him this sage advice: "The matrix cannot tell you who you are." Such advice is also apropos to us.

Religion

Who am I? How important to my personal identity is my religion? I was brought up in a Christian home but kind of sat on the fence during my high school years. It's certainly possible to identify as a Christian but not have it make much difference to your identity. It wasn't until my days as a university student that faith in God took hold of my life.

How about you? How important to your identity is your religion?

Even if organized religion is in decline in many parts of the Western world, and nominalism is rife, for many people religion remains a major factor in their personal

38. See Brian S. Rosner, *Greed as Idolatry: The Origin and Meaning of a Pauline Metaphor* (Grand Rapids: Eerdmans, 2007) and *Beyond Greed* (Waterloo, Australia: Matthias Media, 2004).

39. The word "life" in Matt 6:25 is the Greek *psychē*, often translated "soul" (see chapter four on such terms as they relate to the constitution of human beings). Here it means "the condition of being alive, life itself" (BDAG 1098 [1.b]).

identity. Most government census forms have a box to fill in for religious adherence. Even non-religious people can identify themselves by their non-belief in God.

What does the Bible teach about religion in relation to personal identity? Obviously a book about the Bible's teaching about personal identity will focus on the role of religion, and in one sense this whole book is about how faith in God helps to answer the question, who am I? Still, it is worth noting that the Bible can be quite negative about religion. Religion in itself is not automatically a good thing and does not necessarily lead to a healthy sense of self.

"Christianity isn't exactly a 'religion' in the sense people mean today; it's much bigger than that, much more all-embracing."
N. T. Wright[40]

The Bible is not only critical of "false religion," idolatry, but also of false worship of the true and living God. In the New Testament, words commonly translated "religion" are rarely used in a positive sense. James 1:26 warns of religion that is "worthless." Paul in 1 Timothy 5:4 insists that people must "put their religion into practice." In 2 Timothy 3:5, he cautions against holding "to the outward form of our religion" (GNT), but rejecting "its real power." And in Colossians 2:23, he speaks of religion that is merely "self-made" (NASB). Thus to identify as the adherent of a religion, even the Christian religion, does not necessarily define you positively.

"Religion is a blend of identity, symbol, purpose, behaviour, community and hope."
Michael Bird[41]

"Religion and nationality are but two of the myriad dimensions along which our personal identities are constructed. As human beings, we realize that instinctively. When someone holds open a closing door so we can board an elevator, the component of their identity we value is not that they are Muslim, or American, but rather that they are compassionate. It is when we are frightened, and especially when our fears are played up and redirected and preyed upon, that we tend to reduce others to simplified (and artificial) mono-identities of religion or nationality or race."
Moshin Hamid[42]

Personality and Character

Who am I in terms of my personality and character? When it comes to male stereotypes, I reckon I fall somewhat uncomfortably between rugged individualist and sensitive/urbane. And I don't do either that convincingly. Having said that, others are probably in a better position to judge my enduring personality traits and patterns of behavior.

How about you? How important are your personality and character to your identity?

The Bible has much to say about the personalities of the lives it narrates and the character of certain peoples and individuals. King Saul is paranoid, Queen Esther courageous. Joshua is brave, Samson gullible. Jonah is mean-spirited, Peter tempestuous. Delilah is devious, Ruth loyal. And the main divisions of humanity according to the Bible often refer to character traits; "the righteous" and "the wicked" being the most common and obvious.

40. N. T. Wright, *Revelation for Everyone* (Louisville: Westminster John Knox, 2011), 15.

41. Michael Bird, "Whose Religion? Which Secularism? Australia has a Serious Religious Literacy Problem," *ABC Religion and Ethics*, September 23, 2015, www.abc.net.au/religion/articles/2015/09/23/4318349.htm.

42. Hamid, *Discontent and Its Civilizations*, 92.

However, to say that our personalities and characters are core to our identities is potentially misleading. Your personality and character are an expression of your identity; your true identity is prior to and more stable than your personality and character. After all, someone's personality and character can be changed as they grow older and, among other factors, by circumstances, illness, and medication.

THE DANGER OF IDOLATRY

At the end of the day, it is not only that these foundations of personal identity are inadequate; they are also unsafe and can collapse under their own weight. The problem with building your life on the standard identity markers is that such behavior can lead to idolatry.

Timothy Keller is representative of this view: "Our need for worth is so powerful that whatever we base our identity and value on we essentially 'deify.'"[43] According to Keller, "the human heart" is an "idol factory" that takes good things like a successful career, love, material possessions, and even family and makes them the ultimate things in our lives. This, then, leads to worshipping false gods: "Our hearts deify them as the center of our lives, because, we think, they can give us significance and security, safety and fulfillment, if we attain them."[44] But are such claims overblown? What is idolatry and is it really a danger in these circumstances?

In the Bible there is no more serious charge than that of idolatry: "the central theological principle in the Bible is the refutation of idolatry."[45] Both disdainful polemic and extreme measures of avoidance are directed against idolatry at many points. Idolatry also plays a central role in the Bible's overarching narrative; the history of Israel is the story of the nation's struggle with idolatry, not only in the promised land, but also in exile and in the postexilic period. The new covenant promises of Isaiah and Ezekiel envision the removal of Israel's idols (e.g., Ezek 36:26–36). In the New Testament those who continue to worship idols are excluded from the kingdom of God (1 Cor 6:9–11).

Along with the literal sense of worshipping foreign gods, the concept of idolatry has the capacity for an extended or figurative meaning that makes it fruitful in a range of contexts. The condemnation of greed as idolatry (Eph 5:5; Col 3:5; cf. Matt 6:24) is the clearest example. Idolatry in this sense refers to putting something in the place of God, trusting something instead of God, and loving something more than God.[46]

Idolatry is effectively a confusion of creation with the Creator or the attribution of ultimate value to anything other than God. Hence it is a danger whenever we forget

43. Keller, *Reason for God*, 163.

44. Timothy Keller, *Counterfeit Gods: The Empty Promises of Money, Sex, and Power and the Only Hope that Matters* (New York: Penguin, 2009), xiv.

45. Moshe Halbertal and Avishai Margalit, *Idolatry* (Cambridge: Harvard University Press, 1992), 10.

46. See Rosner, *Greed as Idolatry*.

that we are created beings. Romans 1:23 makes this clear: "[they] exchanged the glory of the immortal God for images made to look like a mortal human being and birds and animals and reptiles." Reinhold Niebuhr argues that when someone refuses to acknowledge their need for self-transcendence, they are in danger of replacing God with that which is finite and contingent.[48] Idolatry occurs when we treat something other than God as ultimate. It is in this sense that the charge of idolatry may be properly applied to making a marker of identity the all-important thing in our lives. Inevitably, we build our sense of self, our value and worth, on something. If it is anything other than God, then we are guilty of idolatry.

"What does it mean to have a god? What is God? My answer is: A god is whatever a person looks to for all good things and runs to for help in trouble.... As I've often said, it's only the trust and faith in your heart which make them both what they are—God and an idol."

Martin Luther, Large Catechism[47]

Two of the ways in which the Bible critiques idolatry are especially relevant to the temptation of defining ourselves without reference to God. First, *idols are gods that fail.*[49] The prophet asks rhetorically, "Of what value is an idol?" (Hab 2:18–19). The main premise of the biblical injunction against idolatry is that idols are ineffectual. Idol worship leads only to the disappointment and embarrassment of those who trust in them. Many pagans believed that certain benefits like fertility, rain, health, and guidance for certain decisions resulted from worshipping idols. Correspondingly, Old Testament idol polemic declares the powerlessness and deceptive nature of idolatry.[50] In Jeremiah 16:19, for instance, idols are described as "worthless things in which there is no profit" (ESV). The same theme continues in the New Testament; Paul condemns idolatry as foolish and futile (Rom 1:21–23) and idols as "lifeless" (1 Cor 12:2 GNT). These insights have obvious implications for the extended senses of idolatry as well. Indeed, one problem with deifying our work, wealth, or relationships is that ultimately they fail to deliver on their promise to give us the lasting sense of significance, security, and satisfaction that each of us craves.

A second problem is that idols are *gods that degrade their worshipers*. It is not just that they lead to disappointment; idols also do us serious harm. This result is based on the universal principle that we become what we worship: "Those who make [idols] will be like them, and so will all who trust in them" (Ps 135:18).[51] Just as idols have "eyes, but cannot see" and "ears, but cannot hear" (Ps 135:16–17), so those who worship them become spiritually blind and deaf as part of God's disciplinary punishment; "what you revere, you resemble, either for ruin or restoration."[52] The same

47. Martin Luther, *Luther's Large Catechism*, translated with introductory essay by Friedemann Hebart (Adelaide, Australia: Lutheran, 1983), 18.

48. Reinhold Niebuhr, *The Nature and Destiny of Man: A Christian Interpretation* (Louisville: Westminster John Knox, 1996), 178.

49. See Vinoth Ramachandra, *Gods that Fail: Modern Idolatry and Christian Mission* (Downers Grove, IL: InterVarsity Press, 1996).

50. The main examples include Pss 115:4–8; 135:15–18; the words of Elijah (1 Kgs 18:27); the prayer of Hezekiah (2 Kgs 19:16–19); and especially the prophets (Isa 41:23–24; 44:9–20; Jer 10:3–4; 14:22; Hos 8:4–6).

51. See G. K. Beale, *We Become What We Worship: A Biblical Theology of Idolatry* (Downers Grove, IL: InterVarsity Press, 2008).

52. Beale, *We Become What We Worship*, 11.

judgment of the "hardening of the heart" can be traced across the New Testament. In Revelation 9:20–21, for instance, idolatrous unbelievers are anaesthetized with spiritual insensitivity, conforming to their lifeless idols.

This is sobering teaching, and we must be careful not to apply it in too exaggerated a fashion. The Bible's polemic has a tendency to present things in absolute terms. The outcome of our lives is not always apparent. And common grace means that God saves many of us from the worst effects of even our own sin. Nonetheless, human beings by nature are inexorably drawn to worship one thing or another. The possibility of idolatry occurring by making one of the markers of personal identity into the main thing is real, and the potential consequences are devastating. Insecure foundations can lead to catastrophic collapse.

"Receiving one's identity from one's God, through a story that one hears, is different from determining one's own identity through idols that the worshiper has created and therefore controls."
Michael Horton[53]

Timothy Keller points to the dangers of defining yourself in terms of your work or family or possessions or even relationships:

- If you build your life and identity on your spouse or partner, you will be emotionally dependent, jealous, and controlling. The other person's problems will be overwhelming to you.
- If you build your life and identity on your family and children, you will try to live your life through your children until they resent you or have no self of their own. At worst, you may abuse them when they displease you.
- If you build your life and identity on your work and career, you will be a driven workaholic and a boring, shallow person. At worst, you will lose family and friends and, if your career goes poorly, develop deep depression.
- If you build your life and identity on money and possessions, you'll be eaten up by worry or jealousy about money. You'll be willing to do unethical things to maintain your lifestyle, which will eventually blow up your life.
- If you build your life and identity on relationships and approval, you will be constantly overly hurt by criticism and thus always losing friends. You will fear confronting others and therefore be a useless friend.[54]

THE FOUNDATIONS OF PERSONAL IDENTITY

The Bible judges the traditional identity markers to be inadequate foundations upon which to build your personal identity and even warns about putting too much weight on them. To recall a couple of the more striking texts, according to Galatians 3:28,

53. Michael Horton, *The Christian Faith: A Systematic Theology for Pilgrims on the Way* (Grand Rapids: Zondervan, 2011), 87.

54. Keller, *Reason for God*, 275–76. This is an abbreviated list. In addition, I have substituted the word "build" for "center" as the third word in each dot point in keeping with the main metaphor of this chapter.

you are more than your race, ethnicity, nationality, culture, and gender, for in Christ Jesus "there is neither Jew nor Gentile, neither slave nor free, nor is there male and female, for you are all one in Christ Jesus."[55] And according to 1 Corinthians 7:29–31, you are more than your marital status, occupation, and possessions, and there is a sense in which you should "live as if you were not married, had no dealings with the world, and did not take full possession of anything that you own."[56]

While the standard markers of identity remain essential for personal identity, they are not the whole story. Ultimately the Bible points to their limitations and questions their sufficiency. Your core identity, which as we will see in later chapters is in one sense a secret identity, is found elsewhere. The traditional identity markers are all important, but none of them is all-important.

A key feature of the Bible's perspective on personal identity is not to regard other people "by what they seem to be" (2 Cor 5:16 CEV), but to consider them from God's point of view. This also goes for how we regard ourselves. It is to this alternative view of human identity that we now turn. The first step will be to consider not who we are, but what we are. What is a human being, anyway?

RELEVANT QUESTIONS

1. How do you introduce yourself? What do you think is important for others to know about you? How does this reflect the way you define yourself?
2. Have you ever had an "identity crisis" or an experience that caused you to question your sense of self? How did this impact your life? Do you live differently because of this?
3. Some traditional markers of identity such as possessions, relationships, and occupation require effort to achieve and maintain. What identity markers are most valued and sought after in your community?
4. Timothy Keller argues that the human heart is an "idol factory" and that human beings are by nature inexorably drawn to worship one thing or another. Do you agree or disagree? In your own life, have you ever felt in danger of being captivated by an "idol" that gave you significance, security, or fulfillment?

55. See also Col 3:11: "Here there is no Gentile or Jew, circumcised or uncircumcised, barbarian, Scythian, slave or free, but Christ is all, and is in all."

56. My own translation.

CHAPTER 4

HUMAN BEINGS ACCORDING TO THE BIBLE

If the rise in gym memberships, cosmetic surgery, the "selfie," body image issues, and eating disorders are anything to go by, the modern world is obsessed with the body. Magazines, newspapers, and advertising are awash with examples of supposedly perfect bodies, most of which have been heavily photoshopped and airbrushed and don't actually exist. And any celebrity who puts on a bit of weight ought to watch out; publication of photos from every conceivable angle are sure to follow.

American actress Jennifer Aniston recently responded to the umpteenth occasion on which she was reported as being pregnant:

> For the record, I am *not* pregnant. What I am is *fed up*. I'm fed up with the sport-like scrutiny and body shaming that occurs daily under the guise of 'journalism,' the 'First Amendment' and 'celebrity news.'. . . If I am some kind of symbol to some people out there, then clearly I am an example of the lens through which we, as a society, view our mothers, daughters, sisters, wives, female friends and colleagues. The objectification and scrutiny we put women through is absurd and disturbing. The way I am portrayed by the media is simply a reflection of how we see and portray women in general, measured against some warped standard of beauty.[1]

Whereas in the past you might see just a few dozen people during your daily activities, these days we are confronted with hundreds of images of beautiful people every day, the vast majority of which are better looking than ourselves. Unsurprisingly, psychiatrists report an alarming rise in body dysmorphic disorder, a condition where people become obsessed with a perceived flaw in their appearance.

Is there more to you than your body? Of what do we consist?

In this and the next chapter, we seek to answer the most basic questions about human beings as a species. What is a human being? What is our constitution? What is our origin? And how are we connected to God?

We begin by looking at the terms the Bible uses to describe us, the so-called

1. Jennifer Aniston, "For the Record," huffingtonpost.com, July 12, 2016, http://www.huffingtonpost.com/entry/for-the-record_us_57855586e4b03fc3ee4e626f.

anthropological terms, in order to examine our essence, limitations, and potential. Then we shall study the opening chapters of the book of Genesis, again considering what these chapters reveal about what it is to be a human being. In chapter five, we will look at what it means for human beings to be made in the image and likeness of God and what we can learn about personal identity from Adam and Eve's transgression in the garden.

THE HUMAN CONSTITUTION

The human constitution is one of those subjects that the Bible treats almost everywhere in passing but nowhere in depth. In the Bible the various aspects of the human constitution are more presupposition and worldview than topic for discussion. Nonetheless, understanding *what we are* is a vital part of our enquiry, and there is much to learn about personal identity from the ways in which the Bible describes us, particularly the anthropological terms it uses.

Old Testament Usage: Made from Dust; Living Beings

What do we learn from the creation narratives about what constitutes a human being?

Genesis 2:7 is the first verse in the Bible to shed any light on this question:

> And the LORD God formed man of the dust of the ground, and breathed into his nostrils the breath of life; and man became a living soul. (KJV)

Apparently we are made of "dust" and have a "soul." While the first reminds us of our connection with everything else on earth, the latter distinguishes us from every other living thing. Or does it?

The use of the word "dust" emphasizes both our physical frailty and the fact that we come from the "ground" and will return to "dust." Kenneth Mathews offers a helpful summary of the significance of being made from dust:

> God is depicted as the potter who forms Israel (Isa 64:8; Jer 18:6; cp. Sir 33:13; Rom 9:20). "Dust" as constitutive of human existence anticipates [Gen] 3:19, where the penalty for the man's sin is his return to "dust" (e.g., Job 34:15). While "dust" may also show that man is fragile physically (e.g., Job 10:8–9; Ps 103:14), the intent of the passage is the association of human life and the basic substance of our making. A play on the words "man" (*'ādām*) and "ground" (*'ădāmâ*) becomes apparent: man is related to the "ground" by his very constitution (3:19), making him perfectly suited for the task of working the "ground," which is required for cultivation (2:5, 15).[2]

2. Kenneth A. Mathews, *Genesis 1–11:26*, NAC 1A (Nashville: Broadman & Holman, 1996), 196.

What are we to make of the idea of the man becoming "a living soul"?

In terms of the human constitution, Genesis 1–2 (and indeed the Old Testament in general) suggest that a human being is a unified whole.[3] As Philip Johnston contends, "it is a mistake to think of the soul as some metaphysical part of us that is separate from our bodies. Indeed the traditional translation of 'soul' is misleading [in texts such as Gen 2:7], since this has connotations of a (later) dualism."[4] The idea of a bodiless soul is a Hellenistic one that turns up in the New Testament period in Jewish authors such as Philo. It is indebted to Plato rather than to the Bible.

"I find the soul a valuable concept, a statement of the dignity of a human life and of the unutterable gravity of human action and experience. I would add that I find my own soul interesting company, if this did not seem to cast doubt on my impeccable objectivity."

Marilynne Robinson[6]

The word translated "soul" is *nephesh* in Hebrew.[5] In Genesis 2:7 most modern English versions, including the NIV (and NKJV), translate the sentence in question as, "the man became a living *being*." *Nephesh* in this verse refers to the whole person and not to some immaterial part of us.[7] As Mathews writes: "In our passage man does not possess a *nepeš* [*nephesh*] but rather *is* a *nepeš* (individual person); 'breath,' not 'soul,' comes closest to the idea of a transcendent life force in man."[8] As it turns out, Genesis also declares that animals are "living creatures" (*nephesh khayya*; 1:20–21, 24; 9:10), using the same language as in Genesis 2:7.

Clearly, the term "soul" does not exhaust the Bible's treatment of our distinctive place in God's creation. The Old Testament uses several other terms to refer to different aspects of human beings, such as "spirit," which is often associated with the capacity for thought,[9] "heart," which is connected with thought and will,[10] and the "liver," "kidneys," and "bowels," which are frequently linked to the emotions.

New Testament Usage: Anthropological Terms in Paul's Letters

What about the New Testament? Does it present humans as being composed of various parts? While the evidence is spread across the New Testament, the letters of Paul are arguably the best texts to answer these questions.[11]

In the following sections we consider seven of the most important anthropological

3. See Philip S. Johnston, "Humanity," in *New Dictionary of Biblical Theology*, ed. T. D. Alexander and B. S. Rosner (Downers Grove, IL: InterVarsity Press, 2000), 564.

4. Johnston, "Humanity," 564.

5. The word *nephesh* is defined in a major Hebrew lexicon (BDB) as "that which breathes, the breathing substance or being, the inner being of man" and is translated by the words "soul, living being, life, self, person."

6. Marilynne Robinson, *The Givenness of Things: Essays* (New York: Farrar, Straus and Giroux, 2015), 9.

7. See also Gen 9:5: "From each human being, too, I will demand an accounting for the life [*nephesh*] of another human being [*adam*]."

8. Mathews, *Genesis 1–11:26*, 197.

9. E.g., Isa 29:24: "Those who are wayward in *spirit* will gain understanding."

10. E.g., Gen 6:5: "The Lord saw how great the wickedness of the human race had become on the earth, and that every inclination of the thoughts of the human *heart* was only evil all the time."

11. Cf. 1 Thess 5:23: "May your whole spirit, soul and body be kept blameless at the coming of our Lord Jesus Christ."

terms in Paul's letters: body, flesh, soul, spirit, mind, heart, and inner being.[13] In line with the Old Testament's anthropology, these are best understood as aspects of a human being rather than parts of a human being. They represent human existence viewed from different angles. Or to put it another way, they refer to the different dimensions in which we function as human beings in God's world.

"I know that little boys are made of frogs and snails and puppy dogs' tails. I know that little girls are made of sugar and spice and all things nice. But what are people *really* made of concerning their material and immaterial constitution?"
Michael Bird[12]

In what follows I will attempt to summarize the usage of these anthropological terms and briefly fill out the nuances of their meanings. The first six key terms are best considered in pairs: body and flesh, mind and heart, and soul and spirit. While these terms throw up many interpretive issues, I shall concentrate on what they tell us about human beings.

Six of Paul's anthropological terms appear in current English usage: (1) "body" and (2) "flesh" refer to the physical substance of a human being; (3) "soul" has a wide range of meaning, denoting everything from the immaterial part of human beings to someone acting with warmth of feeling or bravery; (4) "spirit" signifies the immaterial part of human beings or the typical quality or attitude of a person or group; (5) "mind" is a term for the human intellect or understanding; and (6) "heart" has the figurative sense of having a capacity for sympathy or courage.

Body and Flesh

Not just in our day has society been obsessed with bodily appearance. In the Greco-Roman world there was a widespread view that a perfect exterior was a reflection of an inner perfection. The beautiful were in many contexts equated with the good. What it meant to be beautiful was of course different from our day. In ancient Greece, for example, a beautiful woman was a full-figured redhead. And a beautiful man's face was full-lipped and with high cheekbones.

Where does the body fit in Paul's worldview? Paul uses the Greek term *sōma* to describe the body, although the "body" for Paul is more than simply the physical body. By *sōma* Paul refers to human life viewed from the physical. It is not so much that we have a body, but that we are embodied.[14] *Sōma* is primarily a relational concept. It denotes the person embodied in a particular environment, the means by which the person relates to that environment, and the means of living in and experiencing that environment. Paul sees us as embodied and therefore social beings, defined in part by our social interdependence and responsibility.

That Paul can refer to the whole person with the term "body," and not to some part, is clear from 1 Corinthians 6:19 where he uses the second person pronoun "you" and "body" interchangeably: "Do you not know that *your bodies* are temples of the Holy Spirit, who is in *you*, whom you have received from God?" Similarly,

12. Michael F. Bird, *Evangelical Theology: A Biblical and Systematic Introduction* (Grand Rapids: Zondervan, 2013), 662.

13. The following discussion builds on the excellent summary of Paul's anthropology in James D. G. Dunn, *The Theology of Paul the Apostle* (Edinburgh: T&T Clark, 1998), 51–78. Dunn does not cover "inner being."

14. Paul never uses *sōma* for the human corpse.

when Paul writes to the Christians in Rome "to offer *your bodies* as a living sacrifice" (Rom 12:1), he is telling them to offer themselves. The parallel in Romans 6:13 makes this clear, where he exhorts them to "offer *yourselves* to God" (HCSB). Likewise, when Paul writes of his desire that "Christ will be exalted in my body" (Phil 1:20), "we can hardly think that Paul wanted to glorify Christ through only part of his existence, the body as a subset of his whole being."[15]

The body also has a firm place in the age to come. In 1 Corinthians 15:35–44, where *sōma* occurs nine times, Paul admits that his present bodily existence is unfit for the kingdom of God. But he does not envisage a bodiless existence in the eternal state, but rather a new body suited to the age of the Spirit. Paul's conception of this new, resurrection body of believers ultimately owes its origin to the resurrected Christ, the "life-giving spirit" (15:45), "the heavenly man," to whose "image" believers will conform (15:49).[16]

Paul cannot conceive of a satisfactory human existence without a body. In 2 Corinthians 5:1 he writes, "For we know that if the earthly tent we live in is destroyed, we have a building from God, an eternal house in heaven, not built by human hands."

Moving to a second and related Greek word, the "flesh" for Paul, *sarx* is a controversial term with a wide range of meanings, and it is variously translated. For example, in Romans alone the NIV renders *sarx* as "earthly life" (1:3), "physical" (2:28), "one" (as in "no one," 3:20), "flesh" (4:1; 7:5; 8:3–6, etc.), "human limitations" (6:19), "sinful nature" (7:18), "race" (9:3), and "human ancestry" (9:5). The usage of *sarx* in Paul's letters covers a range of meanings:

The spectrum of meaning of "flesh" runs from human needs, through human weakness and desires, through human imperfection and corruption, to human sin and rebellion against God. The common link between all these uses is the idea of human frailty and mortality. Like his use of *sōma*, Paul uses *sarx* to denote the whole person but from the point of view of our frailty and weakness and our vulnerability to destructive desires.

How do *sōma*, "body," and *sarx*, "flesh," relate to each other? The main difference is that while *sōma* is most often morally neutral, in many cases *sarx* is morally negative.[17]

What is a human being? We are embodied beings, *sōma*, and are therefore social, defined in part by social interdependence and responsibility. And we are also fleshly, *sarx*, that is, frail and weak beings, conditioned by the inevitability of our death and

15. Dunn, *Theology of Paul the Apostle*, 59.

16. Paul makes the same connection elsewhere: at the second coming of Christ "the Lord Jesus Christ . . . will transform our lowly bodies so that they will be *like his glorious body*" (Phil 3:20–21); and "we will certainly also be united with him in a resurrection *like his*" (Rom 6:5b; see also 6:8b). Christ, the eschatological Adam, is the founder of a new and better humanity with new bodies. It is thus no coincidence that the words Paul uses to describe believers' resurrection are roughly the same as when he speaks of the resurrection of Christ. Indeed, some of Paul's key ideas about the resurrection body in 1 Cor 15 can be plausibly seen to derive from the prototypical resurrection of Jesus; specifically, what Paul has to say about the power, glory, and spiritual nature of the resurrection body.

17. Romans 8:13 illustrates well this relationship: "If you live

driven by our desires, many of which are sinful. The recognition that we are embodied and also fleshly runs up against our culture's worship of youth and beauty on the one hand, and its idolizing power and perfection on the other.

"Flesh" / *Sarx* =

NEUTRAL

– The physical body / physical relationships

"I take pride in my ministry in the hope that I may somehow arouse my own people [lit. those who are my flesh] to envy and save some of them" (Rom 11:13–14)

– Mortality, subject to affliction and weakness

"For we who are alive are always being given over to death for Jesus' sake, so that his life may also be revealed in our mortal body [lit. mortal flesh]" (2 Cor 4:11)

– Human weakness in contrast to the power of God

"[God] was pleased to reveal his Son in me so that I might preach him among the Gentiles, my immediate response was not to consult any human being [lit. flesh and blood]" (Gal 1:15–16)

– The sphere of sin's operations

"For I know that good itself does not dwell in me, that is, in my sinful nature [lit. my flesh]" (Rom 7:18)

– Source of corruption and hostility to God

"Those who belong to Christ Jesus have crucified the flesh with its passions and desires" (Gal 5:24)

NEGATIVE

according to the flesh, you will die; but if by the Spirit you put to death the misdeeds of the body, you will live." Note that when *sōma* is used negatively, it is usually combined in a phrase or given an adjective, as in "the body of sin" and "the body of this death." *Sarx*, on the other hand, regularly takes a more negative nuance without any qualification. Interestingly, Col 1:22 and 2:11–12 ESV uses Christ's "body of flesh" to indicate the physical nature of Jesus's bodily death. If in 1 Cor 15 "*flesh* and blood cannot inherit the kingdom of God" (15:50), a "body" certainly will (15:44). Bodies will be transformed and raised from the dead after the pattern of Jesus's own bodily resurrection. Flesh belongs to this world, bodies to this and the next.

The Bible provides a much more realistic assessment of the human condition. As *sōma* and *sarx*, imperfection and weakness are the norm for most of us much of the time, and all of us in the end. To pretend otherwise is to ignore the sick and the weary and the inevitable process of aging. It also puts an enormous strain on maintaining a "shiny" appearance, which over the long term is simply impossible. Failing to acknowledge our frailty will also damage our relationships; flesh and blood can never consistently satisfy our needs. The trend in our day to dispose of relationships when they are not meeting our needs is effectively a denial of the reality of the physical and moral weakness of all human beings. No one satisfies fully the needs of another.

"A recovery of Paul's distinction between human bodiness, to be affirmed and rejoiced in, and human fleshiness, always to be guarded about and against, could be a major contribution to ongoing theological reflection."

James D. G. Dunn[18]

Mind and Heart

The Greek word for "mind" is *nous*. What is the place of *nous* in biblical anthropology?

For Paul, the *nous* is the perceiving, thinking, determining, rational "I." We are rational beings, capable of soaring to the heights of reflective thought. And although not the highest dimension of our being, our minds matter immensely. Indeed, the transformation of our behavior comes via a renewing of our minds so that we affirm that what God wills is thoroughly wholesome and good (Rom 12:2). But the renewal of the mind in the light of God's mercy in the gospel "is not a new capacity to discern God's will by rational means, but the integration of rationality within the total transformation of the person."[19] In place of the depraved human mind (Rom 1:28) and senseless, foolish thinking (Gal 3:1, 3), we have "the mind of Christ" (1 Cor 2:16). And the renewed mind needs to join with the spirit in the worship of God:

> For if I pray in a tongue, *my spirit* prays, but *my mind* is unfruitful. So what shall I do? I will pray with *my spirit*, but I will also pray with *my understanding*; I will sing with *my spirit*, but I will also sing with *my understanding*. (1 Cor 14:14–15)

On the other hand, the "heart," *kardia* in Greek, is the seat of human emotions and will, and overlaps with the mind in that some of the usage locates thought in the heart as well. The heart as the center of emotions is evident in texts such as Romans 5:5 where "God's love has been poured out into our hearts," and in several places where it is said that encouragement or comfort is brought to someone's heart (Eph 6:22; Col 2:2; 4:8; 2 Thess 2:16–17).

The fact that we are less used to the notion of the heart as the place where decisions are made can be seen in the decision of most modern English versions to translate *kardia* as "mind" in texts like 1 Corinthians 7:37, "But the man who has

18. Dunn, *Theology of Paul the Apostle*, 73.

19. Ibid., 74.

settled the matter in his own mind [*kardia*]" (NIV; cf. NRSV; NET; GNT). The HCSB and ESV are exceptions, translating the phrase "in his heart."[20]

As a generalization, the mind is associated with the rational "I" and the heart with the emotional "I." But as we have seen, there is a fair degree of overlap. That human beings are both thinking and feeling beings is clear. That both are necessary is illustrated in Philippians 4:7: "And the peace of God, which transcends all understanding, will guard your hearts and your minds in Christ Jesus."

What is a human being? We are rational beings, *nous*, capable of soaring to the heights of reflective thought. And we are also experiencing beings, *kardia*, capable of emotions, thought, and will. Such perspectives on the human person underline our complexity, both in terms of our remarkable potential and fragile sensitivity. With minds and hearts, human beings are capable of the most astonishing achievements and the deepest feelings.

Soul and Spirit

The Greek *psychē*, "soul" in Paul's letters, regularly refers to the whole person. We are living beings, animated by the mystery of life as a gift.[21] In the following verses it does not refer to a part of a person, but is simply one way of describing human beings, whether the writer or others:

> Let *everyone* [*pasa psychē*; literally, "every soul"] be subject to the governing authorities. (Rom 13:1)
>
> Greet Priscilla and Aquila, my co-workers in Christ Jesus. They risked their lives *for me* [*hyper tēs psychēs mou*; lit., "for my soul"]. (Rom 16:3–4a)

Paul can also use *psychē* to mean "life" or "human vitality." In Romans 11:3 he quotes 1 Kings 19:10 where the prophet Elijah complains that his enemies are "trying to kill *me* [*tēn psychē mou*]"; literally, "they are seeking my soul." In Philippians 2:30 Paul describes Epaphroditus as risking "his *life*" or *psychē*, for Paul.

When it comes to the Greek word *pneuma*, "spirit," what or whom Paul is referring to is not always clear. There are around twenty cases where the referent is clearly the human spirit and well over that where the Spirit of God is in view. Apparently, the human spirit and the Spirit of God are closely related.

The human spirit is that aspect of the human person that relates directly to God.

---

20. Paul in 2 Cor 9:7 uses *kardia* in a similar manner with translations similarly equivocating over whether to translate it as "heart" or "mind." Whereas the NIV translates, "Each of you should give what you have decided in your heart to give" (see also ESV; HCSB; NET), other versions such as the NRSV have, "Each of you must give as you have made up your mind." The related idea of the heart as the source of motivation can be seen in the language of keeping a "pure heart" in 1 Tim 1:5 and 2 Tim 2:22. The heart may also be thought of in terms of the depths of the human person, the place where experience is felt. Faith and obedience must come from the heart (Rom 6:17; 10:9–10).

21. As Dunn, *Theology of Paul the Apostle*, 76, notes, when it comes to *psychē*, "soul," "Paul's usage clearly echoes the typical Hebraic mindset" and is in line with what we observed with the use of Hebrew *nephesh* in Gen 2:7. Paul quotes Gen 2:7 in 1 Cor 15:45.

Paul writes that he serves God with his spirit (Rom 1:9). Correspondingly, when he conceives of God relating to us, he can say that "the Spirit [of God] himself bears witness with our spirit" (Rom 8:16 ESV). The person "who is united with the Lord is one with him in spirit [*hen pneuma*]" (1 Cor 6:17).[22]

"The law of the Lord is perfect, refreshing the soul" (Ps 19:7). Timothy Keller comments: "Since the Hebrew word for 'soul' means one's psyche or self, the Bible has the power to show and restore your true identity."[23]

In terms of distinguishing the human "spirit" from the human "soul," it would appear that for Paul at least, the former denotes the Godward dimension of our existence, and the latter is connected to our life and vitality itself.[24] From our *psychē* we know that we are alive, from our *pneuma* that we can be alive to God. We are both a "psyche," a word used today in psychology for the human mind or personality, and we are also "spirit," connecting us to the realm of the Spirit of God.

What is a human being? We are living beings, *psychē*, animated by the mystery of life as a gift. And we are also spiritual beings, *pneuma*, with the capacity to relate directly to God. The soul and spirit dimensions of the human being remind us that we are more than just smart animals. They explain the perennial human quest for significance, without which we seem doomed to a futile hedonism. It is remarkable that despite the West's widespread commitment to philosophical materialism, a stubborn interest in the "spiritual" dimension of human life persists. Yet the fact that we are spiritual beings does not guarantee that we enjoy a proper connection to the true and living God. Many counterfeits seductively offer a sense of purpose, but they ultimately fail to bring satisfaction. These include everything from folk religion to baseless superstitions.

"For Paul the human being is more than 'soul.' *Psychē* is not sufficient to describe the depths of the individual. Persons exist on and are related to fuller dimensions of reality than just the psychical. At the end of a century which has grown to appreciate the insights of Freud and Jung, then, Paul's anthropology may carry a salutary lesson for us. That lesson would be to warn against thinking that the *psyche* can reveal everything of importance about the inner life of a person. Paul, once again in line with his Jewish heritage, also speaks of the human spirit, a still deeper depth or higher reality of the person. Moreover, he both implies and teaches that it is only by functioning at that level and by opening the human spirit to the divine Spirit that the human being can be whole."

James D. G. Dunn[25]

Inner Being

Paul sees us as whole beings, determined from within. In three places Paul uses the expression, "inner being," *ho esō anthrōpos*:[26]

22. As W. D. Stacey puts it, "The Pauline usage of spirit [is] for the godward side of man" (*The Pauline View of Man* [London: Macmillan, 1956], 137).

23. Timothy Keller with Kathy Keller, *The Songs of Jesus: A Year of Daily Devotions in the Psalms* (New York: Viking Penguin, 2015), 33.

24. See also the related term *psychikos* in 1 Cor 15:44–46, which denotes present bodily existence. In 1 Cor 2:14, the *psychikos* person is not able to receive the things of the *pneuma*.

25. Dunn, *Theology of Paul the Apostle*, 78.

26. The term is rendered differently in English versions as "inner man" (RSV; NKJV), "person" (NET; HCSB), "self" (NAB), "nature" (NRSV), "humanity" (REB), or as "human nature" (NJB).

> In my *inner being* I delight in God's law. (Rom 7:22)
>
> Though outwardly we are wasting away, yet *inwardly* we are being renewed day by day. (2 Cor 4:16)
>
> I pray that out of his glorious riches he may strengthen you with power through his Spirit in your *inner being*, so that Christ may dwell in your hearts through faith. (Eph 3:16–17a)

Once again there are no grounds for taking this expression to mean a particular part of a person. The inner being is simply the whole person viewed from the inside. As Gordon Fee states, the inner being is "the interior of our being . . . the seat of personal consciousness, . . . [and] of our moral being."[27]

We may also define the inner being in connection with other terms that Paul uses. The inner being is another way of talking about the human heart, as Ephesians 3:17 suggests (see above). And it also overlaps with the concept of the human spirit, since it is the place where the Spirit of God strengthens and renews us, as 2 Corinthians 4:16 indicates. Finally, to consider another term, the "spiritual body" of 1 Corinthians 15:44 is not so much equivalent to the inner being as it is its destiny. As Harris puts it eloquently:

> As a result of the final convulsion of resurrection, the butterfly of the spiritual body will emerge from the chrysalis of the renewed "inner person."[28]

What is a human being? From the fact that we have inner beings, we are whole beings determined from within.

Summary

What can we learn about personal identity from the terms the Bible uses to describe us? To sum up, the Bible's anthropological terms highlight our essence, limitations, and potential. We are more than our bodies, but not less than them. Being embodied, we are social beings, defined by our relationships. We are also flesh, that is, frail and weak, driven by our desires, which are often harmful and in opposition to God. As beings with mind and heart, we are capable of the highest thoughts and the deepest emotions. And as souls and spirits, we are alive and have the capacity to connect with the living God. To neglect any one of these dimensions is to distort human identity. Taken together, this multidimensional perspective undermines the dominant materialist view in Western societies today that human beings are simply animals with big brains.

---

27. Gordon D. Fee, *God's Empowering Presence: The Holy Spirit in the Letters of Paul* (Peabody, MA: Hendrickson, 1994), 695–96. An equivalent expression appears in 1 Pet 3:3–4: "Your beauty should not come from outward adornment, such as elaborate hairstyles and the wearing of gold jewelry or fine clothes. Rather, it should be that of your *inner self* [lit. "the hidden person of the heart," *ho kryptos tēs kardias anthrōpos*], the unfading beauty of a gentle and quiet spirit, which is of great worth in God's sight." Leonhard Goppelt's definition of the "inner self" is accurate: "'The hidden person' is not the inner side of the person, but the whole human being as it is determined from within" (*A Commentary on 1 Peter* [Grand Rapids: Eerdmans, 1993], 221).

28. Murray J. Harris, *The Second Epistle to the Corinthians: A Commentary on the Greek Text* (Grand Rapids: Eerdmans, 2005), 360.

GENESIS 1–3 AND WHAT IT IS TO BE HUMAN

What else do we learn about human beings from the famous opening chapters of the Bible? From Genesis 1–3 we learn five things that help to answer the question, what is a human being? Human beings are: (1) special, (2) social, (3) sexual, (4) moral, and (5) spiritual.[29]

Human Beings Are Special

First, human beings are *special.* It is often observed that the main difference between the accounts of creation in Genesis 1 and 2 is that the latter hones in on the creation of a man and a woman and the garden where they live. However, the creation of humanity on the sixth day in Genesis 1:26–31 brings God's work to a definite climax with the creation of human beings. Several features of the text suggest that human beings have a special place in creation. Philip Johnston explains:

> In Genesis 1 the creation of humanity is the longest section and the apex of the account. The important verb *bārā*, 'create' is repeated three times (v. 27; *cf.* vv. 1, 21), and is the only instance when God blesses his creation. Human dominion over all other creatures is noted, and the creation of humanity precedes God's assessment of creation as 'very good'.[30]

As John Lennox notes, the first lesson that Adam was taught "is that he was fundamentally different from *all* other creatures."[31] In Genesis 1:26 Adam is created to rule over every living creature. By being created in God's image and likeness, a point underscored by its repetition in Genesis 1:26–27, humanity is clearly the pinnacle of God's creation.

> "The fact, or at least the degree, of human exceptionalism is often disputed. In some quarters it is considered modest and seemly for us to take our place among the animals, conceptually speaking—to acknowledge finally the bonds of kinship evolution implies. Yet, in view of our history with regards to the animals, not to mention our history with one another, it seems fair to wonder if the beasts, given a voice in the matter, would not feel a bit insulted by our intrusion."
>
> *Marilynne Robinson*[32]

When we come to the second account of creation in Genesis 2, the description of the creation of Adam in Genesis 2:7b sets him apart from the animal kingdom: "God . . . breathed into his nostrils the breath of life." Kenneth Mathews explains the significance of this poignant description:

> The man receives his life force from the breath of the Creator himself, hovering over him. *Breathed* is warmly personal, with the face-to-face intimacy of a kiss and the significance that this was giving as well as making; and self-giving at that. Although both animal (7:22) and human life share in this gift of life (2:7), *human life enjoys a unique relationship with God.* The correspondence between man and his Maker

29. Chapter five looks specifically at the meaning of the description of human beings as made in the image and likeness of God.

30. Johnston, "Humanity," 564.

31. John C. Lennox, *Seven Days That Divide the World* (Grand Rapids: Zondervan, 2011), 71. Emphasis original.

32. Robinson, *Givenness of Things*, 256.

"The question of the origin of human beings—are we made in the image of God, or thrown up on the sea of possible random permutations of matter without any ultimate significance?—is of major importance for *our concept of our human identity*; and it is therefore not surprising that ferocious efforts are being made to minimise the difference between humans and animals on the one hand, and the difference between humans and machines on the other. Such efforts are driven, at least in part, by the secular conviction that naturalism must in the end triumph over theism by its reductionist arguments in removing the last vestige of God from his creation. Human beings must in the end be proved to be nothing but physics and chemistry."

John Lennox[34]

"No man is an island, entire of itself, every man is a piece of the continent, a part of the main; if a clod be washed away by the sea, Europe is the less, as well as if a promontory were, as well as if a manor of thy friend's or of thine own were; any man's death diminishes me, because I am involved in mankind. And therefore never send to know for whom the bell tolls; it tolls for thee."

John Donne[36]

is expressed both by the language of "image" (1:26–27) and by the metaphor of a shared "breath."[33]

More mouth-to-mouth vivification than mouth-to-mouth resuscitation, God breathing directly into the man is another way in which he is set apart from the rest of creation, and it underscores God's intimate and personal connection to him. All of Genesis 1–2, and not just the image of God references, point to the fact that human beings stand apart in creation.

Humans Are Social Beings

Human beings are *social* beings. For a study of personal identity, it is significant that the opening chapters of Genesis include a play on words between the first man's name and the whole of humanity that underscores our profound interrelatedness.

The Hebrew text of the opening chapters of Genesis communicates the individual and collective aspects of humanity in ways that are not easy to translate. The Hebrew word for "Adam," *adam*, can also mean "human" or "mankind." Philip Johnston explains how Genesis exploits this ambiguity:

> The *ādām* in Genesis 1:27 refers to humankind, who are further differentiated as male and female, while *ādām* in Genesis 5:1, 3–5 refers to Adam. However, in Genesis 2–4 *ādām* is used both with and without the article to refer to both humanity and Adam; the demarcation between them is unclear.[35]
>
> Genesis 5:1–2 is a good example:
>
> This is the written account of Adam's [*adam*] family line.
>
> When God created mankind [*adam*], he made them in the likeness of God. He created them male and female and blessed them. And he named them "Mankind" [*adam*] when they were created. (Gen 5:1–2)[37]

33. Mathews, *Genesis 1–11:26*, 196, emphasis added.

34. Lennox, *Seven Days that Divide the World*, 85, emphasis added.

35. Johnston, "Humanity," 564. While English versions differ, the NIV translates *adam* in Genesis 1–5 as follows: "mankind" (1:26, 27; 5:1, 2); "a/the man" (2:7 [2x], 8, 15, 16, 18, 19 [2x], 20, 21 [2x], 22 [2x], 23; 3:8, 9, 12, 22, 24); and "Adam" (2:25; 3:17, 20, 21; 4:1). That God named the first man *adam* makes it clear that at the same time that he was creating Adam, he was also creating humanity.

36. John Donne, "Devotions upon Emergent Occasions—Meditation XVII," in *The Complete English Poems* (London: Penguin, 2004), 242.

37. The Greek translation of the Old Testament, the Septuagint (LXX), resolves the ambiguity at the beginning of verse 1 by using different words for "mankind" and "Adam": "This is the genealogy of human beings [*geneseōs anthrōpon*] in the day in which God made Adam [*adam*]."

We will return to the ideas that Adam represents the race and the corresponding idea of Christ as the second Adam in chapter eight, "Known by God and Christ in the New Testament."

Humans Are Sexual Beings

Humans are *sexual* beings. Genesis 2 is unique among ancient Near Eastern accounts of creation with its focus on the creation of women. Genesis 2:20–25 makes clear not only Adam's need for a mate, but also the differentiation and complementarity of males and females, the incompleteness of one without the other, and the norm of sexual intimacy:

> So the man gave names to all the livestock, the birds in the sky and all the wild animals.
>
> But for Adam no suitable helper was found. So the LORD God caused the man to fall into a deep sleep; and while he was sleeping, he took one of the man's ribs and then closed up the place with flesh. Then the LORD God made a woman from the rib he had taken out of the man, and he brought her to the man.
>
> The man said,
>
> "This is now bone of my bones
> and flesh of my flesh;
> she shall be called 'woman,'
> for she was taken out of man."
>
> That is why a man leaves his father and mother and is united to his wife, and they become one flesh. Adam and his wife were both naked, and they felt no shame.

A similar point is made more concisely in Genesis 1:27 where it is said that in creating humankind, God created "male and female." Kenneth Mathews notes that the "Hebrew terms for 'male' (*zākār*) and 'female' (*nĕqēbâ*), as opposed to man and woman, express human sexuality."[38]

Humans Are Moral Beings

Humans are *moral* beings. God created human beings with a capacity for morally upright behavior, a status Adam and Eve forfeited in their decision to transgress the one command that God had given them.

In Genesis 2 God places Adam in the garden of Eden, sets him to work, and gives him a command that he must not transgress:

38. Mathews, *Genesis 1–11:26*, 173.

> The LORD God took the man and put him in the Garden of Eden to work it and take care of it. And the LORD God commanded the man, "You are free to eat from any tree in the garden; but you must not eat from the tree of the knowledge of good and evil, for when you eat from it you will certainly die." (Gen 2:15–17)

With respect to "the tree of the knowledge of good and evil," it is not that God did not want Adam and Eve to "know" the difference between good and evil. The Hebrew verb "to know," *yadah,* has a wide range of meanings. It can mean "to experience," as in to know happiness or grief, or "to choose," as in God knew = chose Abraham (Gen 18:19). In Genesis 2:17 it means "to determine."

> "Here are the basic ingredients that define human beings as moral beings. God has given them the ability to say 'yes' to him by not eating the prohibited tree, and to say 'no' to him by eating it. In this way the Bible introduces us to the idea that humans are moral beings, with all that implies."
>
> *John Lennox*[39]

Adam is commanded not to eat from the tree of the determination of good and evil. He is not free to determine for himself what is good and what is evil. That prerogative belongs to God alone. When Adam and Eve transgress the command not to eat of that one tree, "they usurp God's authority to reveal—as the reflection of his own character—what is right and what is wrong."[40]

Humans Are Spiritual Beings

Finally, humans are *spiritual* beings. Walter Brueggemann argues that the Old Testament "has no interest in articulating an autonomous or universal notion of humanness."[41] Instead, he insists, humanity is defined entirely in terms of our relationship to God. While this may be slightly overstated, Brueggemann has a point: the relationship of human beings to God is central to the Bible's view of humanity.

In Genesis 1 what God makes is less of a focus than the fact that God makes it. God is the subject of all of the verbs, and his direct activity in creation is underscored repeatedly: "God created" (1:1, 21, 27 [3x]); "God said" (1:3, 6, 9, 11, 14, 20, 22, 24, 26, 28, 29); "God saw" (1:4, 10, 12, 18, 21, 25, 31); "God called" (1:5 [2x], 8, 10); "God made" (1:7, 16, 25, 31); "God set" (1:17); and "God blessed" (1:22, 28). Even in Genesis 2, where God prepares a garden for Adam and Eve in which to live and work, their relationship to him is implicit in the fact that he himself regularly takes walks in that garden (Gen 3:8).

Living in the garden is to live with God and in his presence. A big part of the punishment for Adam and Eve's disobedience in being banished from the garden (Gen 3:23) is the fact that the opportunity to "walk with God" is removed. Looking ahead to God's plan of redemption, Abram is told to "walk" before God (Gen 17:1),

39. Lennox, *Seven Days That Divide the World,* 76–77.

40. John Dickson, *A Doubter's Guide to the Bible: Inside History's Bestseller for Believers and Skeptics* (Grand Rapids: Zondervan, 2014), 39.

41. Walter Brueggemann, *Theology of the Old Testament: Testimony, Dispute, Advocacy* (Minneapolis: Augsburg Fortress, 1997), 450.

and God promises the Israelites that "I will walk among you and be your God, and you will be my people" (Lev 26:12).

According to Genesis 1–3, human beings were created to obey God, to speak with God and to walk with God, to know God and be known by him. But with Adam and Eve's transgression, that intimate and personal relationship with God was broken. They hide from God (Gen 3:10) and are banished from his presence (Gen 3:23). This is the death that God warned would ensue if they transgressed his command not to eat.

BEING HUMAN AND PERSONAL IDENTITY

What is a human being? Two things stand out from our study of the Bible's anthropological terms and the account of the creation of Adam and Eve in Genesis 1–3. Both are of vital importance for our study of personal identity in the following chapters of this book.

First, human beings are relational beings. We are embodied and as such are social by nature, defined by our interdependence and responsibility to and for each other. Our minds and hearts enable us to think and feel and thus to build and sustain relationships. We are sexual beings, made as male and female, with the potential for interpersonal union and procreation. That we are social beings is also seen in the fact that our first parent's name, "Adam," is a play on words for "humankind" and underscores our profound interconnection with each other.

Secondly, human beings are made for intimate relationship with God. We are living beings, souls, given the breath of life by God himself. Even though like other creatures we are made from dust, we have a special place in God's creation. Our first parents were created to know God and be known by him. We are spiritual beings with the capacity to relate personally to God. We are also flesh, that is, frail and mortal, in constant need of God to sustain our lives and to enable us to reach our potential. In the following chapter, we consider the fact that Genesis also asserts that we are made in the image and likeness of God.

RELEVANT QUESTIONS

1. Can you relate to Jennifer Aniston's criticism of our society in terms of the "objectification and scrutiny" the human body is subjected to? How does the biblical concept of *sōma* change the way we view our physical bodies?
2. When it comes to rationality, the Bible describes us both in terms of "mind," *nous*, and "heart," *kardia*. Does this throw fresh light on the way you make decisions?
3. John Lennox argues that naturalism concludes that "human beings must, in the end, be proved to be nothing but physics and chemistry." How does reading Genesis 1–3 challenge this idea?

CHAPTER 5

THE IMAGE AND LIKENESS OF GOD

The word "image" has great currency in our day. It is used in two senses. First, image can mean likeness or resemblance, as in a photograph or painting. A second and overlapping sense of image is what people seek to project about themselves to others. For example, a new phenomenon is the online dating profile that people use to connect with potential romantic partners. Numerous websites give tips for how to project a desirable image, which may or may not bear much resemblance to the reality of who you are. Image in this context is everything.

Intriguingly, the Bible uses "image" to characterize human identity in relation to God. According to the Bible, human beings are spiritual beings, capable of a close relationship with God who is Spirit (cf. John 4:24). This is nowhere more evident than in the declaration that we are made in the image and likeness of God, something stated no less than five times in the opening chapters of Genesis (1:26, 27 [2x]; 5:1; 9:6). It is to the meaning of this intriguing expression that we now turn. In what sense do human beings made in the image of God resemble God? What is it that we reflect of him?

"Human beings are not only sentient but sapient, able not only to have sensations and experiences but to reflect on and interpret them. What distinguishes *homo sapiens* from other creatures is rationality."

Kevin Vanhoozer[2]

Almost all theologians agree that "the image of God is foundational to the biblical concept of humanness."[1] But to what does it refer? Is the image of God an attribute, such as reason or conscience? Or is it our capacity for relationships with God and other human beings? Or is it the task of representing God in having dominion over the rest of creation? Is it all of the above, a combination of the above, or none of the above?

ADAM, THE SON OF GOD

We begin our enquiry with the first occurrences of the expression in the Bible:

1. Philip S. Johnston, "Humanity," in *New Dictionary of Biblical Theology*, ed. T. D. Alexander and B. S. Rosner (Downers Grove, IL: InterVarsity Press, 2000), 564.

2. Kevin Vanhoozer, "Human Being, Individual and Social," in *The Cambridge Companion to Christian Doctrine*, ed. Colin E. Gunton (Cambridge: Cambridge University Press, 1997), 160.

Then God said, "Let us make mankind *in our image, in our likeness,* so that they may rule over the fish in the sea and the birds in the sky, over the livestock and all the wild animals, and over all the creatures that move along the ground."

So God created mankind *in his own image,*
in the image of God he created them;
male and female he created them.

God blessed them and said to them, "Be fruitful and increase in number; fill the earth and subdue it. Rule over the fish in the sea and the birds in the sky and over every living creature that moves on the ground." (Gen 1:26–28)

As regards the two main terms, "image" (Hebrew *tselem*) and "likeness" (Hebrew *demut*) do not appear to be significantly different. If in 1:26 mankind is made in the "image" and "likeness" of God, the parallel statement in 1:27 only mentions being made in the "image" of God. And later biblical references use "image" and "likeness" interchangeably (e.g., "image" in Gen 9:6; "likeness" in Gen 5:1; Jas 3:9). Together and apart, "image" and "likeness" denote the same concept. The GNT translates the two phrases: "They will be like us and resemble us" (Gen 1:26).

Genesis makes it clear that "mankind" in the image of God includes both males and females. The same point is repeated in Genesis 5:2. All people, including both sexes, have the status of bearing God's image.

As a general rule, there are two things that matter most when it comes to biblical interpretation: *context* and *usage.* Together they are the points of reference to look to when understanding a text is difficult. And appeal to context and usage are the best arguments in favor of a particular interpretation. By context I mean both literary context, the place in which the expression in question appears in the text, and historical context, the associations that attach to the expression in the cultural environment in which the text was written. By usage, I mean the way in which the expression functions in other parts of the Bible.

"That strange verse in the first chapter of Genesis, 'in the image of God he created him; male and female he created them,' is meaningless by the standards of positivism or the higher criticism. It is unfalsifiable, undemonstrable, and dependent on terms for which we have no stable definitions. It is dependent as well on a conception of God that compels reverence and will make us reverent of one another. It tells us every essential thing about who we are and what we are, and what we are a part of. It is ontology. It is metaphysics."
Marilynne Robinson[3]

So what does it mean that we are made in the image and likeness of God? In the *literary context* of Genesis 1, the image of God is connected to humanity's role of ruling over creation. In 1:26 God makes mankind in his image and likeness "so that they may rule" over the other creatures in God's world. And in 1:27–28 the

3. Marilynne Robinson, *The Givenness of Things: Essays* (New York: Farrar, Straus and Giroux, 2015), 171.

males and females are created in God's image in order "to fill the earth and subdue it" and to "rule over" it.

Some of the background to the notion of an image in the ancient world ties in with this function. In terms of *historical context*, kings were thought to be the living image of a god and to embody the divine rule, the pharaohs of Egypt being a clear example.[4] And in the ancient Near East, an image or statue of a king was a visible representation of the monarch's rule. Thus, both the context in Genesis 1 and use in the world of Genesis suggest that image language is associated with humanity's rule over creation on God's behalf, perhaps with some royal connotations.

"'Image' describes a relationship between God and humans such that *ādām* can be described as a servant king."

Peter Gentry[5]

What about *usage*? The next mention of the image of God in Genesis is in 5:1–3.[6] If the context of humanity made in the image of God in Genesis 1 suggests that having dominion over creation as God's vice-regent is associated with the concept, the usage of "image and likeness" in Genesis 5 defines it as the language of family relationship:

> This is the written account of Adam's family line.
>
> When God created mankind, he made them *in the likeness of God*. He created them male and female and blessed them. And he named them "Mankind" when they were created.
>
> When Adam had lived 130 years, he had *a son in his own likeness, in his own image*; and he named him Seth. (Gen 5:1–3)

Genesis 5:1–2 contains a clear allusion to the creation of mankind in the image of God in Genesis 1:26–28. Both texts use the language of the "creation" of "mankind" as "male and female" in "the likeness of God." Genesis 5:3 describes Adam's son Seth in language that echoes the creation of the first humans: "Adam . . . had a son *in his own likeness, in his own image*." As his offspring, Seth bears the image and likeness of his father Adam. According to Genesis 5:3, to be made in the image and likeness of someone is to be their son.[7]

Two texts in the New Testament supply further support for the view that human

4. Gordon Wenham, *Genesis 1–15*, ed. David A. Hubbard, Glenn W. Barker, and John D. W. Watts, Word Bible Commentary 1 (Dallas: Word, 1987), 30–31.

5. Peter J. Gentry, "Kingdom through Covenant: Humanity as Divine Image," *SBJT* 12.1 (2008): 28–29.

6. Gavin Ortlund observes that "there has been surprisingly little exploration of the import of Gen 5:3 for the meaning of the *imago Dei*" ("Image of Adam, Son of God: Genesis 5:3 and Luke 3:38 in Intercanonical Dialogue," *Journal of the Evangelical Theological Society* 57.4 (2014): 673.

7. In recent years a number of scholars have written in support of understanding the image of God in terms of sonship, including Henri Blocher, *In the Beginning: The Opening Chapters of Genesis* (Leicester, UK: Inter-Varsity Press, 1984), 89; Gentry, "Kingdom through Covenant," 28–29; John Dickson, *A Doubter's Guide to the Bible: Inside History's Bestseller for Believers and Skeptics* (Grand Rapids: Zondervan, 2014), 28; G. K. Beale, *A New Testament Biblical Theology: The Unfolding of the Old Testament in the New* (Grand Rapids: Baker Academic, 2011), 401; Gavin Ortlund, "Image of Adam, Son of God," 679, 687; Graeme Goldsworthy, *The Son of God and the New Creation*, ed. Dane C. Ortlund and Miles V. Van Pelt, Short Studies in Biblical Theology (Wheaton, IL: Crossway, 2015), 61, 67; and Michael Horton, *The Christian Faith: A Systematic Theology for Pilgrims on the Way* (Grand Rapids: Zondervan, 2011), 388.

beings are children of God by virtue of being made in the image of God. First, in Paul's Areopagus address in Acts 17, he cites the Greek poet Aratus (*Phaenomena* 5) approvingly in saying that "we are his [God's] offspring [*genos*]" (Acts 17:28). Given that Paul elsewhere teaches that Israel and Christian believers are sons of God *by adoption* (e.g., Rom 9:4; Gal 3:26–4:5), it is indeed striking that Paul here affirms that all human beings are children of God. However, as Calvin observes, "The word 'sons' can be diversely taken," and for Paul there is a sense in which "all mortal men are called sons in general."[9] We will return to the theme of sonship in biblical theology in chapter eight, "Known in Christ, the Son of God."

John Calvin does not specifically equate the image of God with being a child of God. However, as Julie Canlis notes: "In the garden, Adam is portrayed by Calvin as the loving son, surrounded with signs of the 'paternal goodness' of God. . . . Adam has no fear at the sight of God, whom he is able to identify as *Father*."[8]

For now it is significant that several commentators appeal to the image of God as the basis for Paul's insistence in Acts 17 that all human beings are part of the family of God. For example, David Peterson writes: "God's commitment to bless 'all peoples on earth' through Abraham's offspring (Gn. 12:3, lit. 'all the families of the earth') shows the Creator's continuing care and concern for everyone made in his image and likeness (Gn. 1:26–27)."[10] And perhaps it is no accident that Paul moves in Acts 17:29 to talk of images: "Therefore since we are God's offspring, we should not think that the divine being is like gold or silver or stone—an image made by human design and skill."

Secondly, and even more significantly, the conclusion of the genealogy of Jesus in Luke 3:38 runs: "The son of Enosh, the son of Seth, the son of Adam, the son of God." The list of people through whom Jesus descended begins with the intimation that Jesus "was the son, so it was thought, of Joseph" (Luke 3:23). The genealogy includes some thirty-seven names, noting the fathers of each. At the end of the list, the reference to Adam as the son of God, as Joel Green writes, "presents the divine origin of the human race and indicates Jesus's solidarity with all humanity."[11] Several commentators including Geldenhuys, Bock, and Ryken link, correctly in my view, Adam's divine sonship with being made in the image of God.[12]

The main argument that the image of God marks human beings as sons of God is the usage of "image and likeness" language in Genesis 5 to denote family relationship, the identification of Adam as the son of God in Luke 3:38, and humanity as "the offspring of God" in Acts 17.

8. Julie Canlis, "The Fatherhood of God and Union with Christ in Calvin," in *"In Christ" in Paul: Explorations in Paul's Theology of Union and Participation*, ed. Michael J. Thate, Kevin J. Vanhoozer, and Constantine R. Campbell (Tübingen: Mohr Siebeck, 2014), 404.

9. John Calvin and Henry Beveridge, *Commentary upon the Acts of the Apostles*, vol. 2 (Bellingham, WA: Logos Bible Software, 2010), 170.

10. David G. Peterson, *The Acts of the Apostles*, PNTC (Grand Rapids: Eerdmans, 2009), 500. See also Calvin, *Commentary upon the Acts of the Apostles*, 170.

11. Joel Green, *The Gospel of Luke*, New International Commentary on the New Testament (Grand Rapids: Eerdmans, 1997), 189.

12. Cited in Ortlund, "Image of God, Son of God," 685.

In terms of usage, there is good evidence for taking the image of God to refer to human beings as children or sons of God. However, this conclusion does not overturn the centuries of Christian reflection on the nature of the image of God. As John Dickson, Simon Smart, and Justine Toh insist, the status of being a child of God made in his image is the basis for our task of ruling the earth:

> This familial dimension of the concept of the image of God accords well with the motif of representative dominion, since children, especially sons, were indeed thought of as subordinate representatives of their fathers, deriving both status and wealth from them.[13]

Stephen G. Dempster rightly points out that both the royal and sonship connotations of the image of God in Genesis are echoed throughout the Old Testament in the portrayals of Abraham, Moses's descent at Sinai, David, Solomon, and Israel as a whole.[14] God's adoption of King David and his dynasty as his sons (see 2 Sam 7:14–15) forges a clear link between the role of the king and divine sonship.

Gavin Ortlund is correct in affirming that, rather than replacing the traditional views, the metaphor of fathering as creating can be seen as "supplementing and potentially unifying them. . . . A child is like his father, represents his father, bears many of his father's characteristics."[15] Indeed, the "son of [something]" is regularly used in the Bible as an idiom for reflecting someone's essential characteristics. For example, in 2 Kings 6:32 NASB a "son of a murderer" is a murderer; in Isaiah 19:11 NASB a "son of the wise" is a wise counselor; and in Mark 3:17 Jesus gives James and John "the name Boanerges, which means 'sons of thunder,'" to refer to their passionate and volatile nature.

For our purposes, recognizing the sonship dimension to the image of God has great potential for a more unified biblical theology of personal identity. The image of God has been rightfully used to insist on the value and significance of all human beings and as the grounds for the just treatment of all people.[16] However, this ethical use of the image of God needs to be supplemented with a biblical-theological use. Our very identity as human beings is tied up with being children of God made in the image of God. And the story of redemption is one of God choosing to bless Abraham and the children of Abraham as the restored children of God.

The image of God then becomes the firm foundation for several topics that we will treat later in this book. These include the imitation of God as his beloved children, the adoption of believers in Christ as children of God with the full rights

13. John Dickson, Simon Smart, and Justine Toh, "Human to the End," 4. Unpublished CPX document.

14. Stephen G. Dempster, *Dominion and Dynasty: A Theology of the Hebrew Bible*, ed. D. A. Carson, NSBT 15 (Downers Grove, IL: InterVarsity Press, 2003), 76, 106, 141, 147, 198, 202, 225.

15. Ortlund, "Image of God, Son of God," 687.

16. See Gen 9:6: "Whoever sheds human blood, by humans shall their blood be shed; for in the image of God has God made mankind," and note Jas 3:9–10.

as heirs of God, and several strands of teaching about Jesus Christ whereby we find new life in him. Once we understand the image of God aright, sonship is seen as a central category not only for redemption but also for creation and new creation. As Henri Blocher states: "In the Son we become sons, an act of grace which fulfills and transcends our primeval quasi-sonship,"[17] a reference to Adam and Eve as image bearers and children of God.

THE LIES OF SATAN ABOUT HUMAN IDENTITY

Before leaving the opening chapters of Genesis, it is worth examining more closely the manner in which our identity as God's children was lost. Adam and Eve's transgression was very much a crisis of identity. Much has been written about the implications of the fall concerning the damage it did to the image of God. Just as important are its ramifications for our status as God's children.

In John 8:44–45 Jesus says of the devil, "there is no truth in him," and describes him as "a liar and the father of lies." Revelation 12:9 describes Satan as the one "who deceives the whole world" (NET). In this section, we compare and contrast the two most famous episodes in the Bible involving satanic deception, namely, the temptations of Adam and Eve and of Jesus.

When the serpent tempted Eve in Genesis 3:1–5, he not only told her lies; he also called God a liar:

> Now the serpent was more crafty than any of the wild animals the LORD God had made. He said to the woman, "Did God really say, 'You must not eat from any tree in the garden'?"
>
> The woman said to the serpent, "We may eat fruit from the trees in the garden, but God did say, 'You must not eat fruit from the tree that is in the middle of the garden, and you must not touch it, or you will die.'"
>
> "You will not certainly die," the serpent said to the woman. "For God knows that when you eat from it your eyes will be opened, and you will be like God, knowing good and evil."[18]

God said not to eat of the fruit of one particular tree in the garden. According to Genesis 2:17, they were not to eat from that tree for their own protection: if they eat, they will "certainly die." Nothing in the narrative to this point has given Adam and Eve any reason to question God's motives for this prohibition. The serpent undermines God's word to Adam and Eve concerning the tree of knowledge of good and evil with three counterclaims, each of which tempts them to seek to

17. Blocher, *In the Beginning*, 90.

18. In the NIV's "you will be like God" (Gen 3:5), "God" translates the Hebrew *'elohim*, which is sometimes rendered "gods" (KJV, NEB, NJB) or "divine beings" (NET). Either way, the point is the same: "Satan promises them [Eve and Adam] divinity" (Calvin, *Commentary upon the Acts of the Apostles*, 151).

establish their own autonomy and an identity independent of God: (1) you will not die; instead, (2) your eyes will be opened; and (3) you will be like God.[19] Each of the three lies contained an element of truth and a tragic irony. We take them in reverse order.

First, in one sense Adam and Eve did become like God: in rebelling against him, they asserted their personal autonomy and independence from God and usurped the place of authority in their lives that God occupied. But ironically, as creatures made in the image and likeness of God, they were already "like God," in the best sense of being his children, made in his image and likeness. In disobeying God, they forfeited the privileges associated with that status, including being known by him intimately and personally in the garden.

Gordon Wenham explains how the first humans experienced "death before death," having cut themselves off from God: "In Israelite worship, true life was experienced when one went to the sanctuary. There God was present. There he gave life. But to be expelled from the camp, as lepers were, was to enter the realm of death. If to be expelled from the camp of Israel was to "die," expulsion from the garden was an even more drastic kind of death. In this sense they did die on the day they ate of the tree: they were no longer able to have daily conversation with God, enjoy his bounteous provision, and eat of the tree of life; instead they had to toil for food, suffer, and eventually return to the dust from which they were taken."[21]

Secondly, Adam and Eve's eyes were actually "opened," but not in a good way. They saw that they were naked, but ironically this realization led to fear and shame rather than liberation (Gen 3:10–11). Prior to their transgression, "Adam and his wife were both naked, and they felt no shame" (Gen 2:25).

And thirdly, Adam and Eve did not die immediately. In fact, according to Genesis 5:5 Adam made it to 930 years of age before dying! But in a more profound and dramatic sense, they did die.[20] They cut themselves off from God.

In the garden, Adam and Eve were known intimately and personally by God. He knew them by name and as his children. He walked with them, conversed with them, and showed them his fatherly care, loving concern, and devoted attention. The presence of God gave the garden its life-giving power (Gen 2:7), an environment in which Adam and Eve experienced true life in knowing God and being known by him. But the serpent undermined their relationship with God by questioning God's motives: "God knows that when you eat from it your eyes will be opened, and you will be like God" (Gen 3:5). As Calvin states, Satan "charges God with malignity and envy, as wishing to deprive man of his highest perfection."[22] The serpent's lies were designed to undermine Adam and Eve's confidence in God

19. "You will not certainly die" (Gen 3:4) is second-person plural in Hebrew, referring to both the woman and the man. Therefore, we are justified in speaking of the temptation of both Eve and Adam.

20. Kenneth A. Mathews calls it a "symbolic death": "They achieved isolation and fear. The couple was cut off as well from the possibility of life, the one feature of divinity for which otherwise they were destined" (*Genesis 1–11:26*, NAC 1A [Nashville: Broadman & Holman, 1996], 237).

21. Wenham, *Genesis 1–15*, 75.

22. John Calvin and John King, *Commentary on the First Book of Moses Called Genesis*, vol. 1 (Bellingham, WA: Logos Bible Software, 2010), 149–50.

and to tempt them to find their identity independently of him. In succumbing to the serpent's lies, they turned from their Father and became disobedient children.

Turning to the New Testament, it is indeed striking that the devil's three temptations of Jesus in the wilderness are also directly related to Jesus's identity as God's Son:

> Then Jesus was led by the Spirit into the wilderness to be tempted by the devil. After fasting forty days and forty nights, he was hungry. The tempter came to him and said, "*If you are the Son of God*, tell these stones to become bread."
>
> Jesus answered, "It is written: 'Man shall not live on bread alone, but on every word that comes from the mouth of God.'"
>
> Then the devil took him to the holy city and had him stand on the highest point of the temple. "*If you are the Son of God*," he said, "throw yourself down. For it is written:
>
> 'He will command his angels concerning you,
> and they will lift you up in their hands,
> so that you will not strike your foot against a stone.'"
>
> Jesus answered him, "It is also written: 'Do not put the Lord your God to the test.'"
>
> Again, the devil took him to a very high mountain and showed him all the kingdoms of the world and their splendor. "All this I will give you," he said, "if you will bow down and worship me."
>
> Jesus said to him, "Away from me, Satan! For it is written: 'Worship the Lord your God, and serve him only.'"
>
> Then the devil left him, and angels came and attended him. (Matt 4:1–11; cf. Luke 4:1–13)

The first two of Satan's tests are prefaced with the taunt, "if you are the Son of God" (Matt 4:3, 6). Satan's tests are designed to see whether or not Jesus will remain God's faithful and obedient Son. What does it mean to be the Son of God? What sort of Son is Jesus? All three probe whether or not Jesus still trusts his Father in his weakened state. In response to the first temptation, to turn the stones into bread, Jesus quotes the Old Testament: "Man shall not live on bread alone, but on every word that comes from the mouth of God" (Matt 4:4; cf. Deut 8:3).

This same pattern is repeated with the second and third tests. In each case, Jesus quotes the Old Testament to indicate that "*listening to God* is that which is life-sustaining."[23]

23. John Nolland, *The Gospel of Matthew: A Commentary on the Greek Text*, NIGTC (Grand Rapids: Eerdmans, 2005), xvii. Emphasis original.

The similarities and contrasts between Genesis 3 and Matthew 4 are striking:

- Both start with temptations to do with eating, but occur in entirely different settings: one in the plenty of the garden, the other in the scarcity of the wilderness.
- Both scenes concern the truth and goodness of the word of God. If Adam and Eve deny what God said and succumb to temptation, Jesus affirms the sufficiency of God's Word and stands firm.
- Both scenes reveal the identity of the ones being tempted. Adam and Eve are known by God intimately and personally as his children, but doubt God's paternal goodness. Jesus, on the other hand, affirms his trust in his Father and proves himself to be God's faithful and obedient Son. Significantly, the scene immediately preceding the temptation of Jesus in Matthew is the baptism of Jesus, which climaxes with the voice from heaven saying, "This is my Son, whom I love; with him I am well pleased" (Matt 3:17).
- Both set the pattern for two different versions of what it means to be a human being. One, following Adam and Eve's example, leads to death, as God had warned; the other sets the course for a new humanity leading to life.

To sum up, in the garden Adam and Eve believed the serpent and became rebellious sons of God, suffering "a symbolic death" as a result.[24] In the wilderness Jesus passed the test and refused to believe Satan's lies; he was indeed the Son of God (see Matt 4:1–11).

Satan continues to tell lies about the identity of human beings in our day, seeking to rob us of the life-giving blessing of being known by God as his children. These lies include:

- God wants to keep your eyes closed and stop you from realizing your potential;
- Independence from God and personal autonomy is the path to life;
- Following the desires of your heart will lead to finding your true self;
- Shutting your ears to God is the key to authentic living;
- Becoming like God will open your eyes and lead to knowing who you really are.

The two archetypal episodes of temptation in the Bible were fought over the issue of personal identity. What is a human being? Who are Adam and Eve? Who is Jesus? Should they establish their identity independently of God? Will self-assertion lead to becoming like God? Does God their Father love them or not? At root, these questions are versions of the most fundamental questions: Are Adam and Eve, and Jesus, truly "sons of God," and if so, how should they behave?

24. Mathews, *Genesis 1–11:26*, 237.

In both cases, the lesson is that true freedom is found in knowing God as your Father, trusting his word, resisting satanic lies, and finding your identity in being known and loved by him. If Adam and Eve failed the test, Jesus Christ proved to be a faithful and obedient Son of God.

CHILDREN OF GOD AND PERSONAL IDENTITY

When Adam and Eve transgressed God's word in the garden by believing the lies of the serpent, they became rebellious children of God, in spite of the fact that they were made in God's image. They suffered death as a result. As a consequence, we also forfeited our status as God's children and became estranged from him, no longer known by him as our Father. The contrasting case of the temptation of Jesus Christ, who withstood the lies of Satan and proved to be God's faithful and obedient Son, gives us hope that our true identity as those known by God as his children can be restored.

RELEVANT QUESTIONS

1. The concept of the "image of God" is often used to explain the value and significance of all human beings. This chapter has argued that there is much more to it than that. How does a biblical-theological interpretation of the term broaden your perspective?
2. The biblical account of Adam and Eve's transgression in the garden can be seen as a crisis of identity. Consider the list of Satan's lies on page 88. Is your sense of identity challenged or restricted by any of these lies? How can you find freedom?
3. If we, both men and women, are now children of God through his act of grace to us in Jesus Christ, how do you see God re-creating you in the image of his Son?

CHAPTER 6

KNOWN BY GOD IN THE OLD TESTAMENT

In our day, personal identity has become a sort of "do-it-yourself project." As sociologist Anthony Elliot observes, "the anything-goes thinking that was fostered by postmodernism has drilled all the way down into the fabric of our identities."[1] Finding, defining, or even designing yourself is almost a moral imperative. And personal autonomy is valued above all other considerations.[2] However, as David Jopling contends, the truth is that "persons come to know themselves in being known by persons other than themselves."[3]

A regular feature in my weekend newspaper is "The Two of Us," which looks at the friendship of two individuals. It's a typical human-interest story that focuses on how two people relate and what they mean to each other. Spouses, parents and children, friends, coworkers, and siblings are the standard fare. One article that stood out for me recently concerned the relationship between two sisters. When talking about her sister Lisa, Bea commented: "Lisa sees the best in me. . . . There's something reassuring and beautiful about someone really knowing you."[4] It is true to say that we often feel "ourselves" when we are around those who know us best.

This has certainly been my experience. In January 2000 I returned to live in Australia having spent sixteen years living overseas. Reentry, let's say, was a bit bumpy. I had less than two weeks to find somewhere to live, set up home, and settle three children into schools before starting a new job teaching high school, for which I had no formal training. As well as these challenges, my sense of self had taken a battering. My personal identity gauge was pointing towards empty and the light was flashing. Slowly getting on top of things and making new friends kept the motor running, but refueling came from renewed contact with those who knew me best.

Two old friends, Frank and Martin, were especially helpful. I had known them most of my life, and we had kept in contact while I was overseas for the previous sixteen years. Martin likes to tell the story of asking me to dice an onion on our

1. Both quoted in John Elder, "We Are Who We Believe We Are," *Sunday Age* (June 21, 2015), 8.

2. In response to such trends, the social sciences are increasingly defining personhood in relational terms. Far from recommending that we "find ourselves," such researchers argue that "the self is too complexly configured to be accessible to a single finite mind inquiring into itself by itself" (David A. Jopling, *Self Knowledge and the Self* [New York: Routledge, 2000], 137).

3. Jopling, *Self Knowledge and the Self*, 166.

4. *Sun Herald*, November 22, 2013.

first bushwalk as teenagers. Not knowing that you had to peel it first left a lasting impression it seems. Frank was a flatmate in my early twenties and happily recalls my early attempts at cooking, which included serving up a relatively raw chili con carne. Back living in Sydney after so many years, Frank called me every Sunday night, and I went on regular overnight bushwalks with Martin. If I was having trouble remembering who I was, being known by Frank and Martin was a great reminder. There is indeed something reassuring and beautiful about someone really knowing you.

> "The self is a network of relationships forged by significant experiences (past and present), actions, and connections with people, places, things and events. The self therefore becomes 'a bundle of relationships.'"
>
> *Michael Allen Fox*[5]

> "The 'self'—understood as an autonomous individual—does not exist."
>
> *Michael Horton*[6]

> "Just as it is impossible for a man to confront himself and to see himself from all sides or for a person who is still developing to know of himself whose child he is, just so certainly does man fundamentally need the meeting with another, who investigates and explains him. But where is the other to whom the being man could put the question: who am I?"
>
> *Hans Walter Wolff*[7]

It was also at this point that I found being known by God to be of great assistance. If knowing God had given my life purpose from my youth, being known by God proved to be a great comfort in a time of confusion and difficulty. In this chapter and the next, we begin looking at how being known by God gives us a secure identity and is also a reassuring and beautiful thing.

What does the Old Testament teach about being known by God? To answer this question, four matters call for attention:

1. The fact that God knows us better than we know ourselves;
2. What it means to be known by God;
3. The kindred ideas of God knowing your name and being remembered by God; and
4. Two key Old Testament texts that expound and apply the theme of being known by God in striking ways.

At a few points I will include some material from the New Testament that relates to an Old Testament topic of interest. However, most of what the New Testament teaches about being known by God, and being known by Christ, will be postponed until the next chapter.[8]

5. Michael Allen Fox, "We're Self-obsessed—But Do We Understand the Nature of the Self?" The Conversation, August 31, 2004, http://theconversation.com/were-self-obsessed-but-do-we-understand-the-nature-of-the-self-30912.

6. Michael Horton, *The Christian Faith: A Systematic Theology for Pilgrims on the Way* (Grand Rapids: Zondervan, 2011), 87.

7. Hans Walter Wolff, *Anthropology of the Old Testament*, trans. Margaret Kohl (Philadelphia: Fortress, 1974), 1–2.

8. I am not assuming that all of the findings from this chapter about the people of God in the Old Testament apply to God's people in the New Testament. While it is safe to say that the blessings of the New Covenant are never eclipsed by those of the Old, the following chapter will test the continuity between the testaments on the theme of being known by God.

GOD KNOWS US INTIMATELY AND PERSONALLY

The most famous passage in the Bible about being known by God is Psalm 139. It opens with the words, "You have searched me, LORD, and *you know me*." The psalmist claims that God is familiar with all his ways (v. 3b). Whether sitting or standing, rising or lying down, speaking or silent, God's knowledge of him is greater even than his knowledge of himself (vv. 2–6).

The psalmist gives two explanations for such wonderful knowledge (v. 6). The first is the fact that God is always present with him (vv. 7–12): "Where can I go from your Spirit? Where can I flee from your presence?" (v. 7). And the second is that God's knowledge of the psalmist originates from and completes a divine knowing begun before he was born (vv. 13–18): "For you created my inmost being; you knit me together in my mother's womb" (v. 13). As artists know their work, so the psalmist infers that God our Creator knows what he has made.

"God is closer to me than I am myself."
Meister Eckhart[9]

There are in fact two sorts of knowledge spoken of in Psalm 139: factual knowledge, the idea that God knows all about me; and relational knowledge, the fact that God knows me personally. In the psalm the two are closely related. God knows about me because he knows me. Some languages mark these two types of knowledge with different words. German, for example, uses *wissen* and *kennen* to refer to knowing *something* and knowing *someone* respectively. The Hebrew, Greek, and English languages use the same verbs "to know" for both.

"God knows me better than I know myself. . . . God knows the true me; the person I really am."
William J. Mander[10]

"How beautiful it is that God knows us better than we know ourselves or anyone else can."
Hawani Tola[11]

God's knowledge of everything and everyone is in fact taught in all of Scripture. God knows our ways, days, thoughts, secrets of our heart, and so on. First John 3:20 affirms God's omniscience bluntly: "he knows everything." "God knows," a phrase repeated three times in Paul's letters, testifies to this conviction. In 2 Corinthians 11:11 Paul uses it to convince his readers that he loves them: "God knows I do!" Even more telling is 2 Corinthians 12:2–3, where Paul affirms that "God knows" something that Paul himself does not know: namely, whether during some mystical experience the apostle was in or out of his body.

But to say that God knows us does not simply mean that God knows about us. If, to use the language of 2 Corinthians 5:11 ESV, God's omniscience means that "*what we are* is known to God," God's relational knowledge means that *who we are*

9. Meister Eckhart, *Sermons and Treatises*, vol. 1 (London: Watkins, 1981), 165.

10. William J. Mander, "Does God Know What It Is Like to Be Me?," *Heythorp Journal* 43.4 (2002): 430–43.

11. Hawani Tola, Ridley College student, social media post (March, 2015).

is known to God. According to the Bible, although God knows all about everyone, he does not know everyone in the intimate sense of personal relationship. Psalm 138:6 can speak of God knowing the proud "from afar" (ESV), but the righteous up close (he "regards" them). Similarly, according to Matthew and Luke Jesus will say to some at the last judgment, "I never knew you" (Matt 7:23; 25:12; Luke 13:27). If God's omniscience is an attribute of God that speaks of his transcendence and overlaps with his omnipresence,[12] his knowing us concerns his immanence and is related to his love.

Knowing things is the principal way of knowing in our day. Justin Thacker notes that

> in the dominant modern view of knowledge today, derived from the Enlightenment, knowledge is seen as objective and detached from the knower. It is possible to "know" something without being in any way engaged or committed to it. The model here is scientific knowing.[13]

However, in contrast to the modern West, relational knowledge is the main framework for knowledge in the Bible. The expression "to know" in the biblical sense originates in "Adam *knew* Eve" (Gen 4:1 ESV; cf. Judg 21:12), a reference to sexual relations, which testifies to the fact that in the Bible to know something can mean to experience it. This knowing by experience can also be seen in descriptions of people "knowing" the loss of children (Isa 47:8), disease (Isa 53:3), and divine punishment (Jer 16:21). Knowing these things is not about having an adequate intellectual grasp of them, akin to our sense of scientific knowledge, but being "acquainted with them existentially, emotionally, socially and cognitively."[14] It is this sort of knowledge with which we are concerned when thinking about being known by God. God knows us intimately and personally. In fact, he knows us better than we know ourselves.

WHAT IT MEANS TO BE KNOWN BY GOD

As with every relationship, our relationship with God has two sides: believers know God and are also known by him. Whereas knowing God is the focus of countless academic and popular books and articles, being known by God has received much less attention.[15] In one sense this is understandable, given that the Bible speaks of God knowing us much less often that it does of us knowing God. However, to measure

12. See also the juxtaposition of omniscience and omnipresence in Ps 139:1–4, "You know when," followed by vv. 5–10, "You hem me in."

13. Justin Thacker, "A Biblical Account of Christian Knowing," *Ethics in Brief* 13.1 (2008): 1.

14. Thacker, "A Biblical Account of Christian Knowing," 2.

15. My own interest in the subject began with an article on isolated remarks in two twentieth-century authors: "Known by God: C. S. Lewis and Dietrich Bonhoeffer," *Evangelical Quarterly* 77.4 (2005): 343–52.

the importance of being known by God by counting references would be a mistake. Although not numerous, texts which speak of being known by God punctuate the canon, turning up from Genesis to 2 Timothy and appearing in every major genre. And these texts refer both to individuals and to the nation Israel and the church.

References to being known by God appear at critical points in the biblical narrative. In the Old Testament, those who are known by God include key figures in God's unfolding plan to save the world:

- In Genesis 18 the explanation that God has chosen *Abraham* to become God's channel of blessing to the nations (v. 18) is that God knows him (v. 19): "*For I have known him*, in order that he may command his children and his household after him, that they keep the way of the LORD, to do righteousness and justice, that the LORD may bring to Abraham what He has spoken to him" (NKJV).
- In Exodus 33 *Moses* is described as God's friend, with whom he speaks face to face (v. 11), and he had told Moses, "*I know you* by name and you have found favor with me" (v. 12).
- In 2 Samuel 7, following the giving of the Davidic covenant, *David* praises God saying, "there is no one like you, and there is no God but you" (v. 22) and confessing to God about himself that "*you know your servant*, Sovereign LORD" (v. 20).
- In Jeremiah 1, *Jeremiah* opens his prophecy with the word of the Lord that establishes his calling: "Before I formed you in the womb *I knew you*, before you were born I set you apart; I appointed you as a prophet to the nations" (v. 5).
- Finally, in Amos 3 the nation of *Israel* itself is said to be known by God: "*You only have I known* of all the families of the earth" (v. 2 NRSV).

"What matters supremely is not, in the last analysis, the fact that I know God, but the larger fact which underlies it—*the fact that he knows me*. I am never out of his mind. All my knowledge of him depends on his sustained initiative in knowing me. I know him because he first knew me, and continues to know me. He knows me as a friend, one who loves me; and there is not a moment when his eye is off me, or his attention distracted from me, and no moment, therefore, when his care falters."

J. I. Packer[16]

As we will see in chapter seven, being known by God is just as significant in the New Testament.

God took the initiative to know Abraham. He knows Moses by name. He knows his servant David. He knew Jeremiah from before he was born. He knows Israel as opposed to other nations. To be known by God is to be known intimately and personally by him. But more can be said. The references to being known by God in the Old Testament

16. J. I. Packer, *Knowing God*, 20th Anniversary ed. (Downers Grove, IL: InterVarsity Press, 1993), 41–42. Emphasis added.

support linking our understanding of the concept to three related ideas: (1) belonging to God; (2) being loved and chosen by God; and (3) being a child of God.

Belonging to God

In the most general sense, to be known by God signals God's ownership of an individual or group. It means that we belong to God. In Numbers 16, the story of the rebellion of Korah and his followers, Moses explains that God will separate the innocent from the guilty before bringing his judgment:

> Then he said to Korah and all his followers: "In the morning the LORD *will show who belongs to him* and who is holy, and he will have that person come near him. The man he chooses he will cause to come near him." (v. 5)

However, the Greek translation of the Old Testament (LXX) renders the verse slightly differently, as "*God knows* those who belong to him." And in the New Testament, Paul in 2 Timothy 2:19 prefers the LXX of Numbers 16:5, quoting almost word for word: "*The Lord knows those who are his.*"[17]

In the LXX translation of Numbers 16, being known by God and belonging to God amount to much the same thing. In defining what it means to be known by God, Walther Eichrodt drew the same conclusion: "God knows his people . . . that is to say, he has introduced them into a permanent relationship of mutual belonging."[18] Adolf Schlatter also concluded that to be known by God is to be "the property of God."[19]

Along with belonging to our families, cultures, friendship groups, and nations, being known by God introduces a new belonging. It is one that is critical to our identity, is not subject to change, and affects everything about us, including our purpose, character, and destiny. We will have more to say about this in part three, "Reflecting on Relevance."

Chosen by God

The link between being known by God and being chosen by God is introduced in the first explicit reference to God's relational knowledge in the Bible. In Genesis 18, in connection with the fulfillment of the Abrahamic promise, God explains his grand plans for the patriarch: "Abraham will surely become a great and powerful nation, and all nations of the earth will be blessed through him" (v. 18). Then he

17. See also NJB: "The Lord knows those who are his own." Twice in Numbers 16 the same thought is expressed with the verb to "choose," a connection we will explore in the next subsection. The one the Lord chooses will be saved (vv. 5 and 7).

18. Walther Eichrodt, *Theology of the Old Testament: Volume Two* (London: SCM, 1967), 292, commenting on Hos 13:5.

19. German: "Gottes Eigentum." Adolf Schlatter, *Paulus, der Bote Jesu: Eine Deutung seiner Briefe an die Korinther* (Stuttgart: Calwer, 1985; orig. 1934), 253.

concludes with the words, "for I have known him" (v. 19 NKJV). That God's choice of Abraham is in view is clear from other numerous references in Genesis pertaining to election and the covenant. In Genesis 12:1–3, for instance, God's promise to Abraham is to make *him* into a great nation, to bless *him*, to make *his* name great, and so on, in distinction from blessing someone else. And God's selection of a particular line of seed turns out to be the backbone of the plot of Genesis 12–50, where the narrative concentrates on Abraham, Isaac, Jacob, and Joseph in succession. Thus it is understandable that English versions, such as the NIV and NRSV, translate Genesis 18:19, "For I have chosen him," even though the original Hebrew is *yadah*, the standard verb "to know" in the Old Testament.

Amos 3:2 is another text that connects being known by God with divine election. There, in the context of reminding Israel of God saving them from slavery in Egypt, the Lord remarks: "You only have I known of all the families of the earth" (ESV). Once again several English translations of the Bible interpret the sense in terms of God's choice of the nation. The NIV, for example, has: "You only have I chosen of all the families of the earth." The NLT does well to capture the close nature of the bond that being known by God suggests in this verse: "From among all the families on the earth, I have been intimate with you alone."

F. F. Bruce observes, "There is no difference between being known by God and being chosen by him."[20] Being known and chosen by God also has an impact on our personal identity. As with Abraham and the nation Israel, God chooses us for a purpose. We are chosen for a vocation, task, and mission. Our election is to be part of something much bigger than ourselves, and puts our otherwise fleeting lives in a different light. More will be said on this in chapter ten, "Shared Memory and Defining Destiny."

Child of God

Both belonging to God and being chosen by God give some content and context to the theme of being known by God. To be known by God is to be singled out as God's special people, those destined for blessing (see Abraham in Gen 18) and not for judgment (see the account of Korah's rebellion in Num 16). Obviously, in these cases being known by God has some considerable advantages!

But is being known by God simply another way of referring to those whom God chooses for blessing? Belonging to God can be a rather general and ambiguous notion. In what realm does the ownership pertain? In what sense do we belong to him? A third more specific definition that overlaps with and sharpens the first two calls for attention. If Eichrodt and Schlatter define being known by God in terms

20. F. F. Bruce, *The Epistle to the Galatians: A Commentary on the Greek Text*, NIGTC (Grand Rapids: Eerdmans, 1982), 202.

of belonging to him, and Bruce locates its meaning in divine election, John Calvin proposed that "to be known by God simply means to be counted among His sons."[21] Compared to the first two definitions, understanding being *known by God as a parent knows their child* deepens our grasp of the concept.

However, it is not the case that being known by God in the Bible refers to three different things. The three definitions are best conceived as more specific versions of the same reality. To belong to God is to be chosen by him. And we belong to God not just as his people, but more specifically as his children. The relationship of the three definitions can be illustrated as concentric circles:

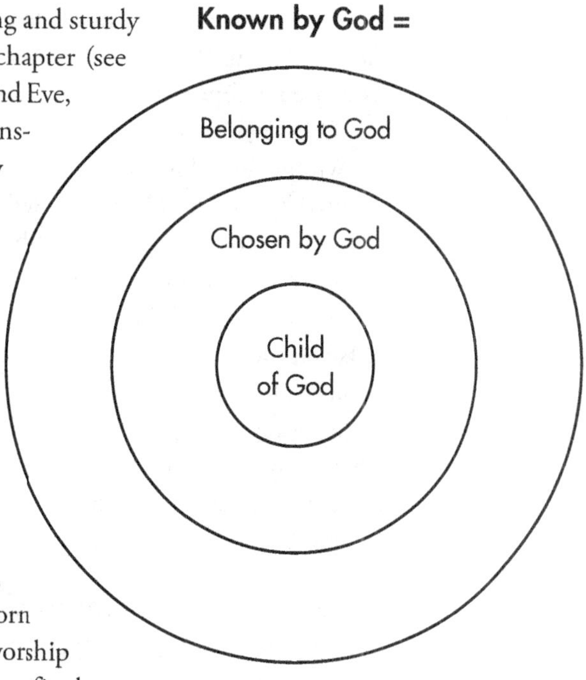

Known by God =

Belonging to God

Chosen by God

Child of God

The identity of being a child of God is a long and sturdy theme in the Bible and deserving of its own chapter (see chapter nine). We have already seen that Adam and Eve, before being ejected from the garden for their transgression, were known by God as his children by virtue of being made in the image of God (see chapter five). It is also the case that the theme of divine adoption in the Old Testament is connected with being known by God.

This theme of being the children of God in the Old Testament is connected to two great moments in salvation history.[22] The first is when *God adopts Israel as his son at the time of the exodus*. In explaining that Egypt's firstborn sons will be killed in judgment God says to Moses: "Say to Pharaoh, 'This is what the LORD says: Israel is my firstborn son, and I told you, "Let my son go, so he may worship me." But you refused to let him go; so I will kill your firstborn son'" (Exod 4:22–23). The prophet Hosea makes the same connection between the exodus and sonship for Israel: "When Israel was a child, I loved him, and out of Egypt I called my son" (Hos 11:1). In the New Testament, Paul reflects a similar understanding when he describes the nation of Israel's blessings as including their "adoption to sonship" (Rom 9:4).

Two references to being known by God in the Old Testament appear in contexts that specifically mention the salvific event of the exodus. When Amos 3:2 refers to God's election of Israel, "you only have I known" (ESV), it is preceded immediately

21. John Calvin, *Calvin's New Testament Commentaries: 1 Corinthians* (Grand Rapids: Eerdmans, 1996), 173.

22. See also Roy E. Ciampa, "Adoption," in *New Dictionary of Biblical Theology*, ed. T. D. Alexander and B. S. Rosner (Leicester, UK: Inter-Varsity Press, 2000), 376.

by the reminder that Israel is the people God "brought up out of Egypt" (3:1b). Additionally, Hosea 13:4–5 sets God's knowing the nation in the context of the same saving event: "I am the LORD your God from the land of Egypt; you know no God but me. . . . It was I who knew you in the wilderness" (ESV).

The second note of adoption in the Old Testament concerns *God adopting the king of Israel as his son in the Davidic covenant*. In 2 Samuel 7:14, God says of the Davidic king: "I will be his father, and he will be my son." The promise is repeated with reference to Solomon in 1 Chronicles 28:6 when God addresses David concerning the question of who will build the temple: "'Solomon your son is the one who will build my house and my courts, for I have chosen him to be my son, and I will be his father." And in Psalm 2:7, a coronation psalm, the Lord says to his anointed king: "You are my son; today I have become your father."

Once again, becoming a child of God in the Old Testament is linked to being known by God. The Davidic covenant in 2 Samuel 7 supports the nexus of being adopted by God and being known by God. Following David's offer to build God's "house" (in the sense of temple) being trumped by God's promise to build David's "house" (in the sense of dynasty), God promises to adopt David's offspring who will succeed him on the throne (v. 14). Amidst the children of God, who are the nation of Israel, the Davidic king will be the son of God *par excellence* (see also Ps 2:7). As we have already noted in chapter two, in the wake of this overwhelming news and the resulting feelings of inadequacy, David asks: "Who am I, Sovereign LORD, and what is my family, that you have brought me this far?" (2 Sam 7:18b). His answer to his own question underscores that he was known by God: "For *you know your servant*, Sovereign LORD" (7:20a).

A Secure Attachment to God

How does being known by God as his child connect to our theme of personal identity? Developmental psychology and psychiatry have some insights to offer.

Loyola McLean explains that when it comes to personal identity, "the self forms within and through relationships and in particular attachment relationships."[23] "Attachment theory" helps explain the key role that parents play in giving their children a stable sense of self:

> In attachment theory our early attachment relationships foster the development of our representations of self and other. Modern theory and much research now demonstrate that it is secure attachment relationships or an internalized secure attachment state of mind that give rise to a positive sense of self.[24]

23. Loyola McLean and Brian S. Rosner, "Theology and Human Flourishing: The Benefits of Being Known by God," in *Beyond Well-Being: Spirituality and Human Flourishing*, ed. Maureen Miner, Martin Dowson, and Stuart Devenish (Charlotte, NC: Information Age Publishing, 2012), 65–83.

24. McLean and Rosner, "Theology and Human Flourishing," 67.

Children develop a secure and positive sense of self when their parents form a secure attachment to them: "Early security fosters a stable self and a coherent narrative about oneself. A relatively coherent and stable personal identity underpinned by a strong and secure sense of self is now being shown to be critical to psychological health and well-being."[25] Significantly for our purposes, a critical factor in a secure attachment between a parent and a child is being known by the parent. McLean explains:

> Involved, loving parents know their children intimately. Indeed, a child's well-being appears to initially depend less on knowing his or her parents than on being known by them. . . . Attachment bonds are vital in both directions, but the caregiver is critical.[26]

In short, *parents give their children their identity by knowing them.* Children are named by their parents and receive their earliest experiences from them. Parents come to know their child's personality, likes and dislikes, physical capabilities, needs and desires. They pass on their own tastes, values, and worldview to their children. Indeed, parents play a big part in the formation and maintenance of their children's identity, especially when they are young.

At my stage of life, the death of a parent is increasingly a regular occurrence among my peers. I recall a conversation with one friend who had lost both of his parents within a couple of months. He reflected that without his parents around, he was beginning to wonder who he was. At best, parents are those who know us well and hold a more complete memory of our lives than anyone else. They establish the settings for our lives and reflect back to us our identity even when we are adults.

> "Similar to the human parent-child relationship, an attachment to God, where it is founded in a lived experience of being known and loved, can lead to a healthy sense of significance and is an effective source of comfort in response to dispiriting difficulties. Being known by God, who is holy and gracious, also offers moral direction, as the child of God seeks to take on the family likeness, and may offer the mental benefits that foster forgiveness and self-reflection that are associated with a secure state of mind."
>
> *Loyola McLean and Brian Rosner*[27]

The idea of receiving your identity as a relational gift from your parents is suggestive for how being known by God as his child contributes to the believer's personal identity. God gives us our identity as his children by knowing us intimately and personally.

KINDRED IDEAS

The Old Testament develops this theme of being known by God not only through explicit references to people being known by him, but also by reminders that God knows our names and is attentive to our lives.

25. Ibid., 68.
26. Ibid., 73.
27. Ibid., 80.

Naming as Knowing

Names in every culture are critical to personal identity. Usually the answer to the question of who you are begins with your name. For this reason, "Who named you?" and "Why?" are regular conversation topics among new acquaintances. Surnames associate you with your family. And saying that someone "knows your name" is another way of saying someone "knows you." Being on first-name terms with someone is an important matter in some cultures and may require some formality like a drink to mark the occasion. Nicknames and pet names indicate the closeness of a relationship. Middle names are often known only to a close circle of family and friends. As it turns out, names have an even greater significance in the Old Testament than in Western culture today.

"The Jewish idea of 'naming' implies more than just nomenclature; it involves the notions of determining the character and exercising authority over what is named (see Gen. 2:19; Ps. 147:4; Eccles. 6:10)."

John Muddiman[28]

Consistently, throughout the Bible God knows his people by name and they know his name. Isaiah 43 contains a message of comfort in which God calling his people by name is equivalent to belonging to God as his children and is set in the context of his work in creating and redeeming them:

> But now, this is what the LORD says . . .
> "Do not fear, for I have redeemed you;
> I have summoned you by name; you are mine. . . .
> Bring my sons from afar
> and my daughters from the ends of the earth—
> everyone who is called by my name,
> whom I created for my glory,
> whom I formed and made." (Isa 43:1, 6b–7)

Similarly, in the New Testament when Jesus compares himself to a shepherd, he makes the point that "he calls his own sheep by name" (John 10:3). However, not only does God know his people by name, he sometimes changes their name as a sign of his thorough involvement in their lives and as an indication of his plans for them. Examples include God changing Abram's name to Abraham, Sarai to Sarah, Jacob to Israel, and in the New Testament, Jesus changing Simon's name to Cephas (Peter).

Even more intriguing is a group of three passages in Isaiah where God gives names to his people, but we are not told what they are. In Isaiah 56 God makes promises to the obedient eunuchs:

28. John Muddiman, *The Epistle to the Ephesians*, BNTC (London: Continuum, 2001), 166–67.

> To the eunuchs who keep my Sabbaths,
> who choose what pleases me
> and hold fast to my covenant—
> to them I will give within my temple and its walls
> a memorial and *a name*
> *better than sons and daughters;*
> *I will give them an everlasting name*
> *that will endure forever.* (Isa 56:4–5)

In an oracle of salvation in Isaiah 62, God promises his people a new name:

> For Zion's sake I will not keep silent,
> for Jerusalem's sake I will not remain quiet,
> till her vindication shines out like the dawn,
> her salvation like a blazing torch.
> The nations will see your vindication,
> and all kings your glory;
> *you will be called by a new name*
> that the mouth of the LORD will bestow. (Isa 62:1–2)

Third, in Isaiah 65 God will give his chosen servants another name:

> Therefore this is what the Sovereign LORD says:
> "My servants will eat,
> but you will go hungry;
> my servants will drink,
> but you will go thirsty;
> my servants will rejoice,
> but you will be put to shame.
> My servants will sing
> out of the joy of their hearts,
> but you will cry out
> from anguish of heart
> and wail in brokenness of spirit.
> You will leave your name
> for my chosen ones to use in their curses;
> the Sovereign LORD will put you to death,
> but *to his servants he will give another name.*" (Isa 65:13–15)

The context of all three passages concerns God's determined intention to *bless* his people beyond their expectations. For this reason, the giving of a new name is reason to "sing out of the joy of their hearts" (Isa 65:14). The intensely personal nature of the giving of the name is underscored ("a new name that the mouth of the LORD will bestow," Isa 62:2) along with its eternal significance ("I will give them an everlasting name" as a memorial within the temple, Isa 56:5). Significantly, in these verses *our identity is not only known by God, but known only to God and then to us when he tells us.*

Despite naming their children on their birth certificates, many parents give their young children "another name," a nickname known only to family members and the closest of friends. Such monikers are generally not used in public. They function as signs of tenderness, intimacy, and affection.

The name of the main character in the popular children's classic *Winnie the Pooh* by A. A. Milne is actually "Edward Bear." He mostly goes by his nickname in the books, "Pooh Bear." However, Tigger calls him "Buddy Bear," and Christopher Robin, "Silly Old Bear."

In the New Testament, we find a similar passage about God giving his people a new name. In Revelation 2:17 two words of encouragement are offered to the members of the church of Pergamum who are suffering persecution. One is "hidden manna"; the other is a reference to "a white stone with a new name written on it, known only to the one who receives it." The consensus among biblical commentators is that "we simply do not know what the white stone signified, though clearly it did convey some assurance of blessing."[29] Whatever else the "new name" reference denotes, its hidden nature, known only to God and its bearer, speaks of intimate interpersonal relationship, a knowledge that encourages the one who overcomes to persevere. Being given a secret name by God is another way of affirming that someone is known personally by God as children are known by their parents.

The theme of naming as knowing is also often reinforced in the Bible's narratives, where the characters who are named are the faithful to whom God is unwaveringly committed. In Exodus 1 the pharaoh is not named—he is just "the king of Egypt." But Shiphrah and Puah, the lowly Hebrew midwives, are named (Exod 1:15). Similarly, in Ruth 4 Boaz is named, but the guardian-redeemer who refuses to buy the land from Naomi for fear of endangering his own estate is not.

In the New Testament, Timothy Keller points to something comparable in the parable of the rich man and Lazarus in Luke 16:

> The rich man, unlike Lazarus, is never given a personal name. He is only called "a Rich Man," strongly hinting that since he had built his identity on his wealth rather than on God, once he lost his wealth he lost any sense of self.[30]

If your life is characterized by faith in and obedience to the Lord, like Shiphrah, Puah, Boaz, and Lazarus, then God knows you by name, and your identity is secure in him. Your name is written in the Lamb's book of life, a book written "from the creation of the world" (Rev 17:8).[31]

29. Leon Morris, *The Book of Revelation*, TNTC (Leicester, UK: Inter-Varsity Press, 1987), 68.

30. Timothy Keller, *The Reason for God: Belief in an Age of Skepticism* (New York: Penguin: 2008), 78.

God's Books

Along with knowing his people by name and even giving them new names, God keeps a list of our names. In both testaments of the Bible is mentioned an "eternal ledger"[32] of those who belong to him, most often termed "the book of life." The existence of such a book ties in with the Bible's consistent interest in genealogies, family lists, and national registers in Israel. In biblical thought, names matter, especially the names of people who are known by God.

An early reference concerns God's wrath in response to the idolatry of the golden calf in Exodus 32:31–33:

> So Moses went back to the LORD and said, "Oh, what a great sin these people have committed! They have made themselves gods of gold. But now, please forgive their sin—but if not, then blot me out of the book you have written." The LORD replied to Moses, "Whoever has sinned against me I will blot out of my book."

The book that God has written seems to contain the names of those whose sins God has forgiven. The rest of the references in the Bible to this book are remarkably consistent on this point.

References in Daniel 12 and Psalm 69 reinforce the idea that those whose names are in the book are destined for salvation and those whose names are not will face judgment:

> At that time Michael, the great prince who protects your people, will arise. There will be a time of distress such as has not happened from the beginning of nations until then. But at that time your people—everyone whose name is found written in the book—will be delivered. (Dan 12:1)

> Charge them with crime upon crime;
> do not let them share in your salvation.
> May they be blotted out of the book of life
> and not be listed with the righteous. (Ps 69:27–28)

The New Testament understands the book of life along similar lines. Those whose names are recorded in the book of life are told to rejoice (Luke 10:20), and "the church of the firstborn" are described as those "whose names are written in heaven" (Heb 12:23), along with Paul's coworkers (Phil 4:3). In Revelation, having your name in the book of life is decisive for whether you are saved or not:

31. In Hebrews 12:23, having your name "written in heaven" is synonymous with being a member of "the church of the firstborn," suggesting once again a link between divine adoption and being known by God.

32. Thomas W. Davis, "Book, Book of Life," in *Evangelical Dictionary of Biblical Theology*, ed. Walter A. Elwell, electronic ed. (Grand Rapids: Baker, 1996).

The Bible has an almost obsessive fascination with names. The first book of the Old Testament contains several genealogies (e.g., Gen 5:1–31; 10:1–32; 11:10–26; 22:20–24; 25:1–4, 12–18; 46:8–27). The first book of the New Testament opens with a list of the names of Jesus's ancestors (Matt 1:1–17; cf. Luke 3:23–38). Censuses play a significant role at different points in biblical history (cf. Exod 38:26; Num 26; 2 Chr 2:17–18; Ezra 2). There are multiple lists of the sons and tribes of Israel (e.g., Gen 46:8–27; Exod 1:1–5; Josh 21:1–8; 1 Chr 2:1–2; 12:24–38; Ezek 48:1–35; Rev 7:1–8). Lists of the disciples of Jesus are also prominent (Matt 10:2–4; Mark 3:16–19; Luke 6:13–16; Acts 1:13). In all, some 2,600 proper names appear in the Bible's sixty-six books.

> And I saw the dead, great and small, standing before the throne, and books were opened. Another book was opened, which is *the book of life*. The dead were judged according to what they had done as recorded in the books. The sea gave up the dead that were in it, and death and Hades gave up the dead that were in them, and each person was judged according to what they had done. Then death and Hades were thrown into the lake of fire. The lake of fire is the second death. Anyone whose name was not found written in *the book of life* was thrown into the lake of fire. (Rev 20:12–15; cf. 3:5; 17:8; 21:27)

What is referred to simply as the "books" (Rev 20:12) are presumably the records of the lives of those whose names are not found written in the book of life, which form the basis of their judgment and condemnation. By contrast, Revelation 13:8 describes the book of life as "the Lamb's book of life, the Lamb who was slain from the creation of the world" as a reminder that the basis of salvation is the cross of Jesus Christ. The book of life being decisive for our acquittal at the last judgment underscores the grace and mercy of God toward those whose names are therein written. Our names matter to God. And the fact that our names are in God's book of life gives our otherwise fleeting lives a reassuring permanence.

Remembered by God

The relationship between being "known" by God and being "remembered" by God is evident in the report of the plight of the people of God in Egypt in Exodus 2:23–25:

> During that long period, the king of Egypt died. The Israelites groaned in their slavery and cried out, and their cry for help because of their slavery went up to God. God heard their groaning and *he remembered his covenant* with Abraham, with Isaac and with Jacob. So God looked on the Israelites and *he was concerned about* [lit., knew] *them*.[33]

When God remembers, he is not simply bringing back to mind something he

33. The Hebrew has simply *yadah*, God "knew," with the object of the verb unexpressed; see also ASV, God "took knowledge of them." The NIV translation, God "was concerned about them," along with most modern translations, understands the object to be the dire situation of the Israelites. See also the NET note: "The idea seems to be that God took personal knowledge of, noticed, or regarded them." A similar use of the verb "to know" appears in Exod 3:7 NIV: "The LORD said, 'I have indeed seen the misery of my people in Egypt. I have heard them crying out because of their slave drivers, and I am concerned about [literally, know] their suffering.'" We will return to Exod 2:25 in chapter thirteen in connection with the comfort that being known by God brings.

has forgotten. The Hebrew verb *zakar* is used in this way but never with God as the subject. Instead, God remembers in the sense that he acts on what he has called to mind. Lindsay Wilson explains the relationship between God remembering his covenant and God knowing us:

> Being remembered by God presupposes God knowing you, but moves on beyond that. It results in God actively treating you according to his promises and purposes, and in light of his past commitments.[34]

God remembering those he knows is grounded in the fact that he made us. As Psalm 103:14 asserts: "he knows how we are formed, he remembers that we are dust." But more often in the Old Testament, God knowing and remembering us has its basis in his redeeming us. God remembers his covenant on numerous occasions and makes good on his promises to bless his people accordingly. In Exodus 6:6, having remembered his covenant, he says to the people of Israel:

> I am the Lord, and I will bring you out from under the yoke of the Egyptians. I will free you from being slaves to them, and I will redeem you with an outstretched arm and with mighty acts of judgment (cf. Lev 26:40–45).

Psalm 106:45 connects being remembered by God with God acting in grace and mercy: "For their sake he remembered his covenant, and showed compassion according to the abundance of his steadfast love" (NRSV; cf. Ps 98:3; 136:23–24).

In the New Testament, when Mary sings her famous song of praise to God in response to the news that she will give birth to "the Son of God" (Luke 1:35), she understands this event as God remembering his covenant: "He has helped his servant Israel, remembering to be merciful to Abraham and his descendants forever, just as he promised our ancestors" (Luke 1:54–55).

God not only remembers his covenant but also individuals within the covenant. There are several examples in the Old Testament of God remembering certain people in the sense that he acted on their behalf and in their best interests:

- In Genesis 19:29 the narrator explains the salvation of Lot from the destruction of Sodom and Gomorrah in terms of God remembering *Abraham*: "So when God destroyed the cities of the plain, *he remembered Abraham*, and he brought Lot out of the catastrophe that overthrew the cities where Lot had lived."
- In Genesis 30:22–23 God gave previously barren *Rachel* a child: "Then *God remembered Rachel*; he listened to her and enabled her to conceive. She

34. Lindsay Wilson, "Remembered by God" (Unpublished paper; Ridley College Theology Conference: Known by God, 29–30 May 2015).

became pregnant and gave birth to a son and said, 'God has taken away my disgrace.'"

- In 1 Samuel 1:19–20 God similarly grants *Hannah's* request for a child: "Early the next morning they arose and worshiped before the LORD and then went back to their home at Ramah. Elkanah made love to his wife Hannah, and *the* LORD *remembered her.* So in the course of time Hannah became pregnant and gave birth to a son. She named him Samuel, saying, 'Because I asked the LORD for him.'"

As Wilson notes, "these examples show that God does not restrict his active remembrance to the people as a whole, but also responds to the individual cries of those among his people who call out to him."[35]

In the Old Testament the cries of the covenant community and individuals within the covenant are regularly framed as calls for God to remember to act:[36]

> Remember, LORD, what has happened to us; look, and see our disgrace. (Lam 5:1)

> O LORD, how long will you forget me? Forever?
> How long will you look the other way?
> How long must I struggle with anguish in my soul,
> with sorrow in my heart every day?
> How long will my enemy have the upper hand? (Ps 13:1–2 NLT)

It is of course not the case that God always answers these cries with acts of deliverance. Nonetheless, the assumption of such prayers is that God knows us and is positively inclined to act on our behalf. As Gerald Wilson comments on the anguished fourfold "How long?" of Psalm 13, "such divine forgetfulness threatens to undo the psalmist, because to be known and remembered by God is to be in the relationship of blessing."[37] The general point is clear: being known by God means that he is attentive to our needs and acts in love and mercy toward us. If there are times when we feel that God has forgotten us, we may know with confidence that God remembers both his covenant and his people forever.

SAMPLE TEXTS: ISAIAH 49 AND MALACHI 3

God knows us as his children. God knows our names. God remembers us and acts towards us in love in keeping with his covenant promises. To round out our study of being known by God in the Old Testament, we consider two case studies in which

35. Wilson, "Remembered by God."

36. Prayers for the people: Exod 32:13; Deut 9:27; 2 Chr 6:41–42; Neh 1:8–9; Pss 74:2–3; 132; Jer 14:21. Prayers of individuals: Judg 16:28; 2 Kgs 20:3; Neh 5:19; Pss 25:7; 106:4; Jer 15:15.

37. Gerald H. Wilson, *Psalms, Volume 1*, NIV Application Commentary (Grand Rapids: Zondervan, 2002), 278.

these elements come together in striking ways. Both have a poignancy befitting descriptions of the intimate bond between God and his people that is signaled in being known by him.

Isaiah 49—God's Tattoo

Isaiah 49:14–18 is a passage in which the Lord seeks to comfort his people who are languishing in exile. In Isaiah 49:13 the exiles are told that "the LORD . . . will have compassion on his afflicted ones" and that they should "shout for joy" and "rejoice" at the prospect, along with the heavens, the earth, and the mountains. Their response to this upbeat message is one of doubt and despondency: "But Zion said, 'The LORD has forsaken me, the Lord has forgotten me'" (Isa 49:14).[38] Sitting in exile, with Jerusalem in ruins, God's people understandably feel abandoned by God. From their perspective, he has not remembered them. They see no sign of his compassion.

In Isaiah 49:15–18 the Lord seeks to quell their doubts and reassure them of his love and concern:

> "Can a mother forget the baby at her breast
> and have no compassion on the child she has borne?
> Though she may forget,
> I will not forget you!
> See, I have engraved you on the palms of my hands;
> your walls are ever before me.
> Your children hasten back,
> and those who laid you waste depart from you.
> Lift up your eyes and look around;
> all your children gather and come to you.
> As surely as I live," declares the LORD,
> "you will wear them all as ornaments;
> you will put them on, like a bride." (Isa 49:15–18)

In verse 15, God's attachment to his people is like that of a mother to a child, only more so. Walter Brueggemann explains:

> It is completely improbable that a nursing mother would forsake her child, improbable but not impossible. For Yahweh, however, such forgetting and forsaking is not even a possibility, for Yahweh's commitment and compassion are stronger and more intense than that of any nursing mother.[39]

38. As Barry Webb explains, "Zion" is code for the people of God: "*Zion* is not just the city of that name, it is its people. Zion is not simply their home, it is their name, their identity" (*The Message of Isaiah*, Bible Speaks Today [Leicester, UK: Inter-Varsity Press, 1996], 196).

39. Walter Brueggemann, *Isaiah 40–66*, Westminster Bible Companion (Louisville: Westminster John Knox, 1998), 116.

Israel may feel forsaken and forgotten by God, but God says, "I will not forget you" (v. 15). God is even more attentive to his people than the most devoted mother to her children.

That God knows his people is affirmed vividly in Isaiah 49:16a: "See, I have engraved you on the palms of my hands." The imagery recalls Isaiah 44:5, where people confess that they belong to the Lord and "write on their hand, 'the LORD's.'" As we have already seen, God knowing your name is analogous to being known by God and can signal belonging to God. Whatever you make of the art of tattooing, there are few more impressive symbols of one person's love for someone else than a permanent bodily reminder. That God has "Israel" tattooed on his hands leaves beyond any doubt that he will remember his people and that he knows their names.

"Tattoos were quite common in the ancient world. People got tattoos for different reasons. Egyptian women tattooed their stomachs and breasts during pregnancy to ensure a safe birth. Slaves got tattoos to identify them as the property of another. Criminals were sometimes forced to get a tattoo to bear the stigma of their crime. The Greeks and Romans got a tattoo to show allegiance to their god. For instance, King Ptolemy IV tattooed his body with ivy leaves to show his devotion to Dionysus, the god of wine. God's tattoo is probably similar to Ptolemy's, only God turns the meaning on its head. While Ptolemy and other kings were running around flaunting their devotion to their god—your God sits on his throne and declares, 'I'm devoted to *you*! And I've put my palms under the needle to prove it.'"

Preston Sprinkle[41]

The second half of Isaiah 49:16 compares God to an architect who thinks constantly about his plans: "your walls are ever before me." The literal meaning is that God plans to rebuild and reclaim the city of Jerusalem. Next, the Lord announces that Zion's children will return to her in overflowing numbers: "you will wear them all as ornaments" (v. 18a). Zion will be like a happy mother whose children have returned. Zion will also be like a father who is exceedingly proud of his daughter at her wedding: "you will put them on, like a bride" (v. 18b). As Barry Webb notes, "the images [here] are mixed and do not always cohere logically, but they all affirm God's love for his people and his tireless commitment to their welfare."[40]

With God's city of Zion in ruins and the identity of the exiled people of God in tatters, God assures the Israelites that they belong to him and that he is lovingly attentive to them as a mother to her children. At the heart of God's reassurances in Isaiah 49 are two themes associated with being known by God in the Old Testament: a comparison of God to a devoted parent and the names of God's people etched into his very being.

Malachi 3—A Scroll of Remembrance

At several points in the Old Testament, the arrogance and prosperity of those who do not honor God is a stumbling block to those who do, which causes them to question the goodness of God. Psalm 73 is one example:

40. Webb, *Message of Isaiah*, 196.

41. Preston Sprinkle, *Charis: God's Scandalous Grace for Us* (Colorado Springs: David C. Cook, 2014), 112.

> Surely God is good to Israel,
> to those who are pure in heart.
> But as for me, my feet had almost slipped;
> I had nearly lost my foothold.
> For I envied the arrogant
> when I saw the prosperity of the wicked. (Ps 73:1–3)

A similar sentiment is expressed in Malachi 3:13–15, which reports some people saying that there is no point in serving God, obeying his commands, or fasting and repenting. Worse still, those who turn their backs on God seem to be getting away with it:

> "You have spoken arrogantly against me," says the Lord. "Yet you ask, 'What have we said against you?' "You have said, 'It is futile to serve God. What do we gain by carrying out his requirements and going about like mourners before the Lord Almighty? But now we call the arrogant blessed. Certainly evildoers prosper, and even when they put God to the test, they get away with it.'"

Those who do seek the Lord are understandably discouraged by this state of affairs. Doesn't God notice when people flout his authority? Is there no difference between those who are faithful to him and those who are not? The issue strikes at the heart of their identity as the people of God. Are they special to him? Does he notice their efforts to live in faith and obedience?

Their first response is to talk things over: "Then those who feared the Lord talked with each other" (Mal 3:16a). While we are not privy to their conversation, Taylor and Clendenen make some plausible suggestions as to what might have been said:

> The content of their speech may have been words of repentance or spiritual encouragement to one another in view of the ruined crops (see Prov 27:17; Jer 31:34). Perhaps they were words of encouragement to do right, such as those of the leprous men in 2 Kgs 7:9—Then they said to each other, "We're not doing right. This is a day of good news and we are keeping it to ourselves. Let's go at once and report this to the royal palace" (see also Jer 36:16). Or perhaps they were simply "speaking the truth to each other, and rendering true and sound judgment in their courts" (Zech 8:16).[42]

Whatever the exact nature of their discussion, "the Lord listened and heard." Moreover, "a scroll of remembrance was written in his presence concerning those who feared the Lord and honored his name" (Mal 3:16).

42. Richard A. Taylor and E. Ray Clendenen, *Haggai, Malachi: An Exegetical and Theological Exposition of Holy Scripture*, NAC 21A (Nashville: Broadman & Holman, 2004), 442–43.

The best background against which to understand this "scroll of remembrance" is God as "the divine King surrounded by his heavenly servants instructing a scribe to record an event in the royal archives."[43] Esther 2:23 notes a recording "in the book of the annals in the presence of the king." In Esther 6:1 "the book of the chronicles, the record of his reign" is ordered for the king. And, in Ezra 5:17 a search of the "royal archives" takes place. As Taylor and Clendenen note, "records of decisions, actions, accomplishments, and various memorable events were kept by royal officials in the ancient world."[44] Significantly, Malachi 1:14 describes God as "a great king," whose name is to be "feared among the nations."

"Helen Bamber, the British campaigner for the care of torture victims, has described the experience of holding a dying woman in her arms after the liberation of the Belsen concentration camp at the end of World War II. As the woman rasped out the horrific account of her experiences in the camp, Bamber said to her: 'I am going to tell your story.' This seemed to calm the distressed woman. 'I think she knew she was going to die,' Bamber said. 'She didn't want to die and [her story] not be told—that nobody would know.' This was a woman anxious, even at her death, not to be ignored or forgotten. When all other desires have left us or become irrelevant, we are left with the desire to be acknowledged, identified, appreciated, and remembered."

Hugh Mackay[46]

The scroll of remembrance is not the same as the book of life, that heavenly register of the faithful (see above in this chapter). Nor is it the record of the deeds of the unrighteous from which God will mete out justice (cf. Dan 7:10; Rev 20:12). Rather, it is "an ongoing account of the words and deeds of the God-fearers."[45] Those who sought to honor God's name needed reassurance that God knew of their plight and that he was taking notice. The same sentiment is present in Psalm 56 where the enemies of the psalmist "are in hot pursuit" (v. 1), and he asks God to "record my misery; list my tears on your scroll—are they not in your record?" (v. 8).

In response to the concern of the faithful that God had not noticed the injustice in their day and their own determination to obey him, "there was written down in a book a record of those who feared the Lord and respected him" (Mal 3:16 GNT). As a further encouragement, the Lord declares his intention to confirm the identity of those who fear him:

> "On the day when I act," says the Lord Almighty, "they will be my treasured possession. I will spare them, just as a father has compassion and spares his son who serves him. And you will again see the distinction between the righteous and the wicked, between those who serve God and those who do not." (Mal 3:17–18)

It is common for people to question their identity in times of hardship and difficulty. In God's response to such a situation in Malachi 3:16–18, we see the same

43. Ibid., 443.

44. Ibid.

45. Andrew Hill, "Malachi," in *Zondervan Illustrated Bible Backgrounds Commentary*, ed. John W. Walton, vol. 5 (Grand Rapids: Zondervan, 2009), 241.

46. Hugh Mackay, *What Makes Us Tick: The Ten Desires that Drive Us* (Sydney: Hachette Australia, 2010), 4.

cluster of ideas that we have noted throughout our study of being known by God in the Old Testament: God's people are those to whom he is attentive—a "scroll of remembrance was written in his presence concerning those who feared the Lord"; they belong to him as his "treasured possession"; and he knows them and relates to them as a father who has compassion on his son (Mal 3:16-18).

Whereas the knowledge of God might sometimes seem ethereal and removed from our daily lives, the fact that we are known by God even in our darkest days is a great comfort. God knows us when our struggles with our own identity feel hidden from everyone else.

The four Gospels in the New Testament are testimony to the fact that the genre of biography goes back to the ancient world. And the first-century Jewish historian Josephus is an early example of someone who wrote his autobiography. However, interest in life stories has never been stronger than in our own day, with politicians, actors, and sports stars leading the way. Ordinary people too are keen to preserve the record of their lives, with social media providing unprecedented opportunities to share everything from the mundane to the profound and extraordinary. Motivations vary. Some wish to bring attention to their accomplishments or unusual experiences, others to record their journey through illness or tragedy. Many wish to pass on their story to subsequent generations of their families. Malachi 3:16 indicates that God is writing the biographies of those who honor his name.

BEING KNOWN BY GOD AND PERSONAL IDENTITY

This chapter opened with a critique of the view that personal identity is a do-it-yourself project. The problem with "defining yourself" is that it ignores the fact that we are social creatures. The self as an autonomous individual does not exist. We are in large measure defined by our relationships. And we come to know ourselves in being known by others.

With this in mind, it is significant, as we saw in chapter two, that one of the Bible's answers to the question of personal identity is that human beings are those who are known by God, those about whom God is mindful (Job 7:17; Pss 8:4; 144:3). And when David asks, "Who am I?" he comes to the conclusion that he is known by God (2 Sam 7:20; cf. 1 Chr 17:18). In contrast to Descartes's dictum, "I think, therefore I am," or "I know, therefore I am," the Bible puts things the other way around: "I am known, therefore I am."[47]

What does it mean to be known by God? And how does being known by God contribute to your personal identity? Our investigation of the theme of being known by God in the Old Testament reveals that to be known by God means to belong to God and to be chosen by him. He knows us intimately and personally and with the love and compassion of a father or mother for their child. He remembers us when we are in trouble, and he knows our name. Being known by God meets our need to be recognized and acknowledged in the most profound manner. Our identity as his

47. See N. T. Wright, who offers a similar revision of Descartes's dictum claiming the support of the apostle Paul, suggesting, "I am loved, therefore I am" (*Paul: In Fresh Perspectives* [London: SPCK, 2006], 173).

children is grounded and sustained by his constant attentiveness. There is indeed something reassuring and beautiful about God really knowing you.

Who am I? I am known and loved by God as his child. In chapter seven, we will consider what the New Testament says about being known by God.

RELEVANT QUESTIONS

1. There is indeed something reassuring and beautiful about someone really knowing you. Do you have people in your life who really know you? How can close relationships be a source of comfort in both good and bad times?
2. "What matters supremely is not . . . that I know God, but the larger fact . . . that he knows me," says J. I. Packer. How can being known by God as his child foster a "healthy sense of significance" and "a secure state of mind" (McLean and Rosner)?
3. What is the story behind your naming, and how do you feel about your name? The words of the old hymn speak of God's remembrance of us: "My name is graven on his hands; my name is written on his heart." What is the significance of being named by God, now and into eternity?
4. In times of hardship and difficulty, it is common for people to question God's goodness and attentiveness. How can God's response to his discouraged followers in Malachi be an encouragement or comfort to us?

CHAPTER 7

KNOWN BY GOD AND CHRIST IN THE NEW TESTAMENT

At one point in C. S. Lewis's *The Voyage of the Dawn Treader*, one of the books in *The Chronicles of Narnia* series, Eustace Clarence Scrubb wanders off to avoid doing his chores and enters a dragon's cave. Greedily plundering its treasures, he finds himself turned into a dragon. Aslan the lion comes to his rescue and "undragons" him, which results in the transformation of the odious Eustace into "a different boy." Following the incident, Eustace asks his cousin Edmund what he knows of Aslan: "But who is Aslan? Do you know him?" Edmund admits to knowing Aslan, but the beginning of his answer is inverted in a surprising way: "Well, *he knows me*."[1] According to Edmund, being known by Aslan is more important than knowing Aslan.

The same applies when it comes to the knowledge of God. God knows us better than we know him, and his knowledge of us precedes and is the basis for our knowledge of him.

Our investigation of the theme of being known by God in the Old Testament in chapter six showed it to be a highly personal truth with deep theological roots. Being known by God characterizes how God related to the nation of Israel as well as to the main characters in salvation history. It connects to several of God's principal saving actions in the Old Testament including the redemption of his people from slavery in Egypt and the establishment of kingship. It has links with Israel's adoption as God's son and the adoption of the Davidic king as God's son. And it emphasizes God's compassionate concern for his people as a loving parent who is attentive to and cares for his children.

What does the New Testament say about the theme of being known by God? Does it have the same shape as in the Old Testament? How important is the theme of being known by God in the New Testament? Is there something reassuring and beautiful about being known by God in the New Testament? What does it contribute to our study of personal identity?

As it turns out, when it comes to the theme of being known by God, there is

1. C. S. Lewis, *The Voyage of the Dawn Treader* (London: Lions, 1980; orig. 1955), 87. Emphasis added.

remarkable consistency between the testaments. Being known by God defines what it means to be a Christian in much the same way it did to be part of Israel as the people of God: those who are known by God belong to God, are chosen by God, and are adopted into his family as his children. However, the New Testament takes things further and develops the theme in two main ways: first, being known by God's Son, Jesus Christ, becomes critical; and second, being known by God and Christ emerges as a defining feature of life in the age to come.

We begin our study of the New Testament with a general look at being known by God, before moving to the idea of being known by Christ. A third major section considers a key New Testament text for our theme, namely the Gospel of John.

THE PRIMACY OF BEING KNOWN BY GOD

As social creatures, we are defined by our relationships. It is thus no surprise that the Bible makes a big deal about the utterly transforming experience and inestimable privilege of knowing God. The prophet Jeremiah declared that knowing the God of kindness, justice, and righteousness is of greater value than having wisdom, strength, and riches: "Let the one who boasts boast about this: that they have the understanding to know me" (Jer 9:23–24). In Philippians, Paul wrote of the "surpassing worth of knowing Christ Jesus my Lord" (3:8). And according to Jesus himself, "This is eternal life: that they know you, the only true God, and Jesus Christ, whom you have sent" (John 17:3).

Notwithstanding the great blessing that it is to know God, on three occasions in Paul's letters the apostle insists that being known by God is even better. In Galatians 4:8–9 Paul reminds gentile Christians of their previous plight before affirming their current blessed status:

> Formerly, when you did not know God, you were slaves to those who by nature are not gods. But now that you know God—*or rather are known by God* . . . .

At first Paul writes of believers knowing God, but then he offers, in the words of F. F. Bruce, a "swift correction."[2] The words "or rather"[3] make it clear that what really matters for the identity of the Christians in Galatia is the fact that they are known by God.

Two other texts that underscore the critical importance of being known by God are in 1 Corinthians. First Corinthians 8:1–3 contain the opening remarks of Paul's lengthy discussion of food offered to idols in chapters eight to ten. Apparently certain

---

2. F. F. Bruce, *The Epistle to the Galatians: A Commentary on the Greek Text*, NIGTC (Grand Rapids: Eerdmans, 1982), 202.

3. See Ernest de Witt Burton on the phrase: "Following a positive expression it introduces an additional and more important fact or aspect of the matter, not thereby retracting what precedes, but so transferring the emphasis to the added fact or aspect as being of superior significance as in effect to displace the preceding thought" (*A Critical and Exegetical Commentary on the Epistle to the Galatians*, ICC [Edinburgh: T&T Clark, 1921], 229). See also Rom 8:34; 1 Cor 14:1, 5; Eph 4:28; 5:11.

Corinthians felt that their knowledge of God and the fact that "an idol is nothing at all in the world" (1 Cor 8:4) meant that they were free to eat food originally sacrificed to idols under any circumstances. Paul warns them about the dangers of becoming proud in their knowledge:

> Now about food sacrificed to idols: We know that "We all possess knowledge." But knowledge puffs up while love builds up. Those who think they know something do not yet know as they ought to know. (1 Cor 8:1–2)

As the alternative to pride, which "puffs up" or "builds up" only oneself, Paul recommends love, which "builds up" others.

A number of commentators have noticed that the next verse contains a surprising twist: "But whoever loves God is *known by God*" (1 Cor 8:3). Whereas we might expect Paul to say, "whoever loves God, knows God," Paul turns things around. The knowledge that counts is not our knowledge of God, but his knowledge of us.[4]

> "Let me know you, for you are the God who knows me; let me recognize you as you have recognized me."
>
> *Saint Augustine*[5]

At the end of his famous poem in praise of love in 1 Corinthians 13, Paul contrasts knowing God with being known by him:

> For now we see only a reflection as in a mirror; then we shall see face to face. Now I know in part; then I shall know fully, even as *I am fully known [by God].* (1 Cor 13:12)[6]

When it comes to knowledge of God, we will only have "complete mutuality of knowledge"[7] when Christ returns and we see him face to face. In the meantime, we "know in part," indirectly as it were, "as in a mirror." We know God truly, but our knowledge of him is hardly exhaustive or complete. God, on the other hand, knows us perfectly and far better than we know him. Paul in 1 Corinthians 13:11 suggests that our knowledge of God is like that of a young child knowing his or her parent. Just as parents know their children much better than the other way around, so God's knowledge of us is much greater than our knowledge of him.

> "The consummation of all things [in 1 Corinthians 13:12] consists in the fact that the cleft between knowing and being known by God is abolished."
>
> *Gunther Bornkamm*[8]

The importance of being known by God is also underscored

4. See Hans Conzelmann, *1 Corinthians: A Commentary on the First Epistle to the Corinthians*, ed. George W. MacRae, trans. James W. Leitch, Hermeneia (Philadelphia: Fortress, 1975), 141. See also Richard B. Hays: "We expect: 'The person who loves God, knows him rightly.' But the thought is deliberately given a different turn" (*First Corinthians*, Interpretation [Louisville: Westminster John Knox, 1997], 139).

5. Augustine, *Confessions* (London: Penguin, 1961), 207.

6. The passive voice of the Greek verb "to know" is used here with God as the obvious, but implicit agent of the action (often labeled a divine passive).

7. C. K. Barrett, *The First Epistle to the Corinthians*, BNTC (London: Black, 1971), 307.

8. Gunther Bornkamm, "The More Excellent Way," in *Early Christian Experience* (New York: Harper & Row, 1969), 185.

in the New Testament with reference to its role on the day of judgment. This is most clear in *not* being known by Christ on that day, which we will discuss in the next section. It is also relevant to another text in 1 Corinthians in connection with whether or not one is known by God. In 1 Corinthians 14:37–38 Paul issues a grave warning to members of the Corinthian church who perceive themselves to have a gift of discernment with respect to Paul's instructions:

> If anyone thinks they are a prophet or otherwise gifted by the Spirit, let them acknowledge that what I am writing to you is the Lord's command. But if anyone *ignores* this, they will themselves be *ignored*.

Verse 38 contains a memorable play on words repeating the verb "to ignore": *ignoring* Paul will result in being *ignored*. The question is, ignored by whom, by God or by someone else? Barrett thinks Paul means that he "does not recognize the man in question as inspired in his opinion, not that he does not recognize him as a Christian."[9] However, the tone of the passage points to a more serious threat. Accordingly, we might translate it: "anyone who disregards (it [i.e., Paul's teaching]), is disregarded (by God)."[10] In other words, Paul intends a covert allusion to God's judgment.

Hays points to similar scriptural statements "announcing God's eschatological punishment on those who reject the word of God," where the terms of judgment correspond to the original rejection by the person being judged:[11]

> You have *rejected* the word of the LORD, and the LORD has *rejected* you as king over Israel! (1 Sam 15:26)

> If anyone is *ashamed of me* and my words in this adulterous and sinful generation, the Son of Man will be *ashamed of them* when he comes in his Father's glory with the holy angels. (Mark 8:38)

Paul is in no doubt writing concerning the divine authority of his message. To deny the prophetic authority of Paul's teaching would not only undermine his authority, but would also reveal that person to be at odds with God. Since what Paul is writing is "the Lord's command" (1 Cor 14:37), to "ignore" it would be tantamount to a denial of the confession that "Jesus is Lord" (1 Cor 12:1–3).[12] To be ignored or not known by God in 1 Corinthians 14:38 is the appropriate punishment for ignoring God and is the equivalent of final rejection by God.[13]

---

9. Barrett, *First Epistle to the Corinthians*, 334.
10. Another divine passive; see footnote on 1 Cor 13:12 above.
11. Hays, *First Corinthians*, 244.
12. See D. A. Carson, *Showing the Spirit: A Theological Exposition of 1 Corinthians 12–14* (Grand Rapids: Baker, 1996), 133.
13. The standard lexicon for New Testament Greek translates the verb in question, *agnoeō*, as "to disregard," "to ignore," and "not to know" (BDAG 12–13).

WHAT IT MEANS TO BE KNOWN BY GOD

Being known by God in the New Testament is equivalent to (1) belonging to God; (2) being chosen by God; and (3) being a child or son of God. These are the same three definitions of being known by God that we encountered in the Old Testament. As in the Old Testament, they are not three discrete notions. Instead they represent more or less specific angles on the identity of being a child of God, which is the heart of the matter (see diagram).

Known by God =

Belonging to God

Chosen by God

Child of God

In defining being known by God in the New Testament, texts from Paul's letters are most enlightening.

Belonging to God

As we saw in chapter six, being known by God is in some contexts the equivalent of belonging to God. We see the same in 2 Timothy 2:16–19, which quotes Numbers 16:5 in the context of God making a division between the faithful and those who have departed from the truth:

> Avoid godless chatter, because those who indulge in it will become more and more ungodly. Their teaching will spread like gangrene. Among them are Hymenaeus and Philetus, who have departed from the truth. They say that the resurrection has already taken place, and they destroy the faith of some. Nevertheless, God's solid foundation stands firm, sealed with this inscription: "*The Lord knows those who are his*," and, "Everyone who confesses the name of the Lord must turn away from wickedness." (2 Tim 2:16–19)

Paul reassures the Christians in Ephesus that obeying the truth and seeking to behave in a godly manner matters to God and does not escape his notice. While at times it may seem that there is no distinction between those who trust God and those who do not, believers rely on the fact that God knows those who belong to him. The quotation from Numbers 16:5 could hardly be given more prominence in the passage; that "the Lord knows those who belong to him" seals God's solid and firm foundation upon which believers may confidently build their lives. Conversely, by implication God does not know the false teachers who deny the truth, and they do not belong to him.

Chosen by God

Being known by God also overlaps with the concept of divine election. In Romans 8:29 Paul forges a connection between being known by God and being chosen by him with just one word: the verb "to foreknow." In Romans 8:28 Paul famously declares that "in all things God works for the good of those who love him." In verses 29–30 he explains that those who love God are those whom God *foreknew*, predestined, called, justified, and glorified. Some have called this "the golden chain of salvation," five unbreakable links in a sequence that spell out the historical outworking of the love of God toward the elect and the grounds of our unshakeable confidence in that love. Foreknowledge stands at the beginning of the series and refers to God knowing and loving us in advance. The Greek lexicon BDAG defines the word translated "foreknew," *proginōskō*, as "know beforehand" or "choose beforehand."[14] Paul uses the word as a synonym for divine election.

God's eternal purpose and love are apparent in the broader context of Romans 8, with the love of God for his people appearing climactically in v. 39 as the complement to the description of believers in v. 28 as those who love God. Both the love of God and predestination are crystallized in the notion of being foreknown by God; to be known by God is to be loved and chosen by him. This can also be seen in Paul's use of the word "foreknew" in Romans 11:2 where his answer to the question of whether God has abandoned the people of Israel is that "God did not reject his people, whom he foreknew"; or we could paraphrase it as "those whom he knew and set his love upon in advance."

Son of God

Two passages from Paul's letters associate being known by God with being sons of God. The broader context of Romans 8:29, being foreknown by God, includes no less than three references to adoption. First, Israel's "adoption to sonship" appears at the head of Paul's list of the nation's privileges in Romans 9:4. Second, in 8:15 believers in Christ receive "adoption to sonship" and cry "*Abba*, Father" by the Spirit. Third, and most importantly for our purposes, the goal of the predestination to which those whom God foreknew are bound in Romans 8:29 is "to be conformed to the image of his Son, that he might be the firstborn among many brothers and sisters." This verse juxtaposes being (fore)known by God and being adopted by God.

The two great moments of adoption in the Old Testament were God's adoption of the nation of Israel and of the kings in the line of David. In Romans 8:29 the two come together in their New Testament fulfillment: the sonship of the new people of God is by virtue of God's unique Son! As Paul puts it in Ephesians 1:5, "he predestined us for adoption to sonship *through Jesus Christ*."

14. BDAG 866.

The second New Testament text to connect being known by God to adoption is Galatians 4:8–9. Most English Bibles start a new section with Galatians 4:8; the NIV for example gives 4:8–20 the heading, "Paul's Concern for the Galatians." However, there are good reasons not to separate 4:8–9 from the preceding verses.

In Galatians 3:23–4:7, Paul expounds the doctrine of God's adoption of believers in Christ. In the NIV the section is accurately entitled, "Children of God," for these verses are indeed the longest exposition of adoption in the Bible. On no less than four occasions, Paul tells the Galatian Christians that they are sons or children of God (3:26; 4:6; 4:7 [twice]):

> For *in Christ Jesus you are all sons of God through faith*. . . . But when the appropriate time had come, God sent out his Son, born of a woman, born under the law, to redeem those who were under the law, *so that we may be adopted as sons* with full rights. And because *you are sons*, God sent the Spirit of his Son into our hearts, who calls "*Abba*! Father!" So *you are no longer a slave but a son*, and if *you are a son*, then you are also an heir through God. (Gal 3:26; 4:4–7 NET)[15]

> "As soon as Paul had declared that the Galatians who formerly knew not God had come to know God, he immediately inverted his statement and added a rhetorical correction—'or rather are known by God.' Paul was here clearly distinguishing the Christian understanding of salvation from the gnostic doctrine of revelation. Just as our adoption by the Father precedes his imparting of the Holy Spirit and our responsive cry, "*Abba*!" so also our knowing God is conditioned upon his prior knowledge of us."
>
> *Timothy George*[16]

When Paul describes the Galatian Christians in Galatians 4:8–9 as those who are known by God, he has not left the theme of adoption behind. The fact that the slavery/freedom motif of 4:1–2, 7 is carried forward in 4:8–9 supports this contention. Paul's preference for "being known by God" over "knowing God" in Galatians 4:8–9 as a description of them is thus perfectly explicable: it fits better with their identity as sons of God, which Paul has just spent so much time expounding.

KNOWN BY CHRIST

The New Testament broadens our understanding of what it means to be known by God in one unmistakable way: believers are not only known by God, but are also known by Jesus Christ.

The theme of being known by Christ will prove to be of critical importance as our study proceeds. In the chapters following, we will see that our personal identity

15. The NIV translates the Greek *huioi* as "children" instead of "sons" in 3:26 and 4:4–7 to indicate that the term in context is gender inclusive; it refers to both male and female believers in Christ. While this is true in the present discussion, I prefer "sons" to preserve the technical distinction between children and sons, the latter in the ancient world being heirs with full rights (see 4:7). The difference between children and sons will be further clarified in chapter eight.

16. Timothy George, *Galatians: An Exegetical and Theological Exposition of Holy Scripture*, NAC 30 (Nashville: Broadman & Holman, 1994), 314.

is inextricably tied up with Jesus Christ and with his identity. The defining moments of his life define our lives as well. And his destiny is our destiny. To begin laying the foundations for these profound and weighty matters, we will consider two things about being known by Christ in this section: (1) the extent of Christ's knowledge of us; and (2) the role of being known by Christ at the last judgment.

Jesus Christ Knows Us Intimately and Personally

Revelation 2–3 contains a series of brief letters from the risen Christ to seven churches. The letters have an identical fourfold structure, as George Beasley-Murray explains:

> (1) an introductory statement from the risen Christ, drawn from the opening vision [in Rev. 1] and usually pertinent to the contents of the letter; (2) praise for the good qualities of the church and/or criticism of its faults; (3) a promise to the victor relating to the blessings to be bestowed in the kingdom of Christ; and (4) an exhortation to listen to what the spirit is saying to the churches.[17]

All seven of the churches faced considerable challenges. Following the introductory statement, significantly for our purposes each letter begins with the same two words from the Lord Jesus: "I know." Recognition and acknowledgement are among the first things that a person in difficulty needs. In the cases of five of the churches in Asia Minor, Jesus knows their perseverance, afflictions, poverty, faithfulness, love, faith, and service:

> The Church in Ephesus
>
> *I know* your deeds, your hard work and your perseverance. *I know* that you cannot tolerate wicked people, that you have tested those who claim to be apostles but are not, and have found them false. You have persevered and have endured hardships for my name, and have not grown weary. (Rev 2:2–3)
>
> The Church in Smyrna
>
> *I know* your afflictions and your poverty—yet you are rich! *I know* about the slander of those who say they are Jews and are not, but are a synagogue of Satan. (Rev 2:9)
>
> The Church in Pergamum
>
> *I know* where you live—where Satan has his throne. Yet you remain true to my name. You did not renounce your faith in me, not even in the days of Antipas, my faithful witness, who was put to death in your city—where Satan lives. (Rev 2:13)

---

17. George R. Beasley-Murray, "Book of Revelation," in *Dictionary of the Later New Testament and Its Developments*, ed. R. P. Martin and P. H. Davids, electronic ed. (Downers Grove, IL: InterVarsity Press, 1997), 1030.

The Church in Thyatira

I know your deeds, your love and faith, your service and perseverance, and that you are now doing more than you did at first. (Rev 2:19)

The Church in Philadelphia

I know your deeds. See, I have placed before you an open door that no one can shut. *I know* that you have little strength, yet you have kept my word and have not denied my name. (Rev 3:8)

Like the "book of remembrance" in Malachi 3 (see chapter six), Jesus reassures the churches that he knows them in their suffering and is attentive to their plight. And like the new names given to God's people in Isaiah 56, 62, and 65 (see "Naming as Knowing" in chapter six), God promises to the church in Pergamum a new name: "To the one who is victorious. . . . I will also give that person a white stone with a new name written on it, known only to the one who receives it" (Rev 2:17).

"Jesus is promising to each faithful disciple, to each one who 'conquers,' an intimate relationship with himself in which Jesus will use the secret name, which, as with lovers, remains private to those involved."

N. T. Wright[18]

Boxall notes the color "white functions elsewhere in Revelation as the color of heaven (1:14; 14:14; 20:11) and of victory (3:4–5, 18; 6:2, 11; 7:9, 13; 19:14)."[19] Whatever else the "new name" implies, its hidden nature, known only to God and its bearer, speaks of intimate, interpersonal relationship, a knowledge that would encourage the one who overcomes to persevere. Being given a secret name by God is another way of affirming that a person is known by God.[20] The value of being known in our afflictions will be a focus in chapter thirteen when we consider the comfort of being known by God.

What Jesus knows of the other two churches is less comforting:

The Church in Sardis

I know your deeds; you have a reputation of being alive, but you are dead. (Rev 3:1)

The Church in Laodicea

I know your deeds, that you are neither cold nor hot. I wish you were either one or the other! So, because you are lukewarm—neither hot nor cold—I am about to spit you out of my mouth. (Rev 3:15–16)

18. N. T. Wright, *Revelation for Everyone* (Louisville: Westminster John Knox, 2011), 23.

19. Ian Boxall, *The Revelation of Saint John*, BNTC (London: Continuum, 2006), 61. The reference to a new name in Rev 2:17 remains obscure. The consensus among biblical commentators is still that "we simply do not know what the white stone signified, though clearly it did convey some assurance of blessing" (Leon Morris, *The Book of Revelation*, TNTC (Leicester, UK: Inter-Varsity Press, 1987), 68.

20. See also Rev 3:12: "The one who is victorious I will make a pillar in the temple of my God. Never again will they leave it. I will write on them the name of my God and the name of the city of my God, the new Jerusalem, which is coming down out of heaven from my God; and I will also write on them my new name."

With respect to the church in Sardis, as in Malachi 3, a distinction "between those who serve God and those who do not" (Mal 3:18) is fundamental to being known by Christ. Jesus warns some of those in Sardis to repent: "But if you do not wake up, I will come like a thief, and you will not know at what time I will come to you" (Rev 3:3). As we discovered in chapter five, you can be *known about* without *being known* (in the sense of being known intimately and personally). Jesus's words to those who are "dead" in Sardis are the equivalent of a call to repentance and faith and indicate that they are not yet known by him in the fullest sense. To others in Sardis, Jesus offers more reassuring words that confirm their identity as those who belong to him: "Yet you have a few people in Sardis who have not soiled their clothes. They will walk with me, dressed in white, for they are worthy" (Rev 3:4).

In the case of the church of Laodicea, Jesus delivers a confronting message of correction: "I counsel you to buy from me gold refined in the fire, so you can become rich; and white clothes to wear, so you can cover your shameful nakedness; and salve to put on your eyes, so you can see" (Rev 3:18). Jesus's knowledge of them enables him to rebuke them as a father would correct his son: "Those whom I love I rebuke and discipline" (Rev 3:19).[21]

We learn one more thing about being known by Jesus in the letters to the seven churches: to be known intimately and personally by Jesus leads to knowing Jesus. Each letter begins with a revealing description of Jesus:

> These are the words of him who holds the seven stars in his right hand and walks among the seven golden lampstands. (Rev 2:1)
>
> These are the words of him who is the First and the Last, who died and came to life again. (Rev 2:8)
>
> These are the words of him who has the sharp, double-edged sword. (Rev 2:12)
>
> These are the words of the Son of God, whose eyes are like blazing fire and whose feet are like burnished bronze. (Rev 2:18)
>
> These are the words of him who holds the seven spirits of God and the seven stars. (Rev 3:1)
>
> These are the words of him who is holy and true, who holds the key of David. (Rev 3:7)
>
> These are the words of the Amen, the faithful and true witness, the ruler of God's creation. (Rev 3:14)

21. See Deut 8:5: "Know then in your heart that as a man disciplines his son, so the LORD your God disciplines you"; Prov 3:12: "the LORD disciplines those he loves, as a father the son he delights in"; see also Heb 12:5–6 which quotes Prov 3:11–12.

To the faithful in the church in Thyatira Jesus promises: "I will also give that one the morning star" (Rev 2:28). N. T. Wright regards this as another indication of the intimacy that Jesus offers his disciples: "He will share his very identity with them."[22] Indeed, later in Revelation we learn that "the bright Morning Star" is Jesus himself (Rev 22:16).

Known and Not Known at the Last Judgment

The critical importance of being known by Christ is nowhere better seen than in three last judgment scenes in the Synoptic Gospels. In each case, the concluding solemn verdict of condemnation includes the denial by Jesus the Judge of ever having known the individuals concerned:

> The Sermon on the Mount, in the judgment of false prophets by their fruit:
> "Then I will tell them plainly, '*I never knew you.* Away from me, you evildoers!'" (Matt 7:23)
>
> The parable of the ten virgins, in response to the foolish virgins:
> "He replied, 'Truly I tell you, *I don't know you.*'" (Matt 25:12)
>
> The parable of the narrow door, in response to those knocking outside:
> "He will reply, '*I don't know* you or where you come from. Away from me, all you evildoers.'" (Luke 13:27)[23]

In all three texts the seriousness of Jesus's not knowing those he condemns is reinforced by various means, including their description as "evildoers," Jesus's insistence that his words must not be taken lightly (he speaks the truth, "plainly") and the stern words of dismissal, "Away from me."

Three more texts underscore not only the tragedy of some not being known at the last judgment but also the joyful reassurance of others being known by him on that day:

> Whoever acknowledges me before others, *I will also acknowledge before my Father in heaven.* But whoever disowns me before others, I will disown before my Father in heaven. (Matt 10:32–33)
>
> I tell you, whoever publicly acknowledges me before others, *the Son of Man will also acknowledge before the angels of God.* But whoever disowns me before others will be disowned before the angels of God. (Luke 12:8–9)

22. Wright, *Revelation for Everyone*, 27.

23. See also Ps 9:4–6: "For you have upheld my right and my cause, sitting enthroned as the righteous judge. You have rebuked the nations and destroyed the wicked; *you have blotted out their name for ever and ever.* Endless ruin has overtaken my enemies, you have uprooted their cities; *even the memory of them has perished.*"

> The one who is victorious will, like them, be dressed in white. I will never blot out the name of that person from the book of life, *but will acknowledge that name before my Father and his angels.* (Rev 3:5)[24]

Making Jesus's not knowing someone the decisive criterion of judgment is particularly disturbing. The verdict "I never knew you" is highly personal, shatteringly brief, yet comprehensive, and it places the decision fully out of the reach of the person being condemned. What can they do about not being known? Any appeal against this judgment would be futile. Davies and Allison refer to "I never knew you" as a formula of renunciation equivalent to "I never recognized you as one of my own."[25]

In terms of other New Testament depictions of the last judgment, to be told "I never knew you" ranks alongside the great white throne judgment of Revelation 20 for severity. In that passage, people are condemned for not having their name written in the book of life, a synonym for not being known by God. This situation underscores the grace of God as the sole grounds for those who are saved; you can hardly take any credit for having your name in a list compiled before you were born or for being known by Christ (see chapter twelve on "Humility").

SAMPLE TEXT: THE GOSPEL OF JOHN

Knowing Christ and being known by him is a major theme in John's Gospel and makes a substantial contribution to a biblical theology of personal identity. To trace the theme, we will follow two strategies that I generally recommend for reading the Fourth Gospel:

- Read John with the prologue (John 1:1–18) and the purpose statement (John 20:30–31) in mind;
- Read John cumulatively.

The Prologue and Purpose Statement

John's prologue, 1:1–18, is a remarkably effective introduction to the Gospel of John. The major themes of John are introduced in the prologue, especially the identity and mission of Jesus, his rejection by Israel, and the blessings of faith in him. In addition, Mark Stibbe points out that the main movements of the Gospel's plot are also anticipated in the prologue:

> Many scholars have noticed that vv. 10–13 encapsulate the plot of the whole Gospel. Verses 10–11 point to the lack of recognition of Jesus and to his rejection

24. G. K. Beale states, "Christ will confess the names of believers to his Father and to the angels. The idea may be that he will read the believers' names out of the book of life in recognition of their final salvation. . . . Those who confess Christ's name have their own name confessed by Christ before the Father" (*The Book of Revelation*, NIGTC [Grand Rapids: Eerdmans, 1999], 280–81).

25. W. D. Davies and D. C. Allison, *Matthew 1–7*, ICC (London: T &T Clark, 1988), 717.

by his own race in chs. 1–12 (part one of the Gospel story). Verses 12–13 point to the adoption and acceptance of the disciples as the children of God in chs. 13–21 (part two of the story). Something of the whole plot of John's story is therefore indicated at this stage.[26]

With respect to the theme of knowing and being known by Christ, the prologue anticipates the rest of the Gospel in predicting that even though "he was in the world, and the world came into being through him; yet the world did not know him" (John 1:10 NRSV). The fact that the Word made the world (see also 1:3) implies that he knew the world, something that is confirmed explicitly elsewhere in John in two places. To explain Jesus's reluctance to entrust himself to certain people who had supposedly put their trust in him, the narrator explains that Jesus "*knew all people*" (2:24). And in a conversation with Peter, the risen Jesus asks Peter three times whether he loves him. The third time, Peter replies with some exasperation: "Lord, *you know all things*; you know that I love you" (21:17). But Jesus's knowledge of others is not usually reciprocated, as many scenes throughout John attest; Jesus's true identity was hidden from many of the characters with whom he interacts: "*The world did not know him*" (1:10 NRSV).

Nonetheless, according to the climax of the prologue, the purpose of the Word becoming flesh was to make himself and God known: "No one has ever seen [or known] God, but the one and only Son, who is himself God and is in closest relationship with the Father, has made him known" (1:18). To be known by and to come to know Jesus as the light of the world (1:9) is to be given "the right to become children of God" (1:12), the same personal identity that we have been exploring in this chapter and explored in chapter six in connection with being known by God.

The purpose statement of the Gospel of John makes clear that John's overall goal is that readers might come to know the true identity of Jesus:

> Jesus performed many other signs in the presence of his disciples, which are not recorded in this book. But these are written that you may believe that Jesus is the Messiah, the Son of God, and that by believing you may have life in his name. (John 20:30–31)

Combined with the prologue, John's purpose is summed up as having his readers come to know Jesus as Messiah and Son of God and to know themselves as children of God (1:12). With reference to having "life in his name," it is significant that elsewhere Jesus explains that to know God and himself is the equivalent of eternal life: "Now this is eternal life: that they know you, the only true God, and Jesus Christ, whom you have sent" (17:3).

26. Mark W. G. Stibbe, *John* (Sheffield: JSOT Press, 1993), 26.

Cumulative Reading

A second recommendation for reading John is not to read the Gospel in piecemeal fashion. For any passage in John, the context is the entire Gospel, which is framed by the prologue and purpose statement. The best way to read John is to read cumulatively, recalling what has gone before, and on second and subsequent readings anticipating what follows in the Gospel. Reading a narrative like John is thus a process of retrospection and prospection, looking back and looking forward across the book and making connections. As I tell students, read like a snowball rather than a bowling ball!

"Whenever we read past segments must be retained in each present moment. The new moment is not isolated, but stands out against the old, and so the past will remain as a background to the present, exerting influence on it and, at the same time, itself being modified by the present. . . . Reading does not merely flow forward, but recalled segments also have a retroactive effect, with the present transforming the past."

Wolfgang Iser[27]

Known by Christ in John

The most significant passages in John for the topic of personal identity are those in which Jesus has an extended conversation with an individual. Richard Bauckham notes that there are seven such encounters, and they "represent a distinctive feature of John's Gospel, one of its many differences from the Synoptics":

1. Nathanael (1:47–51)
2. Nicodemus (3:1–21)
3. The Samaritan woman (4:7–26)
4. Martha (11:20–27)
5. Pilate (18:33–19:12)
6. Mary Magdalene (20:14–17)
7. Peter (21:15–22).[28]

There are several ways in which these conversations can be studied. These include how they contribute to the larger narrative in John; the manner in which the individuals are representative of larger groups (the Samaritan woman, her village; Nicodemus, the Jewish establishment; Martha, her family; and so on); how they draw readers to identify with the characters in question; and the way in which some of the characters are models of faith.

For our purposes they illustrate the theme of individuals being known by Jesus. Indeed, the distinctive manner in which Jesus interacts with the individuals concerned shows that Jesus knows them from the start. As Bauckham observes:

27. Wolfgang Iser, *The Act of Reading: A Theory of Aesthetic Response* (Baltimore: Johns Hopkins University Press, 1978), 114, 116.

28. Richard Bauckham, *Gospel of Glory: Major Themes in Johannine Theology* (Grand Rapids: Baker, 2015), 14.

> It is not only, as has so often been noticed, that they respond differently to Jesus, but that Jesus deals with each of them differently, according to their individual circumstances. Sometimes he initiates the dialogue, as, for example, rather shockingly in the case of *the Samaritan woman*, or tenderly, as a familiar friend, in the case of *Mary Magdalene*. Sometimes he responds to an approach, as with Nicodemus or Pilate. He does not deal with them according to some standard formula, but rather engages the particular point in their lives at which he encounters them. . . . The particularities of each encounter determine the themes of the dialogues, different in each case.[29]

The seven individuals relate very differently to Jesus. If Nicodemus is his Jewish interrogator and Pilate is his gentile judge, Martha, Mary Magdalene, and Peter are Jesus's disciples, and Nathanael and the Samaritan woman become his disciples during their conversation with Jesus. We will focus on three who demonstrate Jesus's intimate and personal knowledge of individuals who are among those who received him (John 1:12), namely, Nathanael, the Samaritan woman, and Mary Magdalene.

In a fourth section following the exposition of Jesus's conversations with Nathanael, the Samaritan woman, and Mary Magdalene, we will focus on the Good Shepherd discourse in John 10 as the hermeneutical key to the theme of being known by Jesus in John's Gospel. In each of the three cases, we will observe how Jesus's comparison of himself to a shepherd in John 10 explains his profound personal knowledge of his followers. Jesus "calls his own sheep by name and leads them out" (John 10:3b). Speaking of himself, Jesus says: "I am the good shepherd; I know my sheep and my sheep know me" (10:14).

Jesus and Nathanael

The immediate context for Jesus's conversation with Nathanael in John 1:47–51 is 1:19–46, the unit immediately following John's prologue. The passage is characterized by an interest in questions of the personal identity of John the Baptist and Jesus, and also of his earliest followers.

In John 1:20 John the Baptist confesses to the delegation from the Jewish leaders in Jerusalem that he is "not the Messiah." This prompts them to ask him, "Then who are you?" (1:21), and "What do you say about yourself?" (1:22). He replies cryptically that he is "the voice of one calling in the wilderness" (1:23) and then shifts the focus to the identity of someone else, namely, "the one who comes after me" (1:27).

The identity of Jesus takes center stage in the rest of the chapter. In fact, the Gospel of John is frontloaded with a veritable cascade of answers to the question, who is Jesus? John the Baptist confesses: "I myself did not know him" (1:33). However,

29. Bauckham, *Gospel of Glory*, 15–16. Emphases added.

Jesus's identity was revealed to John by God at Jesus's baptism when the Spirit descended on Jesus like a dove. On that basis, John the Baptist identifies Jesus as "the Lamb of God" (1:29, 36) and "God's Chosen One" (1:34). In the rest of the chapter, other characters also reveal Jesus's identity:

- Andrew calls Jesus "the Messiah (that is, the Christ)" (1:41).
- Philip describes Jesus as "the one Moses wrote about in the Law, and about whom the prophets also wrote" (1:45).
- Nathanael declares to Jesus "you are the Son of God; you are the king of Israel" (1:49).
- Jesus calls himself "the Son of Man" (1:51).

John 1:11–12 ◀ John 1:35–51

The identity of Jesus's disciples is also a focus in John 1:35–51. As D. A. Carson explains, "the chapter provides concrete examples of a point made in the prologue: although in general his own people did not receive him, yet some did, believing on his name and gaining from him the authority to become children of God (1:11–12)."[30] First of all, we are introduced to Andrew and his brother Simon Peter, whom Jesus renames Cephas (1:40–42). This action looks forward to John 10:3 where Jesus explains that "he calls his own sheep by name."

Next in line for introductions are Philip and then Nathanael. Nathanael's experience illustrates what it means to know and be known by Jesus:

> When Jesus saw Nathanael approaching, he said of him, "Here truly is an Israelite in whom there is no deceit."
>
> "How do you know me?" Nathanael asked.
>
> Jesus answered, "I saw you while you were still under the fig tree before Philip called you."
>
> Then Nathanael declared, "Rabbi, you are the Son of God; you are the king of Israel." (John 1:47–49)

Jesus sees Nathanael and offers a brief summary of his character: he is truly an Israelite "in whom there is no deceit" (1:47). The description itself calls to mind a passage in the Old Testament. In Genesis 28:10–15 and 32:24–30, Jacob is called Israel after encounters with God that transform his devious character. Jesus recognizes that Nathanael is an "Israel" not a "Jacob."

Nathanael's question "How do you know me?" in John 1:48 confirms that Jesus's assessment of him is accurate. Jesus replies that he simply saw him under the fig tree. What Nathanael was doing under the fig tree is open to conjecture:

30. D. A. Carson, *The Gospel according to John*, PNTC (Leicester, UK: Inter-Varsity Press, 1991), 157.

"In the Old Testament the fig tree is sometimes almost a symbol for 'home' or for prosperity (e.g. 1 Ki. 4:25; Is. 36:16; Zc. 3:10); occasionally in rabbinic literature its shade is associated with a place for meditation and prayer."[31] However, the point is not Nathanael's location so much as Jesus's precise and penetrating knowledge of Nathanael. Jesus knew him before he had even met him.

John 1:49 ▶ John 20:31

In response to being known by Jesus, Nathanael declares Jesus's own identity with remarkable clarity: "you are the Son of God; you are the king of Israel" (John 1:49). If Jesus's knowledge of Nathanael points back to the prologue's prediction that some will receive him (1:12), Nathanael's confession points forward to the Gospel's purpose statement. John wrote that his readers might come to know Jesus as "the Messiah, the Son of God" (20:31). As Andrew Lincoln observes, "Nathanael's believing confession is in line with the Gospel's statement of purpose (see also 20:31)."[32] Not only does Nathanael know Jesus as "the Son of God,"[33] his confession that Jesus is "the king of Israel" is equivalent to calling him "the Messiah" since "the title King of Israel was used by Palestinian Jews for the Messiah."[34] In John the titles "Son of God" and "Messiah" or its equivalents ("Christ" or "King of Israel") only occur together in 1:49 and 20:31.

From the Nathanael episode in John 1:47–49, we learn that Jesus's piercing knowledge of his own is prior to and elicits their accurate knowledge of him. Jesus knows us before we know him and knows much better than we will ever know him.

John 1:16 ◀ John 1:51

Nathanael's conversation with Jesus and confession of Jesus as God's Son and King is not merely for his own benefit. Being known by Jesus turns Nathanael into a disciple of Jesus. And as we will see with the Samaritan woman and Mary Magdalene, others benefit when we enter into a living relationship with Jesus.

In John 1:50–51 Jesus moves from addressing Nathanael alone to addressing the group of disciples. Notice the change from singular to plural Greek pronouns in Jesus's final words to Nathanael:

> Jesus said, "You [singular] believe because I told you [singular] I saw you [singular] under the fig tree. You [singular] will see greater things than that."

31. Carson, *Gospel according to John*, 161.

32. Andrew T. Lincoln, *Gospel according to Saint John*, BNTC (London: Continuum, 2005), 121.

33. Lincoln notes the startling nature of Nathanael's knowing Jesus as "Son of God" when compared to the Synoptic Gospels: "Luke does not use 'Son of God' as a title addressed to Jesus by his followers; neither does Mark, though he has the title on human lips for the first time when the centurion witnesses Jesus's death (Mark 15:39). Matthew also employs it in the centurion's confession (Matt 27:54) but is willing to use it earlier in the disciples' recognition of Jesus after he has walked on the water and in Peter's confession at Caesarea Philippi (Matt 14:33; 16:16). John's Gospel, however, has Jesus recognized by his followers as Son of God from the outset of his ministry and then develops this category as the key to understanding Jesus's true identity" (*Gospel according to Saint John*, 121).

34. Carson, *Gospel according to John*, 161–62.

He then added, "Very truly I tell you [plural], you [plural] will see heaven open, and the angels of God ascending and descending on the Son of Man."

John 1:51 is the climax of John 1:19–51. It is the first time Jesus teaches in John. It is the first of many times that Jesus refers to himself as "the Son of Man" in John. And it is the first of twenty-five sayings introduced with the solemn words, "Very truly I tell you." The words "you will see heaven open, and the angels of God ascending and descending on the Son of Man" are an allusion to Jacob's dream in Genesis 28:12: "he saw a stairway resting on the earth, with its top reaching to heaven, and the angels of God were ascending and descending on it."

All Jews acknowledged Jacob/Israel, the father of the twelve tribes, as one who had received a critical revelation from God. In John 1:51 we learn that Jesus replaces and surpasses that revelation. He bridges heaven and earth. As John 1:16 says, "Out of his fullness we have all received grace in place of grace already given." Carson writes: "What the disciples are promised, then, is heaven-sent confirmation that the one they have acknowledged as the Messiah has been appointed by God."[35]

Jesus and the Samaritan Woman

John 4 contains another example of Jesus knowing someone deeply and that knowledge leading this person to a saving knowledge of him. The passage in question is known for several things, not least Jesus's evocative promise of "living water. . . . welling up to eternal life" (4:10, 14). For our purposes, the passage deals with questions of the identity of both Jesus and a potential follower.

In John 4:1–7, Jesus arrives in Sychar, a town in Samaria, where he meets a Samaritan woman. Jesus meets her at Jacob's well and asks her to draw water for him to drink (4:6–7). Focusing on his ethnic and religious identity, she is reluctant, pointing out that Jews do not associate with Samaritans (4:9). Jesus runs with the subject of his own identity and counters that if she "knew who it is that asks you for a drink" (4:10), she would have asked him for a drink!

John 2:24 ◀ John 4:17–19 ▶ John 6:70–71

The two then talk at cross-purposes about wells and springs of water before Jesus tells her to "go, call your husband and come back" (4:16). She replies concerning her marital status that she has no husband (4:17a). Jesus's responds unnervingly: "You are right when you say you have no husband. The fact is, you have had five husbands, and the man you now have is not your husband. What you have just said is quite true" (4:17b–18).

That Jesus has supernatural insight into the character of people is also attested in two other places in the Gospel. In John 2:24–25 it is affirmed that Jesus "knew

35. Carson, *Gospel according to John*, 163–64.

all people" and that "he knew what was in each person." And in John 6:70–71 Jesus predicts his betrayal by Judas: "Have I not chosen you, the Twelve? Yet one of you is a devil!" (6:70).

Jesus's precise knowledge of her past understandably prompts the woman to reflect on his identity. She responds, "I can see that you are a prophet" (4:19). While grammatically it is possible that she meant that Jesus was *the* coming prophet like Moses (see Deut 18:15–19), a title for the Messiah, she probably meant no more than "prophet" in the sense of someone with a special gift of insight. (As John 4:25–26 indicates, she comes to know Jesus as the Messiah at a later point in the conversation.)

John 4:25–26, 28 ▶ John 20:30–31

Having demonstrated his keen knowledge of the woman, Jesus finally reveals to her that he is in fact the long-awaited Messiah: "I, the one speaking to you—I am he" (4:26). Like Nathanael, being known by Jesus led to knowing Jesus and being useful to him as a disciple and witness. The woman returned to the town in exuberant astonishment: "Come, see a man who told me everything I ever did. Could this be the Messiah?" (4:29). The result of her testimony to Jesus's identity was that those to whom she spoke "came out of the town and made their way towards him" (4:30).

Just as in John's purpose statement, the promise of life is premised on believing that Jesus is the Messiah: "whoever drinks the water I give them will never thirst. Indeed, the water I give them will become in them a spring of water welling up to eternal life" (John 4:14). Jesus's encounter with the Samaritan woman serves as a case study of his deep knowledge of an individual leading to mutual positive recognition. Being known by Jesus leads to knowing Jesus the Messiah. And in the context of John 4, as identities go, being known by Jesus and knowing Jesus as Messiah is of greater significance for a person's identity than that individual's own ethnicity (Jew or Samaritan) and marital status (married or divorced):

> A time is coming when you will worship the Father neither on this mountain nor in Jerusalem. . . . a time is coming and has now come when the true worshipers will worship the Father in the Spirit and in truth. (John 4:21, 23a)

Jesus and Mary Magdalene

The third extended conversation in John in which an individual is known by Jesus is the post-resurrection appearance of Jesus to Mary Magdalene outside the garden tomb. A climactic scene in the Gospel, Mary is the first person in John to encounter the risen Jesus and also the first to proclaim to others the good news of the resurrection. The passage opens with a focus on Mary's grief:

> Now Mary stood outside the tomb crying. As she wept, she bent over to look into the tomb and saw two angels in white, seated where Jesus' body had been, one at the head and the other at the foot.
>
> They asked her, "Woman, why are you crying?"
>
> "They have taken my Lord away," she said, "and I don't know where they have put him." (John 20:11–13)

Mary's tears are mentioned four times; twice by the narrator (20:11), once by the angels (20:13), and once by Jesus (20:15). The tender pathos of the scene is unmistakable. Jesus comes to Mary and knows her in her time of sorrow and despair. Bauckham makes the intriguing suggestion that "Jesus's encounter with Mary Magdalene in the garden is intended to recall Isaiah 25:8": "He will swallow up death forever. The Sovereign LORD will wipe away the tears from all faces."[36]

John 1:38 ◀ John 7:34 ◀ John 20:15

At this point Jesus engages Mary in conversation:

> At this, she turned around and saw Jesus standing there, but she did not realize that it was Jesus. He asked her, "Woman, why are you crying? Who is it you are looking for?" (John 20:14–15a).

The Greek verb "to look for" (*zēteō*) in v. 15a is often translated "to seek" in other parts of John. As it turns out, there is a lot of "seeking" in the Gospel. The "search" begins in John 1:38 where Jesus asks Andrew and Philip, "What do you seek?"[37] Their answer is given in 1:41, "We have found the Messiah," and in 1:45, "We have found the one Moses wrote about in the Law, and about whom the prophets also wrote."

The successful "seeking" of Andrew and Philip contrasts with that of the Jewish leaders, about whom Jesus lamented, "You will seek me, but you will not find me" (John 7:34). Up until Mary's "search" in John 20:15a, "most examples of people seeking Jesus in the Gospel show them doing so for wrong or inadequate reasons."[38] When it comes to the theme of seeking Jesus in John, the Gospel opens with Jesus asking Andrew and Philip, "What do you seek?" (1:38), and it closes with Jesus asking Mary, "Whom do you seek?" (20:15). As Bauckham notes, in John "only the last occurrence of the verb ["to seek"] corresponds to the first."[39] In both cases "what is found exceeds what is sought."[40] They find the Messiah who loves them and lays down his life for them (John 10:11).

36. Bauckham, *Gospel of Glory*, 72.
37. My own translation.
38. Bauckham, *Gospel of Glory*, 148.
39. Ibid.
40. Ibid.

John 10:3–4 ◀ John 20:16

The two questions from Jesus are not enough for Mary to recognize him. In fact in John 20:15b, she mistakes him for someone else:

> Thinking he was the gardener, she said, "Sir, if you have carried him away, tell me where you have put him, and I will get him."

To clear up the misunderstanding, Jesus utters a single word, Mary's name:

> Jesus said to her, "*Mary.*" She turned toward him and cried out in Aramaic, "Rabboni!" (which means "Teacher"). (John 20:16)

Don Carson draws out the significance of this exquisite moment and makes a connection to the Good Shepherd discourse in John 10:

> Whatever the cause of her blindness, the single word *Mary*, spoken as Jesus had always uttered it, was enough to remove it. The good shepherd "calls his own sheep by name . . . and his sheep follow him because they know his voice" (10:3–4). Anguish and despair are instantly swallowed up by astonishment and delight.[41]

Mary answers Jesus in her customary manner, "Rabboni," indicating her relationship to Jesus as his disciple and acknowledging his authority. As Lincoln notes, "the first disciples had responded to Jesus's question in 1:38 by calling him Rabbi, and Rabboni is an extended form of this address."[42] Jesus knows those who belong to him intimately and personally; he knows them by name.

> "It is the human tenderness of Jesus's love for his friends that John's exquisitely told narratives are able to evoke as nothing else could. We see it incomparably in the story of his meeting with Mary Magdalene in the garden (20:11–18). It is a reunion of friends, the reunion that Jesus had promised his friends after his supper (16:16–22). For Jesus, it is a reunion with one of only four friends who stood by him in the extremity of his giving his life for them (19:25–26). Moreover, very significantly, the encounter echoes the parable of the good shepherd. Like the sheep in the parable (10:3, 14), Mary recognizes Jesus's voice when he says her name. She is one of his own who knows him personally, as he knows her."
>
> *Richard Bauckham*[43]

John 1:12 ◀ John 20:17

This "touching" scene continues with Jesus insisting that Mary not touch him. Their intimacy and friendship will have to continue in a different form in the light of his resurrection:

41. Carson, *Gospel according to John*, 64. See also Lincoln, "The revelation to Mary of Jesus's identity takes place through the personal address with its utterance of her name, 'Mary,' in contrast to 'Woman,' which had introduced the previous questions. As the good shepherd, Jesus calls his own sheep by name, and Mary turns to face him directly because now she knows his voice (cf. 10:3–4)" (*Gospel according to Saint John*, 493). Murray J. Harris writes, "Jesus proceeds to call one of his sheep by name (cf. 10:3)" (*John*, Exegetical Guide to the Greek New Testament [Nashville: Broadman and Holman Academic, 2015], 327).

42. Lincoln, *Gospel according to Saint John*, 493.

43. Bauckham, *Gospel of Glory*, 68–69.

> Jesus said, 'Do not hold on to me, for I have not yet ascended to the Father. Go instead to my brothers and tell them, "I am ascending to *my Father and your Father*, to my God and your God." (John 20:17)

Jesus's response to Mary contains a hint of what he has done for her in laying down his life (John 10:11): his Father is now her Father, and his God, hers! John has around one hundred and twenty references to God as the Father of Jesus, and this is the only one where that filial relationship is extended to his disciples.

Throughout the Gospel, Jesus's relationship to his Father has been a constant focus and, at times, a bone of contention (see John 10:30). And that relationship has been exclusive; even his disciples have not shared in it and do not address God as Father. But back in the prologue in John 1:12, it was promised that all who believe in Jesus's name would be given "the right to become children of God." Jesus's words to Mary indicate the fulfillment of that promise. In John 20:15–17 this new identity as a child of God is tied up with being known by Jesus.

As with Nathanael and the Samaritan woman, being known by Jesus leads to Mary being enlisted in his service. She immediately goes and proclaims the resurrection of Jesus from the dead:

> Mary Magdalene went to the disciples with the news: "I have seen the Lord!" And she told them that he had said these things to her. (John 20:18)

Jesus and His Sheep

Three times in John, Jesus surprises individuals with his intimate and personal knowledge of them. Nathanael asks in bewilderment: "How do you know me?" (1:48). The Samaritan woman exclaims in amazement: "I can see that you are a prophet" (4:19). And Mary Magdalene turns to embrace Jesus when he addresses her by name (20:16). In each case, being known by Jesus led to knowing Jesus and remarkable confessions about his identity. And in each case, being known by Jesus led to Jesus being known by others.

Individual	Known by Jesus	Knowing Jesus	Others Know Jesus
Nathanael	Jesus knows his character to be without guile	"the Son of God" and "the king of Israel"	All of the disciples will receive a revelation of Jesus's true identity
The Samaritan Woman	Jesus knows her personal history	"the Messiah"	Many Samaritans respond to her witness and acknowledge Jesus as "the Savior of the world"
Mary Magdalene	Jesus calls her by name	"Rabboni" and "Lord"	She tells the disciples that the Lord is risen

The cycle of evangelism can be conceived of as a two-step process: people come to know Jesus and then make him known to others. However, this cycle misses a crucial first step that makes the other two steps possible. These three conversations of Jesus with individuals in John teach us that *being known by Jesus* leads to knowing him and making him known. And being known by Jesus is the critical and initial step in the process.

How are we to understand Jesus's extraordinary and transforming knowledge of his disciples? The parable of Jesus as the Good Shepherd in John 10 provides a good explanation.[44] In John 10:1–21 Jesus tells a parable of sheep and shepherds to teach about the relationship between the people of God and their leaders. His purpose is not only to depict his own role as the true leader of God's people but also to criticize the behavior of the Pharisees toward the blind man whom Jesus had healed in John 9. If Jesus is the Good Shepherd (10:11, 14), the Pharisees are the thieves and robbers who climb into the sheep pen and do not use the gate (10:1). The passage opens with Jesus addressing the Pharisees (10:1) and closes with a reference to Jesus's healing of the blind man (10:21b). The stark contrast between Jesus's leadership and that of the Pharisees is also underscored by the repetition of the Greek verb "to send out," *ekballō*:

In John 9:34 the Pharisees "send out" or "throw out" of the synagogue the man who was born blind and had been healed by Jesus.

In John 10:4 Jesus "sends out" or "brings out" of the sheep pen "all his own," lovingly going before them.

The picture that Jesus paints in John 10 is one of several flocks of sheep in a fold. Shepherds in the ancient Near East were known to stand in a familiar place and call to their sheep in such folds. The sheep would then recognize their own shepherd's voice and gather around him. In the parable Jesus goes a step further and calls his sheep by name:[45]

> The gatekeeper opens the gate for him, and the sheep listen to his voice. *He calls his own sheep by name* and leads them out. When he has brought out all his own, he goes on ahead of them, and his sheep follow him because they know his voice. (John 10:3–4)

It is not only Nathanael and Mary Magdalene whom Jesus knows by name; the same is true for all who are "his own" (10:4), those who belong to him.[46]

In the flow of John's narrative, the parable teaches that Jesus comes to the

44. "I am the Good Shepherd" is one of seven "I am" sayings in John.

45. Bauckham, *Gospel of Glory*, 69. Bauckham notes, "John 10:3 is the only reference in the Bible to animals having names."

46. The same language is used in 3 John 14 in the context of personal relationship and friendship: "Greet the friends there *by name*."

sheep pen of Judaism and "calls his own sheep out individually to constitute his own messianic 'flock.'"[47] However, Jesus has others in mind also; we are not merely spectators when it comes to being known by Jesus. Jesus also addresses the readers of the Gospel to reassure them that the same intimate, mutual knowing and loving relationship applies to them if they believe in Jesus: "I have other sheep that are not of this sheep pen" (10:16). John 17:20 strikes a similar note: "My prayer is not for them alone. I pray also for those who will believe in me through their message."

The parable goes on to compare the relationship of Jesus to his sheep to the relationship of Jesus to God:

> I am the good shepherd; *I know my sheep and my sheep know me—just as the Father knows me and I know the Father*—and I lay down my life for the sheep. (John 10:14–15)

The key clauses of the passage form a chiastic structure, where the first and fourth elements correspond to each other, as do the second and third:

A I know my sheep and
B my sheep know me—*just as*
B¹ the Father knows me
A¹ and I know the Father—
and I lay down my life for the sheep.

Jesus's relationship with his Father illustrates the shape and nature of his relationship with his sheep; he knows them "just as" the Father knows him. Unlike the Pharisees, Jesus knows the people of God intimately and personally. The relationship of mutual knowing that believers have with Jesus is modeled on the relationship of mutual knowing of Jesus and his Father.[48] Or as Don Carson puts it, the intimacy of the relationship between Jesus and his sheep is "grounded upon the intimacy between the Father and the Son."[49] The language of Father and Son knowing each other underscores the closeness of their relationship. The passage also links Jesus's knowledge of his sheep with his care for his sheep. He is willing to die for them, unlike a Pharisee who "abandons the sheep and runs away" if any danger arises (John 10:11–12, 15).

> "The love between the Father and the Son, their unsurpassable intimacy, is the source from which relationship between God and humans derives."
>
> *Richard Bauckham*[50]

The intimacy of Jesus's relationship to his Father is in fact introduced in John's prologue where 1:18 says that the Son is "in the bosom of the Father" (KJV), meaning "near the Father's heart" (NLT). Significantly, a similar expression is used of the

47. Carson, *Gospel according to John*, 383.

48. See also Luke 10:22: "No one knows who the Son is except the Father, and no one knows who the Father is except the Son and those to whom the Son chooses to reveal him."

49. Carson, *Gospel according to John*, 387.

50. Bauckham, *Gospel of Glory*, 19.

beloved disciple's closeness to Jesus at the Last Supper: "Now there was *leaning on Jesus' bosom* one of his disciples, whom Jesus loved" (John 13:23 KJV). The same thing is said of the intimacy of Jesus's relationship to his Father and of Jesus's intimacy with his disciples. Jesus is close to God's heart, and we are close to his.

Being known by Jesus produces an intimate and abiding relationship between Jesus and the individual believer modeled on the relationship of Jesus and his Father. John's Gospel develops this notion with its profound teaching about what Bauckham calls the "in-one-anotherness" or "personal coinherence"[51] between individual believers and Jesus, which is also modeled on the Father and the Son being in one another. This language, along with the notes of mutual knowing, underscores the special bond that exists between two persons.

A few texts highlight the extraordinary closeness of the Father and the Son with in-one-another language:

> The Father is in me, and I in the Father. (John 10:38)

> Don't you believe that I am in the Father, and that the Father is in me? (John 14:10)

The parable of the vine and branches in John 15, on the other hand, teaches a reciprocal in-one-another relationship for believers and Christ:

> Remain in me, as I also remain in you. (15:4; see also 15:5, 7)

In terms reminiscent of John 10:14–15, Jesus sums up the analogous nature of this mutual indwelling in John 14:20:

> I am in my Father, and you are in me, and I am in you.

BEING KNOWN BY GOD AND CHRIST AND PERSONAL IDENTITY

According to the Bible, in order to know who you are, you have to know *whose you are*. We are defined by our relationships, by who we know, and who knows us. And when it comes to personal identity, both the Old and New Testaments agree that being known by God is of critical importance. Being known by God introduces a new belonging. We belong to God as his children. We are part of his family. But the New Testament brings that relationship into sharper focus. We are not only known by God, but also known by Jesus Christ.

Does Jesus Christ know you intimately and personally? Does he know your personality, your character, and your particular circumstances? Does he know you

51. Bauckham's terms; see *Gospel of Glory*, 11.

Eustace asked Edmund: "Do you know him?" He replied: "Well, he knows me. He is the great Lion, the son of the Emperor-beyond-the-Sea, who saved me and saved Narnia."[53]

If you were to ask Nathanael, the Samaritan woman, and Mary Magdalene if they knew Jesus, they might have replied: "Well, he knows me. And he is the Messiah, the Son of God, and by believing in him we have life in his name."

by name? As Bauckham notes, three remarkable conversations in John's Gospel between Jesus and Nathanael, the Samaritan woman, and Mary Magdalene "encourage hearers or readers to expect Jesus to meet them and direct them in the particularity of their individual lives and circumstances."[52] The three conversations are recorded so that we might know that we too are known by Jesus, just as intimately as the Father knows the Son and the Son knows the Father.

To be known by Jesus is to come to know Jesus as God's Son and King (John 20:30–31) and to be given a new identity as his disciple and as God's child. The connections between belonging to Jesus, being known by Jesus, and being a child of God are evident when texts from John 1, 10, and 20 are compared:

To all who did receive him, to those who believed in his name, he gave the right to become *children of God.* (John 1:12)	"He calls his own sheep by name. . . . *I know my sheep* and my sheep know me." (John 10:3b, 14)	Jesus said to her, "Mary". . . . "I am ascending to *my Father and your Father.*" (John 20:16, 17)

John Calvin wrote that the conversation with Mary Magdalene in John 20 is a model for what all believers can expect from Jesus Christ:

> Jesus had formerly addressed her, but his discourse seemed to be that of an unknown person; he now assumes the character of the Master, and addresses his disciple by name, as we have formerly seen that the good shepherd calls to him by name every sheep of his flock (John 10:3). That voice of the shepherd, therefore, enters into Mary's heart, opens her eyes, arouses all her senses, and affects her in such a manner, that she immediately surrenders herself to Christ. Thus in Mary we have a lively image of our calling; for the only way in which we are admitted to the true knowledge of Christ is, when he first knows us, and then familiarly invites us to himself, not by that ordinary voice which sounds indiscriminately in the ears of all, but by that voice with which he especially calls the sheep which the Father hath given to him. Thus Paul says, "After that you have known God, or rather, after that you have been known by him" (Gal 4:9).[54]

The New Testament expands the theme of being known by God to being known not only by God but also by Jesus Christ. To the church in Sardis Jesus wrote:

52. Bauckham, *Gospel of Glory*, 17.
53. Lewis, *Voyage of the Dawn Treader*, 87.
54. John Calvin and William Pringle, *Commentary on the Gospel according to John*, vol. 2 (Bellingham, WA: Logos Bible Software, 2010), 257–58.

> The one who is victorious will, like them, be dressed in white. I will never blot out the name of that person from the book of life, but will acknowledge that name before my Father and his angels. (Rev 3:5)

If earlier in this chapter we noted the dark and gloomy verdict of not being known by Jesus at the last judgment, here we read of the sublimely joyful occasion of being *known by name by both Jesus and God*.[55] As N. T. Wright observes: "To be acknowledged by Jesus himself will be amazing. To have him acknowledge us before his father will be the moment of all moments."[56]

RELEVANT QUESTIONS

1. The idea that "the Lord knows those who are his" is a solid and firm foundation upon which believers can confidently build their lives (2 Tim 2:19). Does this reflect the way you currently live? Or do you find this a challenge? Why?
2. How is our personal identity tied up with Jesus Christ and his identity?
3. All the letters to the churches in Asia Minor (Rev 2–3) include the phrase "I know." If Jesus were to write you a similar letter stating "I know," what might he write about you? How do you feel about the fact that Jesus knows you intimately and personally?
4. Contrast the leadership of Jesus (particularly shown in the parable of the Good Shepherd) with the leadership of the Pharisees. What difference does his deep and transforming knowledge of us make?
5. Have you ever considered that the way we are known by Jesus is modeled on the extraordinary closeness between the Father and the Son? How does this idea of "mutual knowing" help us to work out who we are?

55. See also Matt 10:32: "Whoever acknowledges me before others, I will also acknowledge before my Father in heaven."

56. Wright, *Revelation for Everyone*, 32.

CHAPTER 8

KNOWN IN CHRIST, THE SON OF GOD

What is there to learn about personal identity from the identity of Jesus Christ? With respect to what it means to be a human being, Pontius Pilate proclaimed at Jesus's trial: "Behold the man!" (John 19:5; RSV). And Martin Luther described Jesus as "God's proper man."[1] With respect to the question of personal identity, the apostle Paul could say: "I have been crucified with Christ and I no longer live, but Christ lives in me" (Gal 2:20).

Thus far in this biblical theology of personal identity, we have investigated two interrelated biblical concepts: being made in the image of God (chapter five) and being known by God (chapters six and seven). In both cases the notion of being God's child proved to be central to human and personal identity: as those made in the image of God, we are God's offspring; and as believers in Christ, we are known by God as a father knows his child. We now turn to the question of what Jesus Christ has to do with the subject of personal identity. There is in fact much to learn about who we are by looking at who Jesus is. Jesus Christ, as God's unique and beloved Son, brings together the themes of being made in the image of God, being known by God, and becoming a child of God.

In our day, when personal autonomy and individual choice are paramount and "being yourself" is a moral imperative, it is countercultural, to say the least, to suggest that you need to find your identity in connection with someone else. And yet that is a big part of what the Bible urges on the subject of personal identity. We find our true identity in connection with Jesus Christ. As Richard Bauckham puts it: "It is 'in Christ' that Christians understand their true self to be found."[2]

In this chapter, we begin to explore the significance of Jesus Christ for a biblical theology of personal identity by looking at Paul's notion of finding your identity "in Christ." Being "in Christ" is arguably Paul's most comprehensive answer to the question of personal identity. The goal of Paul's ministry is to "present everyone

1. Cited in Philip E. Hughes, *The True Image: The Origin and Destiny of Man in Christ* (Grand Rapids: Eerdmans, 1989), viii.

2. Richard Bauckham, *The Bible in the Contemporary World: Hermeneutical Ventures* (Grand Rapids: Eerdmans, 2015), 143. Comparable notions to union in Christ in the Bible include imagery drawn from agricultural, marriage, and biological spheres: Jesus as the vine and believers as branches in John 15:1–16; Jesus as husband and believers as his wife in Eph 5:31–32; and believers as parts of the body of Christ in 1 Cor 12.

fully mature *in Christ*" (Col 1:28). Being in Christ is one of Paul's standard ways to describe both himself (e.g., 2 Cor 12:2) and other believers (e.g., Rom 16:7, 11b). And Paul makes no small claims about it: "If anyone is *in Christ*, the new creation has come: The old has gone, the new is here!" (2 Cor 5:17).

What does it mean, then, to be "in Christ" and to find your own identity in him? And how does this identity help in the quest to find a fulfilling sense of self? In order to answer these questions, we will look at four things:

1. The identity of Jesus Christ as the Son of Man and the Son of God;
2. The fact that Jesus is himself known by God as his Son;
3. The link between divine adoption and union with God's Son; and
4. The ways in which being in union with the Son of God gives us our identity.

"But what *is* man? What does it mean to say, as the Gospel writers say and insist, that Jesus was indeed a human being? What we are remains a very open question. Perhaps some part of the divine purpose in the Incarnation of the Son of Man was and is to help us to a true definition."

Marilynne Robinson[3]

THE IDENTITY OF JESUS CHRIST

Who is Jesus Christ? No person's identity has been more disputed than that of Jesus Christ.

At a critical turning point in the narratives of the three Synoptic Gospels is the scene at Caesarea Philippi in which Jesus addresses directly the question that has been bubbling along from the beginning of his public ministry, that of his personal identity:

> When Jesus came to the region of Caesarea Philippi, he asked his disciples, "*Who do people say the Son of Man is?*"
>
> They replied, "Some say John the Baptist; others say Elijah; and still others, Jeremiah or one of the prophets."
>
> "But what about you?" he asked. "*Who do you say I am?*"
>
> Simon Peter answered, "You are *the Messiah, the Son of the living God.*" . . .
>
> Then he ordered his disciples not to tell anyone that he was the Messiah (Matt 16:13–16, 20; see also Mark 8:27–30; Luke 9:18–20).

The disciples report that people are saying Jesus is to be identified as John the Baptist, Elijah, Jeremiah, or one of the other prophets. We could add magician, demon-possessed man, and insurrectionist to this list from other parts of the Gospels. And in our day, the number of alternatives for Jesus's identity has grown to even more,

3. Marilynne Robinson, *The Givenness of Things: Essays* (New York: Farrar, Straus and Giroux, 2015), 257.

including Jesus as itinerant cynic philosopher, prophet of the end times, agitator for social change, clever sage, or marginal Jew.

The Son of Man

Before we get to Peter's answer to the question of Jesus's identity, it is worth noting that there is a partial answer to Jesus's question in the way he frames it: "Who do people say *the Son of Man is*?" The Son of Man is in fact Jesus's favorite way of referring to himself in all four Gospels. It was cryptic in Jesus's day, and its meaning is still debated among scholars today. Does it refer to Jesus's heavenly origin, as its use in Daniel 7:13–14 suggests? Or is it a reference simply to Jesus as a human being, as in the name God frequently calls the prophet Ezekiel? Probably the answer is both, depending on the context.

> In my vision at night I looked, and there before me was one like *a son of man*, coming with the clouds of heaven. He approached the Ancient of Days and was led into his presence. He was given authority, glory and sovereign power; all nations and peoples of every language worshiped him. His dominion is an everlasting dominion that will not pass away, and his kingdom is one that will never be destroyed. (Dan 7:13–14)

In Mark 14 for example, Jesus alludes to Daniel 7 at his trial when he responds to the question of the high priest concerning his identity:

> Again the high priest asked him, "Are you the Messiah, the Son of the Blessed One?"
>
> "I am," said Jesus. "And you will see the Son of Man sitting at the right hand of the Mighty One and coming on the clouds of heaven." (Mark 14:61–62)

In this case Son of Man refers to his heavenly origin. However, in the majority of verses in the Gospels, the title is a reference to Jesus's humanity, as in Luke 9:58: "Foxes have dens and birds have nests, but the Son of Man has no place to lay his head."

In the Greek of Matthew 16:13, the word for "man," *anthrōpos*, is repeated, suggesting that Jesus as a human being is in fact the point in this context of speaking to his disciples. The NKJV translates the verse: "Who do men [*hoi anthrōpoi*] say that I, the Son of Man [*ton huion tou anthrōpou*], am?" Either way, for our purposes it is significant that Jesus talks about himself in a manner that emphasizes his humanity.

The Son of God

In Matthew 16:16 Peter answers Jesus's question on behalf of the disciples: "You are the Messiah, the Son of the living God" (NRSV). As titles for Jesus, Messiah and Son of God are sometimes synonymous. This seems to be the case here. Son of God, as we will see below, can refer to the coming king in the line of David, who is also the Messiah. Jesus reflects this understanding when he tells his disciples not to tell anyone that he is the Messiah, but feels no need to mention not passing on that he is the Son of God.[4] In Mark 8:29 and Luke 9:20, the parallel passages to Matthew 16, Peter identifies Jesus only as "the Messiah" and "God's Messiah," respectively. And the two identities are also paired in the high priest's question to Jesus in Mark 14:61: "Are you the Messiah, the Son of the Blessed One?"

What does it mean that Jesus is the Son of God? To answer this question, we need to know what the Old Testament says about the theme of son (or sons) of God. What is the backstory of the identity of God's Son? There are three human sons of God in the Old Testament that set the background for the use of the term with reference to Jesus.[5]

First, as we saw in chapter five, Adam is God's first son (Luke 3:38), so to speak, and all human beings as God's image bearers are also God's offspring. In this connection, Jesus is the new and better Adam, the last Adam, who begins humanity afresh and sets a new course for the race (1 Cor 15:20–24, 45–49).

Second, following Adam's transgression, by which he and all human beings after him lost the full status of being God's son, God adopted Israel as his children (Exod 4:22–23; Deut 14:1; Isa 43:6; Jer 3:19). In this connection, the Gospels, especially Matthew, portray Jesus as the new and better Israel, recapitulating key events from the nation's history. For example, with reference to the nation Israel's exodus from Egypt, Matthew writes: "So [Joseph] got up, took the child and his mother during the night and left for Egypt, where he stayed until the death of Herod. And so was fulfilled what the Lord had said through the prophet: 'Out of Egypt I called my son'" (Matt 2:14–15, quoting Hos 11:1).

Third, the most relevant background to Jesus as the Son of God in Matthew 16 is the teaching that King David and his royal descendants are "sons" of God (see 2 Sam 7:14–16; Pss 2:6–7, 12; 89:26–29; Isa 9:6–7; Rom 1:3–4). And Jesus is the new and better Davidic King or Messiah who comes to rule forever in fulfillment of God's covenant with David (Luke 1:32–33; Heb 1:5; Rev 22:16). Ultimately, as the ideal Davidic king Jesus is not only the Son of God, but in the words of Isaiah 9:6 he is "Mighty God." Jesus as the Son of God, especially in John's Gospel, is also God the Son.

As Son of God, then, Jesus is the "new Adam," the "true Israel," the ideal "king," and even deity. This is why Jesus

Jesus was called the Son of God at his death on the cross, ironically, by his executioner: "With a loud cry, Jesus breathed his last. The curtain of the temple was torn in two from top to bottom. And when the centurion, who stood there in front of Jesus, saw how he died, he said, '*Surely this man was the Son of God!*'" (Mark 15:37–39)

4. See also Nathanael in John 1:49: "Rabbi, you are the Son of God; you are the king of Israel"; Martha in John 11:27: "I believe that you are the Messiah, the Son of God"; and the purpose statement of John's Gospel in 20:31: "These are written that you may believe that Jesus is the Messiah, the Son of God."

5. Angels are also called sons of God (e.g., Job 1:6; 2:1; 38:7; Pss 29:1; 89:6). In the NIV the Hebrew for "sons of God" is translated "angels" or "heavenly beings." Even Satan is among the "sons of God" in Job 1:6 and 2:1.

as the Son of God is arguably the most comprehensive identity of Jesus revealed to us in the Gospels. Its backstory spans biblical theology and salvation history. For this reason, Jesus as the Son of God is the key concept for our own identity in him.

THE SON OF GOD KNOWN BY GOD

It is not only Peter who identifies Jesus as the Son of God in the Gospels. Others recognize him as such, including the angel to Mary (Luke 1:32, 35), Nathanael (John 1:49), Martha (John 11:27), the unclean spirits (Mark 3:11) and the demons called "legion" (Mark 5:7), and the centurion at Jesus's crucifixion (Mark 15:39). However, most striking of all is the fact that at three key points of his life, Jesus's identity as the Son of God is confirmed by God. Jesus, like those who trust in him, is known by God:

1. **The baptism of Jesus:**

   At that time Jesus came from Nazareth in Galilee and was baptized by John in the Jordan. Just as Jesus was coming up out of the water, he saw heaven being torn open and the Spirit descending on him like a dove. And a voice came from heaven: "*You are my Son, whom I love; with you I am well pleased.*" (Mark 1:9–11; see also Matt 3:13–17; Luke 3:21–22)

2. **The transfiguration of Jesus:**

   After six days Jesus took with him Peter, James and John the brother of James, and led them up a high mountain by themselves. There he was transfigured before them. His face shone like the sun, and his clothes became as white as the light. Just then there appeared before them Moses and Elijah, talking with Jesus.

   Peter said to Jesus, "Lord, it is good for us to be here. If you wish, I will put up three shelters—one for you, one for Moses and one for Elijah."

   While he was still speaking, a bright cloud covered them, and a voice from the cloud said, "*This is my Son, whom I love; with him I am well pleased.* Listen to him!" (Matt 17:1–5; see also Mark 9:2–7; Luke 9:28–35)

3. **The resurrection of Jesus:**

   Paul, a servant of Christ Jesus, called to be an apostle and set apart for the gospel of God—the gospel he promised beforehand through his prophets in the Holy Scriptures regarding his Son, who as to his earthly life was a descendant of David, and who through the Spirit of holiness was *appointed*[6] *the Son of God* in power by his resurrection from the dead: Jesus Christ our Lord. (Rom 1:1–4)

6. The Greek verb behind "appointed" is in the passive voice with God as the implied agent of the action.

> We tell you the good news: What God promised our ancestors he has fulfilled for us, their children, by raising up Jesus. As it is written in the second Psalm:
>
> "*You are my son;*
> *today I have become your father.*" (Acts 13:32–33)

Also back in chapter seven, we looked at the Good Shepherd discourse in John 10 and noted how Jesus compared knowing his sheep and being known by them to knowing his Father and being known by him: "I am the good shepherd; I know my sheep and my sheep know me—just as the Father knows me and I know the Father" (John 10:14–15a).

In the above texts, we see that at three of the most critical junctures in Jesus's adult life, when he was baptized, transfigured, and raised from the dead, he is known by God as his Son. Not only is Jesus Christ's identity critical for our identity, the manner in which he receives his identity is the same as ours; in both cases we are known by God.

Intriguingly, in 1 Peter 1 both Jesus and believers are said to be known by God:

> To God's elect . . . who have been *chosen according to the foreknowledge of God the Father*, through the sanctifying work of the Spirit, to be obedient to Jesus Christ and sprinkled with his blood. (1 Pet 1:1–2)

> [Jesus] was *foreknown* before the foundation of the world but was made manifest in the last times for the sake of you who through him are believers in God, who raised him from the dead and gave him glory, so that your faith and hope are in God. (1 Pet 1:20–21; ESV)

While no New Testament text says it explicitly, Jesus being known by God as his Son may well be the grounds by which we are known by God as his sons and daughters. Either way, the related point that our identity as God's children arises from being in union with God's Son is affirmed in Scripture.

UNION WITH THE SON OF GOD

Several scholars believe that our identity as God's sons and daughters is based on the fact that if we trust in Jesus Christ, we are *in* God's Son. John Murray believed that "we cannot think of [divine] adoption apart from union with Christ."[7] Henri Blocher contends that "in the Son we become sons, an act of grace which fulfills and transcends our primeval quasi-sonship."[8] Grant Macaskill writes that "in [John]

7. John Murray, *Redemption: Accomplished and Applied* (Grand Rapids: Eerdmans, 1961), 170.

8. Henri Blocher, *In the Beginning: The Opening Chapters of Genesis* (Leicester, UK: Inter-Varsity Press, 1984), 90. "Our primeval quasi-sonship" is a reference to Adam as the son of God by virtue of being made in the image of God; see chapter five.

> "We are actually incorporated into Christ's own life—that is what union with Christ is. In union with Christ, we receive forgiveness, which enables adoption and new life as adopted children, by the Spirit's power."
>
> *J. Todd Billings*[11]

Calvin's account of adoption . . . it is because believers are ingrafted into Christ through faith that they are adopted [into God's family]."[9] And J. Todd Billings asserts that "our true identity, our real identity" is "our identity as adopted children in union with Christ."[10]

Two texts in Paul's letters demonstrate that a link exists between union with Christ and the adoption of believers in Christ into God's family. First, in Ephesians 1:3–6 Paul lists a number of spiritual blessings that belong to God's people who are found in Christ, adoption being among them:

> Praise be to the God and Father of our Lord Jesus Christ, who has blessed us in the heavenly realms with every spiritual blessing in Christ. For he chose us in him before the creation of the world to be holy and blameless in his sight. In love he predestined us for adoption to sonship through Jesus Christ, in accordance with his pleasure and will—to the praise of his glorious grace, which he has freely given us in the One he loves.

As Trevor Burke explains, "adoption in Ephesians 1:5 is situated within the context of a plethora of spiritual blessings that are ours only in and through God's Son, Jesus Christ."[12] In particular, as Peter O'Brien notes, the description of Jesus Christ as "the one whom God loves" refers implicitly to his status as God's Son and indicates that our own "sonship" is due to being found in him:

> The term "Beloved" ["the one he loves"] here in v. 6 shows that God's election of believers to be his sons and daughters is intimately related to their being in Christ the Chosen One (cf. v. 5), and that the bounty which he lavishes on them consists in their being caught up into the love which subsists between the Father and the Son.[13]

A second text that links adoption to union with Christ is Galatians 3:26–29:

> *So in Christ Jesus you are all children [sons] of God through faith,* for all of you who were baptized into Christ have clothed yourselves with Christ. There is neither Jew nor Gentile, neither slave nor free, nor is there male and female, for you are all one in Christ Jesus. If you belong to Christ, then you are Abraham's seed, and heirs according to the promise.[14]

---

9. Grant Macaskill, *Union with Christ in the New Testament* (Oxford: Oxford University Press, 2013), 87.

10. J. Todd Billings, *Union with Christ: Reframing Theology and Ministry for the Church* (Grand Rapids: Baker, 2011), 30.

11. Billings, *Union with Christ*, 31.

12. Trevor J. Burke, *Adopted into God's Family: Exploring a Pauline Metaphor*, ed. D. A. Carson, NSBT 22 (Downers Grove, IL: InterVarsity Press, 2006), 124.

13. Peter T. O'Brien, *The Letter to the Ephesians*, PNTC (Grand Rapids: Eerdmans, 1999), 105.

14. In v. 26, the Greek is *huioi*, "sons."

We have already encountered this passage in chapter three, noting there with reference to Galatians 3:28 how the standard identity markers of race, ethnicity, social status, and gender are reduced in importance in light of our new identity of belonging to Christ. Here we notice Paul's elaboration of that new identity in terms of being "in Christ Jesus" and clothing "yourself with Christ" (or putting on Christ). And for our purposes the thing to notice is that according to v. 26, all of those who have faith in Christ become children of God "in Christ Jesus."[15]

"Believers in Christ are united with him, participate in him, are incorporated into him, and as he is God's Son inherently, so in him they become God's sons and daughters by adoption."

F. F. Bruce[16]

Grant Macaskill draws out the implications of becoming children of God in Christ Jesus and underscores the critical nature of the identity of Jesus Christ, the Son of God, for our own identity as God's sons:

> The description in Galatians 3:27 of those baptized into Christ being "clothed" with him is reflective of the extent to which the believer's identity is now defined by the personhood of Jesus. The statement is paired with a negation of other grounds of identity or status ("there is no Jew nor Greek, slave nor free, male nor female," 3:38) and with a declaration of unity in Christ ("you are all one in Christ Jesus"). . . . The clothing metaphor here, then, is one that is intended to present believers in the identity of Christ as sons of God. It is subordinated to the imagery of adoption, but it is vital to note that the grounds of this is the categorically different sonship of Jesus: believers are baptized into *him*, and clothe themselves with what *he* is as constituent of his own identity. Their identity is derivative of his.[17]

The notion of being in union with Jesus Christ, the Son of God, draws together several threads of a biblical theology of personal identity. If in Adam we lost our status as God's children and damaged the image of God, in Christ we are being conformed to and renewed in the image of God's Son (Rom 8:29; Col 3:10). Indeed, it is Christ's purpose "to create *in himself* one new humanity" (Eph 2:15).

---

15. There is debate among commentators and translations as to whether Gal 3:26 should be translated: (1) "*in Christ Jesus* you are all sons/children of God through faith" (ESV, GNT, NET, NIV, NRSV); or (2) "you are all sons of God through faith *in Christ Jesus*" (HCSB, NASB, NKJV, NLT). The issue concerns whether the phrase "in Christ Jesus" is governed by "sons of God" or by "faith." F. F. Bruce points out that Paul usually expresses faith in Christ using an objective genitive (see 3:22; *The Epistle to the Galatians: A Commentary on the Greek Text*, NIGTC [Grand Rapids: Eerdmans, 1982], 184). In response, Constantine R. Campbell cites three texts where an expression similar to "faith in Christ Jesus" appears (*Paul and Union with Christ: An Exegetical and Theological Study* [Grand Rapids: Zondervan, 2012], 118). However, none of the examples matches Gal 3:26 perfectly: Col 1:4 has "*your* faith in Christ"; and 1 Tim 3:13 and 2 Tim 3:15 include an article functioning as a relative pronoun (lit., "faith *which is* in Christ Jesus"). The grammar does not decide the issue. On balance, context favors understanding Gal 3:26 as asserting that believers become sons of God by way of union with Christ Jesus: the reference in 3:27a to being baptized into Christ likely recalls and explains the reference to union with Christ in v. 26 (see explanatory *gar* in the Greek at the beginning of v. 27).

16. Bruce, *Epistle to the Galatians*, 183–85.

17. Macaskill, *Union with Christ in the New Testament*, 196–97, emphases original. See also Stephen E. Fowl: "We only obtain our share in this adoption through the true son, Christ" (*Ephesians: A Commentary*, ed. C. C. Black, M. E. Boring, and J. T. Carroll [Louisville: Westminster John Knox, 2012], 42).

UNION WITH THE SON OF GOD AND PERSONAL IDENTITY

If being known by others is a key to identity, as I have argued throughout this book, our relationship with God and being known by him is critical to personal identity. Being in union with the Son of God means that *God knows us in his Son*. Union with Christ also contributes to the Bible's account of the relational self in explaining how in knowing us God can look on us so favorably and not reject us because of our sinfulness.[18] Jesus Christ is God's Son whom he loves and with whom he is well pleased. In Christ we enjoy the same blessed status.

> "For [John] Calvin, that little phrase 'in Christ' signals an altered identity. Not a religious platitude, this phrase requires a new self-understanding in which the Christian can no longer separate his or her identity from being 'in Christ' or, indeed, from those who join together forming Christ's body. Calvin's term 'adoption' can be seen as shorthand for this pneumatological sphere in which we, *en Christō* [in Christ], are relating to God from the transformed reality of adoptive sonship, able to cry '*Abba*' like the Son. Our cry of '*Abba*' is not sentimental but pneumatological, as 'the Spirit testifies to our heart respecting the paternal love of God' (Calvin, *Commentary on Romans* 8:16). Calvin insists that the self can only be understood in its *relation* to God."
>
> *Julie Canlis*[20]

Union with God's Son implies our participation in the major events of Christ's life. If the defining events of his life are his death, resurrection, and ascension, it follows for those in Christ that when we were "dead in [our] transgressions and sins. . . . God raised us up with Christ and seated us with him in the heavenly realms *in Christ Jesus*" (Eph 2:1, 6). The Christian practice of baptism reinforces our status as people who find our identity in Christ.[19] Paul, for example, states:

> Or don't you know that all of us who were *baptized into Christ Jesus* were baptized into his death? We were therefore buried with him through baptism into death in order that, just as Christ was raised from the dead through the glory of the Father, we too may live a new life. (Rom 6:3–4)

It is not that union with the Son of God cancels the significance of our own life events. We do not lose our past stories. We remain individuals in the fullest sense. Life's ups—such as getting married, having children, getting a job, buying a house—along with life's knocks, our family histories, and so on remain significant for our life stories. But ultimately these events don't define us. As Bauckham explains:

> Finding our true selves in Christ, we identify with him who loved us, follow his way of self-giving for God and for others, and thus continually find ourselves afresh in him.[21]

18. Theologically, justification by faith and union with Christ are closely related. See Campbell, *Paul and Union with Christ*, 388–405.

19. For more on this, see chapter fifteen.

20. Julie Canlis, "The Fatherhood of God and Union with Christ in Calvin," in *"In Christ" in Paul: Explorations in Paul's Theology of Union and Participation*, ed. Michael J. Thate, Kevin J. Vanhoozer, and Constantine R. Campbell (Tübingen: Mohr Siebeck, 2014), 414–15.

21. Bauckham, *Bible in the Contemporary World*, 143.

In chapter ten, we will think further about the significance of our shared memory of Christ's death and resurrection and our hope of rising to new life in him. But before that, we need to dig deeper into the Bible's teaching about our new identity as children of God.

RELEVANT QUESTIONS

1. Jesus Christ answered questions about his own identity by describing himself as the Son of Man, a term that emphasised his humanity. Is Jesus's humanity important to you? And if so, in what ways?
2. As believers in Christ we are united with him and "caught up" in the love between the Father and the Son. How does participating in this perfect love affect your concept of who you are?
3. This chapter has presented the idea that while we remain individuals with our own significant stories, ultimately life events do not define us. Our true self can only be found in our union with the Son of God. How do you respond to this idea? How does it help you reorder or re-evaluate the foundations of your personal identity?

CHAPTER 9

SON OF GOD AND CHILD OF GOD

When it comes to your personal identity, many things change throughout your lifetimes. Your age, job, where you live, and even your personality and character can be different from one decade to another. For most people, families are among the few constants that stay with us from the beginning to the end of our lives. Without the most drastic of actions, and despite fractured relationships, among your most influential relationships are your relatives, and most significantly your parents. And this is especially the case when one of your parents is noteworthy for some reason; it's hard not to live in the shadow of a famous (or infamous) father or mother. While being a son or a daughter is foremost when you are growing up, the impact of your parents on your identity goes the distance. How many of us have said to ourselves long into adulthood, often with some irritation: "Oh dear, I'm turning into my father/mother"?

Who are we? The Bible has a number of metaphorical ways of talking about the identity of God's people. God's relationship with us is compared to that of king and subject, master and servant, husband and wife, shepherd and sheep, potter and clay, and so on. In this chapter we investigate what is arguably the most powerful and pervasive of such identity metaphors: father and child.

What you call yourself is of fundamental importance in forming your identity. What does it mean to say that God is our Father and that we are God's children? In order to answer this question, we must begin by considering how to interpret a metaphor.[1] Sometimes people regard metaphors as sort of decorative additions to the more important direct communication, more "icing on the cake" than the cake itself. This view is mistaken, and it leads

"Words, including self-designations, have an ability to lead to a radical reinterpretation of identity."

Paul Trebilco[2]

1. Some question whether or not being a child of God is actually a metaphor. They argue that the primary reality is God's family, after which human families are the reflection. However, we are better to take being a child of God as a spiritual reality that the Bible expounds in comparison to the more familiar concept of human families. As D. A. Carson notes, while there are "many instances in the Bible where sonship is entirely natural and biological . . . [divine] sonship is metaphoric" (*NIV Zondervan Study Bible* [Grand Rapids: Zondervan, 2015], 2664). Even John Calvin, who understood "the relationship of the Father and the Son to be the root of all reality," writes of God in relation to humanity as being "*like* a father." Cited in Canlis, "The Fatherhood of God and Union with Christ in Calvin," 403.

2. Paul Trebilco, *Self-Designations and Group Identity in the New Testament* (Cambridge: Cambridge University Press, 2012), 300.

to a seriously stunted reading of the Bible, which is "full to the brim" of figurative language. Metaphors communicate *more* meaning than literal modes of speaking, not less.

With a clear understanding of metaphorical language in place, we will then consider the two sides of the father/child metaphor: (1) being a child or son of God; and (2) being brothers and sisters in God's family. This metaphor is widely used in the Bible.

UNDERSTANDING METAPHORS

What is a metaphor? What does it mean to say that I am a child of God or that we are brothers and sisters in God's family?

Janet Martin Soskice contends that the many theories of how metaphors work fall into three basic groups. The first regards metaphors as decorative ways of saying what could be said literally. But this view is clearly mistaken in ignoring the emotive responses that metaphors arouse. Simply to "translate" a metaphor into straightforward language is to miss the metaphor's dynamism. A second group stresses the affective impact a metaphor exerts, the feelings it evokes. But this view goes too far in the other direction in denying that a metaphor contributes any increment to meaning. For if thoughts and feelings can be expressed in words, then at least part of a metaphor's meaning may be expressed literally, even if by doing so one risks blunting the affective impact. An adequate account of metaphors must consider both their cognitive meaning and emotive effect. Thus, a third group considers metaphors to be unique cognitive vehicles enabling one to say something that can be said in no other way.[3]

Here are some examples of biblical metaphors:

God is a rock.
The Lord is my shepherd.
The Lord God is a sun and a shield.
Jesus is the door.
Jesus is the true vine.
Judah is a lion's cub.
Herod is a fox.
You are the salt of the earth.
You are God's children.
You are brothers and sisters in God's family.

3. Janet Martin Soskice, *Metaphor and Religious Language* (Oxford: Clarendon, 1987), 24–53.

My own definition of a metaphor points to three essential elements:

Metaphors are a form of communication that uses a familiar image to (1) say something (2) memorably (3) with feeling.

Metaphors communicate more meaning than propositional or literal language in that, rightly understood, they both *inform* and also *move* the hearer. And by appealing to something that is concrete and known, like all figurative language, a good metaphor sticks in the mind and is easily recalled. The trick with interpretation is to determine what feelings the metaphor evokes, its *affective impact*, as well as what we learn from the metaphor, that is, its *cognitive meaning*.

There are two things to consider for accurate interpretation of metaphors. The first is *context*—sometimes clues are given in the literary context of a metaphor that help explain its meaning. And secondly, *milieu*—we need to determine the cultural setting of the image in question to ascertain its regular associations. The milieu of biblical metaphors can be ascertained both from extra-biblical texts and from the Bible itself.

"Metaphors are incongruous conjunctions of two images—or two semantic fields—that turn out, upon reflection, to be like one another in ways not ordinarily recognized. They shock us into thought by positing unexpected analogies."
Richard Hays[4]

Paul's use of family metaphors, for example, is explicitly tied to Old Testament texts. In Romans 9:25–26, Paul claims that gentile Christians have the privilege of being called "*children* of the living God" on the basis of Hosea 1:10. In Galatians 4:27–31, Paul quotes Isaiah 54:1 to support the Galatian Christians' new familial status as "*children* of the promise" (Gal 4:28). And in 2 Corinthians 6:18, Paul's supports his description of the Corinthian community as God's "sons" and "daughters" by a quotation of 2 Samuel 7:14.

"Metaphor consists in bringing two sets of ideas close together, close enough for a spark to jump . . . so that the spark, in jumping, illuminates for a moment the whole area around, changing perceptions as it does so."
N. T. Wright[5]

As a case study in understanding metaphors, consider "God is a rock"—a biblical metaphor with a long history. This metaphor is a conjunction of two apparently incongruous things. Yet after reflecting on their respective semantic fields, they turn out to be alike in certain ways. What is the comparison of God to a rock saying? The difficulty in interpreting a metaphor is working out which features of each semantic field are being drawn upon in the comparison.[6] Which associations are being highlighted and which are being suppressed? In other words, what is the

4. Richard B. Hays, *The Moral Vision of the New Testament: Community, Cross, New Creation, A Contemporary Introduction to New Testament Ethics* (New York: HarperCollins, 1996), 300.

5. N. T. Wright, *The New Testament and the People of God*, Christian Origins and the Question of God 1 (Philadelphia: Fortress, 1992), 40.

6. As Steven J. Kraftchick puts it, "Metaphor is not an isomorphic mapping of all relationships within one field to another, but a highlighting of some and suppression of others" ("A Necessary Detour: Paul's Metaphorical Understanding of the Philippian Hymn," *Horizons in Biblical Theology* 15.1 [1993]: 23).

metaphor's cognitive meaning? And how is God being compared to a rock meant to make us feel? What is its affective impact?

The use of this metaphor in the Psalms is revealing:

> The LORD is my rock, my fortress and my deliverer;
> *my God is my rock*, in whom I take refuge,
> my shield and the horn of my salvation, my stronghold. (Ps 18:2; see also 2 Sam 22:2–3, 32–33; Ps 62:2)

The point of comparing God to a rock is to highlight God's strength and protection. Rocks withstand pressure, enduring even when massive force is brought against them. In line with this understanding, the Aramaic translations of the Pentateuch take God being a rock in Deuteronomy 32 to refer to his strength and paraphrase the verses in question as describing God as "the Strong One."[7] Given that everyone has some experience of rocks, comparing God to a rock is memorable. And this carries with it feelings of security and safety that would be lacking if it were reduced to a literal utterance about God.

We may present an understanding of the metaphor of God as a rock in a diagram:

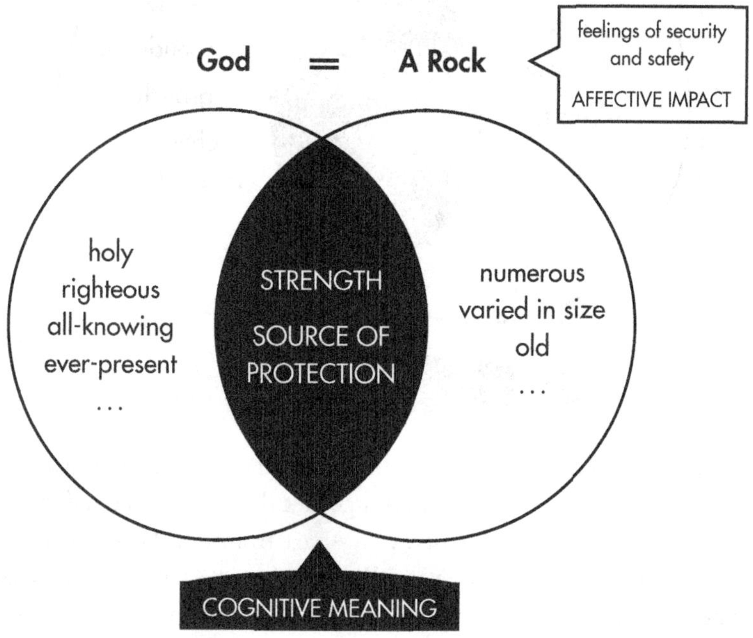

7. See Brian S. Rosner, "'Stronger than He?': The Strength of 1 Corinthians 10:22b," *Tyndale Bulletin* 43.1 (1992): 171–79.

DIVINE ADOPTION

As we noted in chapter three, the family to which you belong is of critical importance to your identity. And as we will see, being a member of God's family picks up on many of these associations.

What then are we to make of the "family of God" metaphor? Clearly it communicates memorably, since having parents and siblings is such a common human experience. But which associations of the imagery are the points of the comparison? What feelings are communicated by the family metaphor? What do we learn from its use in various literary contexts? What is its milieu? What cultural associations did fathers, sons, children, and siblings carry in Bible times?

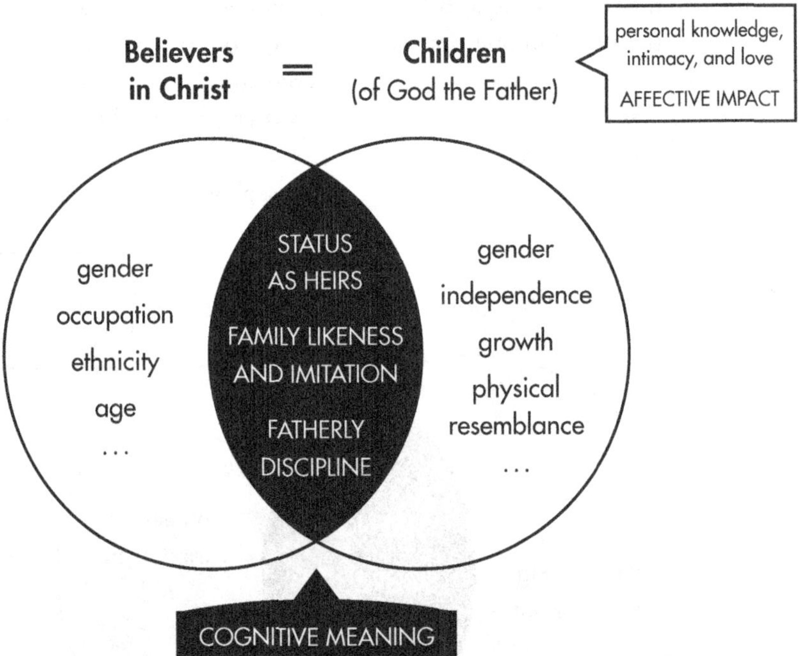

In 1973, J. I. Packer pointed to the surprising lack of interest in the topic of divine adoption. He lamented "the strange fact that the truth of adoption has been little regarded in Christian history. . . . Apart from two last-century books, now scarcely known . . . there is no evangelical writing on it, nor has there been at any time since the Reformation."[8] Fortunately, the tide has turned in recent times with several major contributions to investigating the topic appearing.[9] Our focus in this

8. J. I. Packer, *Knowing God*, 20th Anniversary ed. (Downers Grove, IL: InterVarsity Press, 1993), 149.

9. See for example James M. Scott, *Adoption as Sons of God*, WUNT 2.48 (Tübingen: Mohr Siebeck, 1992); Trevor J. Burke, *Adopted into God's Family: Exploring a Pauline Metaphor*, ed. D. A. Carson, NSBT 22 (Downers Grove, IL: InterVarsity Press, 2006); and Peter Balla, *The Child-Parent Relationship in the New Testament and its Environment*, WUNT 155 (Tübingen: Mohr Siebeck, 2003).

book is on the critical importance of God adopting us into his family for the subject of the personal and corporate identity of believers in Christ.

The family of God metaphor is both remarkably widespread in the Bible and impressively flexible in its application. By way of preview, we may present the main features of the metaphor as it relates to our status as children of God in the diagram above. The second major section in this chapter will consider our identity as brothers and sisters in God's family.

Which associations are being highlighted and suppressed in this metaphor? In other words, what is the metaphor's cognitive meaning? And how is being compared to children of God meant to make us feel? What is its affective impact?

The following two sections expound the major aspects of the metaphor: 1) its affective impact, namely, personal knowledge, intimacy, and love; and 2) its cognitive meaning with reference to becoming heirs of God, displaying the family likeness, and receiving fatherly discipline.

The Affective Impact

The affective impact of saying that God is our Father is easily determined. In the biblical cultures as well as throughout the Bible, parents are those who love and care for their children. Jesus took this for granted in teaching about our heavenly Father:

> Which of you fathers, if your son asks for a fish, will give him a snake instead? Or if he asks for an egg, will give him a scorpion? If you then, though you are evil, know how to give good gifts to your children, how much more will your Father in heaven give the Holy Spirit to those who ask him! (Luke 11:11–13; see also Matt 7:9–11)

When God declares that Jesus is his Son at Jesus's baptism and transfiguration, as we saw in chapter eight, he identifies him as the one "whom I love." And when Paul speaks of our adoption into God's family, he mentions God's love for both his adopted sons and his only begotten Son:

> *In love* he predestined us for *adoption to sonship through Jesus Christ*, in accordance with his pleasure and will—to the praise of his glorious grace, which he has freely given us in *the One he loves*. (Eph 1:4–6)

Jesus drew out another dimension of the father-child relationship in the Good Shepherd discourse in the Fourth Gospel in a text we considered in chapter seven:

> I am the good shepherd; *I know my sheep and my sheep know me—just as the Father knows me and I know the Father*—and I lay down my life for the sheep. (John 10:14–15)

Jesus compared the knowledge he has of his "sheep" to the intimate and personal knowledge a father has of his children. And as we saw in chapters six and seven, to be known by God is be known intimately and personally as his children.

Thus, the metaphor of believers in Christ as God's children carries with it feelings of love, intimacy, and personal knowledge. These are not things to do or even learn, but rather things to sense and embrace—that is, the affective impact of the metaphor.

The Cognitive Meaning

What does the identity of being a son or child of God entail? When it comes to cognitive meaning, there are three regular uses to which the metaphor of believers as members of God's family is put in the Bible. Put another way, three things are highlighted as common to both believers in Christ and children. (See the common set in the Venn diagram above.)

Heirs with an Inheritance

The first regular use is this: *as children of God, believers have the status as God's heirs and coheirs with Christ awaiting an eternal inheritance.*

The theme of heirs and inheritance has a long and colorful history in the Bible. Abraham's first response to God's call in Genesis 15 concerns his heir:

> Abram said, "Sovereign Lord, what can you give me since I remain childless and the one who will inherit my estate is Eliezer of Damascus?" And Abram said, "You have given me no children; so a servant in my household will be my heir." (Gen 15:2–3)

Later in Genesis, conflict erupts between Sarah and her maidservant Hagar over whether Ishmael or Isaac would be Abraham's heir. Sarah said to Abraham: "Get rid of that slave woman and her son, for that woman's son will never share in the inheritance with my son Isaac" (Gen 21:10).

Paul deals with believers as heirs at length in Galatians 3:7–4:7. In response to the Judaizing opponents, who insisted that the Abrahamic inheritance was restricted to those who put themselves under the law by being circumcised, Paul argues that Abraham's true children are those who put their faith in Jesus: "those who have faith are children of Abraham" (Gal 3:7). In Galatians 5:21, Paul indicates that the inheritance in view is the kingdom of God (see also 1 Cor 6:9–10; Eph 5:5). In Titus 3:7, on the other hand, Paul defines our inheritance in a different but related manner: by grace believers "become heirs having the hope of eternal life."

Paul links believers being children and heirs with Jesus Christ being the Son of God:

> When the time came to completion, God sent His Son, born of a woman, born under the law, to redeem those under the law, so that we might receive adoption as sons. And because you are sons, God has sent the Spirit of His Son into our hearts, crying, "*Abba*, Father!" So you are no longer a slave but a son, and if a son, then an heir through God. (Gal 4:4–7 HCSB)

In Paul's view, Christ the Son of God is the true heir (see also Matt 21:38), and believers become co-heirs by being united to him.

The language of sonship raises a major problem of interpretation and translation. Are those who are in union with Christ God's sons or his children? Does it matter? Is the language of sonship necessary to communicate the notion that we are heirs of God? Many modern translations, including the NIV, render the Greek *huios* in Galatians 4:7 (and elsewhere) as "child" rather than as "son": "So you are no longer a slave, but God's child; and since you are his child, God has made you also an heir." While Greek *huios* in this verse is clearly generic and includes believers of both genders, there are two possible reasons for retaining "son" in translation. The first is the fact that in Bible times, it was the right of the eldest son in the family to be the primary heir (see, e.g., Deut 21:15–17). However, while technically the language of sonship does forge a link to Christians being heirs, we should note that Paul himself does not always insist on using it. In Romans 8:16–17, he discusses Christians being heirs, describing us as God's "children," *tekna*. Other New Testament books, such as the Gospel of John, talk in terms of believers as "children of God" (John 1:12) with Jesus as "the one and only Son" (John 1:18; 3:16).

Different authors in the New Testament develop the metaphor of believers as God's children and part of God's family in different ways. Nonetheless, there is a second reason for retaining the language of sonship, at least in some contexts, so long as it is understood that the term is gender inclusive: it reminds us that we are part of God's family and heirs thanks to the Son of God. In other words, we are sons of God precisely because he is the Son of God. Julie Canlis writes: "I am unwilling to drop the gendered term 'sonship,' as our 'sonship' is founded upon Christ's own Sonship. For those who find the term suspect, I do not think it can be interchanged with all sorts of terms like 'becoming children of God' or 'being adopted' . . . these lose christological clarity."[10]

My policy in this book is to use the language of "children of God" rather than "sons of God" unless the notion of sonship has a direct bearing on the point I am making. In those cases readers should be aware that "sons of God" carries a generic sense and refers to all believers in Christ, both male and female.

> "The concept of the believer's inheritance highlights the dignity of the family relationship of the believer in Christ. No higher position or greater wealth can an individual acquire than to become an heir of God through faith in Christ."
> *William E. Brown*[11]

Family Likeness and Imitation

As children of God, believers have the status as God's heirs and coheirs with Christ awaiting an eternal inheritance. A second cognitive meaning of the metaphor of the family of God is this: *As children of God, believers are to imitate the Father and the*

10. Canlis, "The Fatherhood of God and Union with Christ in Calvin," 404.

11. William E. Brown, "Inheritance," in *Evangelical Dictionary of Biblical Theology*, ed. Walter A. Elwell, electronic ed. (Grand Rapids: Baker, 1996).

Son. On this point we see the profoundly formative nature of the identity of being children of God for our behavior and character.

In terms of the milieu of fathers and sons, D. A. Carson notes:

> In the ancient world, the overwhelming majority of sons took up the same vocation as that of their fathers. The sons of farmers became farmers, the sons of fishermen, became fishermen—and in both cases the sons learned their trade from their fathers. . . . These realities established their identity. That is why Jesus can be identified as "the carpenter's son" (Matt 13:55) and, presumably after the death of his (apparent) father Joseph, as himself "the carpenter" (Mark 6:3).[12]

With this in mind, it makes perfect sense for Jesus to say, "whatever the Father does the Son also does" (John 5:19).

The very language of "son of [something]" itself points to a relationship of resemblance. In 2 Kings 6:32 a "son of a murderer" is a "murderer" and is translated as such (cf. NASB and NIV). Likewise, the "son of might" is a "fighter" (2 Sam 17:10), and Jesus names James son of Zebedee and his brother John, "Boanerges, which means 'sons of thunder'" (Mark 3:17), presumably to match their passionate and volatile character. In John 8:44 Jesus says of those opposing him: "You belong to your father, the devil, and you want to carry out your father's desires."

Like it or not, fathers shape the identity of their sons. On one occasion, my nine-year old son said something that was mildly offensive. When I corrected him, my wife pointed out a certain similarity with me. Toby responded in his own defense: "You taught me to be myself!"

In this light, not surprisingly, the Bible has so much to say about imitating God and Christ. To be God's child is to reflect the family likeness. Ephesians 5:1–2 mentions the imitation of both God and Christ:

> *Follow God's example*, therefore, *as dearly loved children* and walk in the way of love, just as Christ loved us and gave himself up for us as a fragrant offering and sacrifice to God.

Let's begin with the imitation of God. This theme goes back to Leviticus where God tells his people to "be holy, because I, the Lord your God, am holy" (Lev 19:2; see also 20:7, 26; 1 Pet 1:16). Jesus carried on the tradition by telling his disciples to love their enemies, "that you may be children of your Father in heaven" (Matt 5:44–45), and to "be perfect, therefore, as your heavenly Father is perfect" (Matt 5:48). To avoid a superficial survey of the subject, we will focus on one text, the letter to the Ephesians. As Ephesians 5:1 indicates (see above), imitating God is clearly linked to the child/parent relationship.[13]

12. Carson, *NIV Zondervan Study Bible*, 2664. Even in our day, some surnames reflect this tradition: Baker, Smith, etc.

13. This section builds on Roy E. Ciampa, "*Missio Dei* and *Imitatio Dei* in Ephesians," in *New Testament Theology in Light of the Church's Mission: Essays in Honor of I. Howard Marshall*, ed. Jon C. Laansma, Grant Osborne, and Ray Van Neste (Bletchley, UK: Paternoster/Eugene, OR: Cascade, 2011), 238–42.

The theme of imitating God is subtly present in the second half of Ephesians and has links to the first half. In general terms, it is noteworthy that believers are "created to be like God in true righteousness and holiness" (Eph 4:24). And the call to unity in Ephesians 4:3, to "make every effort to keep the unity of the Spirit," is based on the oneness of God, that there is "one Lord" and "one God and Father of all" (Eph 4:5–6).

Moreover, the theme of unity is expanded with a call to "be completely humble and gentle; be patient, bearing with one another in love" (Eph 4:2). As Roy Ciampa notes, "it does not take much reflection to realize that the first half of the letter had made it clear that those same qualities had marked God's own treatment of the readers"[15]—it was out of God's great mercy and love that he had given them new life in Christ. Likewise in Ephesians 4:32, Paul tells the Ephesian Christians to "be kind and compassionate to one another, forgiving each other, just as in Christ God forgave you." Ciampa writes: "It is natural and expected that children will imitate their parents. . . . What God has modeled for believers is his loving nature."[16]

"How can we be sure that we are adopted children of God? The Spirit is the answer. The Spirit jointly bears witness with our spirits that we are children of God (Rom 8:16). . . . The very fact that the Christian can pray as a child of the Father rather than address God like a slave addressing a master is evidence of the Spirit's witness and adoption."

Graham A. Cole[14]

The theme of imitating God is also implicit in the pervasive "walking" motif in Ephesians 4–6, using the Greek word *peripateō* as a metaphor for daily conduct.[17] Believers are not to "walk as the Gentiles do" (Eph 4:17 ESV), as you "once walked, following the course of this world" (Eph 2:2 ESV). Instead, we are to "walk in love" (Eph 5:2 ESV); "Walk as children of light" (Eph 5:8 ESV); and walk in wisdom (Eph 5:15 ESV). Significantly, love, light, and wisdom "were all well-known divine attributes,"[18] and hence the call to walk in love, light, and wisdom is a call to walk in God's footsteps. Equally, Paul lists "the fruit of the light" as "all goodness, righteousness and truth" (Eph 5:9), which are also qualities associated with God himself.

Imitating Christ is even more prominent in the New Testament than imitating God.[19] Following the example of Jesus Christ is enjoined in many texts. Jesus told his disciples: "Whoever wants to be my disciple must deny themselves and take up their cross daily and follow me" (Luke 9:23). Having washed his disciples' feet, he said, "I have set you an example that you should do as I have done for you" (John 13:15). Paul exhorts the Corinthians, "Follow my example, as I follow the example of Christ" (1 Cor 11:1). He commends the Thessalonians who "became imitators of us and of the Lord" (1 Thess 1:6a). And he instructs the Philippians, "In your relationships

14. Graham A. Cole, *He Who Gives Life: The Doctrine of the Holy Spirit* (Wheaton, IL: Crossway, 2007), 269–70. See also Rom 8:15: "The Spirit you received brought about your adoption to sonship."

15. Ciampa, "*Missio Dei* and *Imitatio Dei* in Ephesians," 239.

16. Ibid.

17. This is the source of the English word "peripatetic," which is used for teachers and other occupations whose work moves between more than one school or college.

18. Ciampa, "*Missio Dei* and *Imitatio Dei* in Ephesians," 240.

19. For a thorough study of this theme, see for example Richard A. Burridge, *Imitating Jesus: An Inclusive Approach to New Testament Ethics* (Grand Rapids: Eerdmans, 2007).

with one another, have the same mindset as Christ Jesus" (Phil 2:5). Accordingly, Peter reminds his readers, "Christ suffered for you, leaving you an example, that you should follow in his steps" (1 Pet 2:21).

But is the imitation of Christ Jesus connected to the metaphor of believers as members of God's family? In many cases it is. In Romans, for example, being conformed to the image of God's Son is an integrative theme for Paul's teaching about the Christian life.[20] The key text is Romans 8:29:

> For those God foreknew he also predestined to be conformed to the image of his Son, that he might be the firstborn among many brothers and sisters.

The older brother Jesus is the model for his younger siblings. Leon Morris puts it well:

> It is God's plan that his people become like his Son, not that they should muddle along in a modest respectability. We should be in no doubt as to the high standard that Paul sets for Christian people. We have been admitted to the heavenly family; we are *brothers* [and sisters] in that family and we call God "Father". We are accordingly to live as members of the family, and that means being made like our elder Brother. This is all part of God's predestination; he predestined us not only to be released from an unpleasant predicament, but in order that we might become like his Son.[21]

That Jesus is the template to which his brothers and sisters are to conform is evident across Romans. The language of obedience lies at the heart of the Christian life. The letter is framed by two references to "the obedience that comes from faith" (Rom 1:5 and 16:26). Paul describes his own obedience in Romans 15:17–19 and calls for Christians not to obey sin but rather to live lives of "obedience, which leads to righteousness" (Rom 6:16; see also 6:12). He also commends the Roman Christians in that "Everyone has heard about your obedience" (Rom 16:19). It is no accident that when Paul explains the basis of our justification, he points to the obedience of Jesus Christ: "For just as through *the disobedience of the one man* the many were made sinners, so also through *the obedience of the one man* the many will be made righteous" (Rom 5:19). As God's children, we are to be obedient because Jesus the Son of God obeyed God.

Significantly, Paul's practical teaching in Romans 12–15 is driven by the goal of conformity to the pattern of God's Son. The call in Romans 12:2 not to "conform to the pattern of this world," but to "be transformed by the renewing of your mind" signals the beginning of the major section of explicit exhortation in the letter. Michael

20. This section builds on Richard Gibson's unpublished notes on Romans.

21. Leon Morris, *The Epistle to the Romans* (Grand Rapids: Eerdmans, 1988), 333. Emphasis original.

Thompson observes that the call to mind renewal recalls the depraved mind of Romans 1:18–32 and represents its reversal.[22] According to Thompson, "underpinning 12:1–2 is Jesus's foundational and exemplary sacrifice. For Paul, Christ's image is the goal of the transforming process."[23] Offering ourselves as "living sacrifices" in Romans 12:1 recalls the application of cultic language to Jesus's atoning death in Romans.[24] Whereas Jesus's sacrifice necessitated his death, Paul points out that ours is a living sacrifice. Furthermore, the language of being "transformed" (*metamorphousthe*) in our behavior in Romans 12:2 echoes the goal of being "conformed" (*summorphos*) to the image of God's Son in Romans 8:29.

The closing verse of Romans 13 confirms that Paul had Jesus in mind in Romans 12–13 as he shares his vision of humanity: "Clothe yourselves with the Lord Jesus Christ, and do not think about how to gratify the desires of the flesh" (Rom 13:14). Likewise, Paul's advice in Romans 14:1–15:7 about the need to accept one another in disagreements over disputable matters is reinforced by the example of Jesus:

> Each of us should please our neighbors for their good, to build them up. For even Christ did not please himself but, as it is written: "The insults of those who insult you have fallen on me." (Rom 15:2–3)

Fatherly Discipline

As children of God, believers have the status as heirs of God and must imitate the Father and the Son. A third dimension of the metaphor is this: *as children of God, believers are disciplined by God, our loving heavenly Father, so that we might grow into full maturity.*

One of the main associations of what it means to be a father in the Old Testament is the task of disciplining children. In Proverbs, father-like sages make frequent reference to the need to be careful to "discipline" your children (Prov 13:24), to "rebuke" them when necessary (1:25; see also 10:17), and on occasion to use "the rod of discipline" (22:15; see also 10:13; 23:13–14). The responsibility to discipline was based on the premise that fathers were to be obeyed: "A wise son heeds his father's instruction" (Prov 13:1a; see also 15:5). In Proverbs 3:12, the Lord is compared to a caring father who "disciplines those he loves."

Such discipline is underscored with respect to the Davidic king in 2 Samuel 7:14: "I will be his father, and he will be my son. When he does wrong, I will punish him with a rod wielded by men." And God promises to do the same for all of his people to bring them to maturity: "Know then in your heart that as a man disciplines his son, so the Lord your God disciplines you" (Deut 8:5).

22. Michael B. Thompson, *Clothed with Christ: The Example and Teaching of Jesus in Romans 12.1–15.13*, Journal for the Study of the New Testament Supplement Series 59 (Sheffield: JSOT Press, 1991), 78–82.

23. Thompson, *Clothed with Christ*, 85.

24. See also Rom 3:24–25; 5:8–9; 8:3–4.

Hebrews 12:5–11 exhorts readers along these lines, quoting Proverbs 3:11–12 as support.[25] Notice how the passage is explicitly framed by the identity of God's people as sons of God their Father:

> And have you forgotten the exhortation addressed to you as sons?
> "My son, do not scorn the Lord's discipline
> or give up when he corrects you.
> For the Lord disciplines the one he loves
> and chastises every son he accepts." [Prov 3:11–12]
>
> Endure your suffering as discipline; God is treating you as sons. For what son is there that a father does not discipline? But if you do not experience discipline, something all sons have shared in, then you are illegitimate and are not sons. Besides, we have experienced discipline from our earthly fathers and we respected them; shall we not submit ourselves all the more to the Father of spirits and receive life? For they disciplined us for a little while as seemed good to them, but he does so for our benefit, that we may share his holiness. Now all discipline seems painful at the time, not joyful. But later it produces the fruit of peace and righteousness for those trained by it. (Heb 12:5–11 NET)

"The Christian's sonship is derived from our relationship with Christ as adopted sons. On this basis New Testament believers typically identified one another as 'brothers' [and 'sisters']."
R. A. Taylor and E. R. Clendenen[26]

BROTHERS AND SISTERS IN THE FAMILY OF GOD

Who did the first Christians think they were? What did they call themselves? In his study entitled *Self-Designations and Group Identity in the New Testament*, Paul Trebilco lists the following titles and descriptions favored by the first Christians: believers, saints, the church, disciples, the Way, Christians, and brothers and sisters (Greek *adelphoi*). It is significant for our investigation of personal identity that "*adelphoi* is the most common term in use as a designation for Christians in the New Testament."[27] In fact, as Trevor Burke notes, "the frequency with which the early Christian movement in general, and the apostle Paul in particular, employed this expression [brothers and sisters] is unprecedented."[28]

The extensive use of sibling language in the early church stood out in the ancient world, with the one exception being Jews whose kinship could be traced in

25. See also Prov 19:18; 29:17.

26. Richard A. Taylor and E. Ray Clendenen, *Haggai, Malachi: An Exegetical and Theological Exposition of Holy Scripture*, NAC 21A (Nashville: Broadman & Holman, 2004), 322–23.

27. Trebilco, *Self-Designations and Group Identity in the New Testament*, 65. See also 300: "When early Christians called themselves 'brothers and sisters' . . . they were creating and shaping their identity and their ongoing life as well as reflecting their experience of what was significant for them."

28. Trevor Burke, *Family Matters: A Socio-Historical Study of Kinship Metaphors in 1 Thessalonians* (London: T&T Clark, 2003), 174.

general terms through blood lines.[29] While the language of brother and sister was not unheard of in pagan philosophical circles, groups like the Epicureans or Cynics preferred the language of friendship. Paul, on the other hand, avoids calling Christians his friends. Abraham Malherbe notes that "Paul does not speak of friends or friendship but of brotherly love. He was familiar with the conventional discussions about friendship but studiously avoided using the word itself."[30]

A possible reason for Paul's preference for sibling language is his concern not just for individual morality but also for the corporate life of God's family. Wayne Meeks writes: "We cannot begin to understand the process of moral formation [in Paul's letters] until we see that it is inextricable from the process by which distinctive communities were taking shape. Making morals means making community."[31] The use of *adelphoi* shows that a child of God is not only an individual identity, but also a corporate one.

> "The very widespread use of *adelphoi* across the New Testament shows how widely it was in use amongst the earliest Christians, and that it can be seen as a unifying factor across the movement. Its importance can be related to the pervasive ethos of being fictive kinship groups in early Christianity. . . . This speaks of a sense of love, mutuality, togetherness, and belonging and also testifies that the early Christians saw themselves as a distinctive group over against other groups. This use of *adelphoi* both reflects and enhances the identity and cohesion of early Christian groups."
>
> *Paul Trebilco*[32]

> While Jesus was still talking to the crowd, his mother and brothers stood outside, wanting to speak to him. Someone told him, "Your mother and brothers are standing outside, wanting to speak to you." He replied to him, "Who is my mother, and who are my brothers?" Pointing to his disciples, he said, "Here are my mother and my brothers. For whoever does the will of my Father in heaven is my brother and sister and mother." (Matt 12:46–50; see also Mark 3:31–35; Luke 8:19–21)

> "Because the English language does not distinguish between the second-person singular and plural, translations do not communicate that Paul's letters are a dialogue between him and the entire community. . . . Even private correspondence to Philemon addresses the whole church."
>
> *Michael B. Thompson*[33]

What gave rise to the widespread use of the language of brother and sister in the early church? It seems that four factors worked together to make the language stick:

1. Historically, there was a strong precedent of the same language in the Old Testament for Israel as the people of God.[34]
2. Jesus taught that his followers were a new family.[35]

---

29. See many examples in 1 and 2 Macc and generally in rabbinic texts.

30. Abraham Malherbe, *Paul and the Thessalonians: The Philosophic Tradition of Pastoral Care* (Philadelphia: Fortress, 1987), 104.

31. Wayne A. Meeks, *The Origins of Christian Morality: The First Two Centuries* (New Haven: Yale University Press, 1993), 5.

32. Trebilco, *Self-Designations and Group Identity in the New Testament*, 65.

33. Thompson, *Clothed with Christ*, 27.

34. See Malherbe, *Paul and the Thessalonians*, 49: "It is generally agreed that the Christian concept of brotherhood developed out of Judaism. Pagans, in fact, took offense at the intimacy that Christians expressed with such language, and scorned it."

35. See Matt 12:46–50.

3. "The members of the communities were *adelphoi* [brothers and sisters] because Jesus is the firstborn Son (Rom 8:29)."[36]
4. The early church had a "powerful experience of community as 'a new family.'"[37]

If a metaphor is a form of communication that uses an image to say something memorably with feeling, what is the affective impact of the comparison of believers in Christ to brothers and sisters? And what is its meaning?

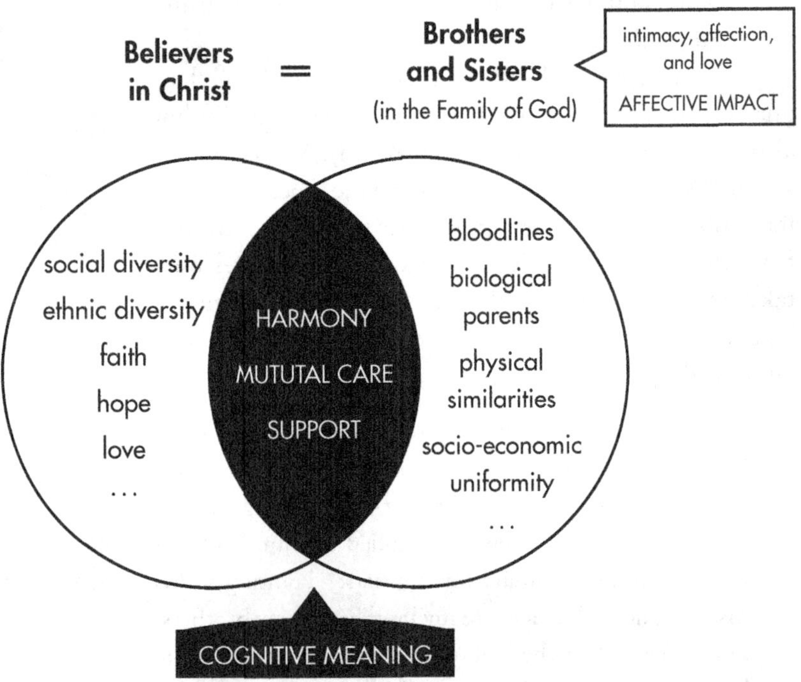

Affective Impact: Love and Intimacy

The feelings elicited by the family of God metaphor are not hard to discern. If the affective impact of having God as your Father is the experience of love and intimacy with God (see above), a corresponding love for and intimacy with fellow believers is communicated by the family of God metaphor.

The compound Greek word *philadelphia*, "love for brothers and sisters," combines the words for "love" and "sibling."[38] It appears five times in the New Testament. Modern translations concerned to not misrepresent its gender inclusiveness sometimes translate it as "love" or "mutual love" (e.g., Rom 12:10, NIV and NET, respectively). But its connection to the family metaphor should not be missed. An alternative

36. Trebilco, *Self-Designations and Group Identity in the New Testament*, 66.

37. Ibid., 65.

38. BDAG 1055.

translation might be "family affection," especially in contexts where the word "love" is also present. Christians should have the closeness and love for one another that characterize siblings (in their better moments):

> Love one another with *brotherly [and sisterly] affection.* (Rom 12:10 ESV)
>
> Now concerning *love of the brothers and sisters,* you do not need to have anyone write to you, for you yourselves have been taught by God to love one another. (1 Thess 4:9 NRSV)
>
> Keep on *loving one another as brothers and sisters.* (Heb 13:1 NIV)
>
> Having purified your souls by your obedience to the truth for a sincere *brotherly [and sisterly] love,* love one another earnestly from a pure heart. (1 Pet 1:22 ESV)
>
> Make every effort to supplement your faith with goodness, goodness with knowledge, knowledge with self-control, self-control with endurance, endurance with godliness, godliness with *brotherly [and sisterly] affection,* and *brotherly [and sisterly] affection with love.* (2 Peter 1:5–7 HCSB)

Paul also connects love and brothers and sisters in his distinctive address: "My beloved brethren" (1 Cor 15:58; Phil 4:1 NASB), Greek *adelphoi mou agapētoi.* Likewise, John connects being brothers and sisters in Christ with the response of love:

> Anyone who loves their brother and sister lives in the light. (1 John 2:10)
>
> This is how we know who the children of God are and who the children of the devil are: Anyone who does not do what is right is not God's child, nor is anyone who does not love their brother and sister. (1 John 3:10; see also 3:18; 4:20).

Psalm 133:1 gives us a glimpse of the background for such sentiments in the Old Testament: "How good and pleasant it is when brothers [and sisters] live together in harmony!" (Ps 133:1 HCSB).

Cognitive Meaning: Harmony, Mutual Care, and Support

If love and intimacy are the emotive effect of living out the metaphor of the family of God, what is this metaphor's cognitive meaning? What does the New Testament say about the identity of believers as brothers and sisters? In general terms, two things stand out.

First, *sibling language is used to call for avoiding conflict*: "Is it so, that there is not among you one wise man who will be able to decide between his *brethren,* but *brother* goes to law with *brother,* and that before unbelievers?" (1 Cor 6:5–6 NASB). Brothers and sisters are not to squabble.

Second, *being brothers and sisters is the grounds for exercising mutual care and support*:

> "The sibling metaphor relates to social relations, to emotional ties, to harmony and concord, as well as to a common ancestry through the work of Christ, and so has a rich range of links to Christology, ecclesiology, ethics, and so on."
> *Paul Trebilco*[39]

Brothers and sisters, if someone is caught in a sin, you who live by the Spirit should restore that person gently. But watch yourselves, or you also may be tempted. Carry each other's burdens, and in this way you will fulfill the law of Christ. (Gal 6:1–2)

Old Testament precedents include the ban on charging interest to fellow Israelites: "Do not charge *your brother* [or sister Israelite] interest on money, food, or anything that can earn interest. You may charge a foreigner interest, but you must not charge *your brother* [or sister Israelite] interest" (Deut 23:19–20 HCSB). Such language recalls Cain's excuse that he was not his "brother's keeper" (Gen 4:8–10). As brothers and sisters in Christ, we in fact are our brother's and sister's keepers.

SAMPLE TEXTS: HEBREWS AND THE SERMON ON THE MOUNT

To this point in this chapter, we have been looking broadly at the meaning of the metaphors of believers in Christ as God's children and members of his family across a range of biblical texts. In order to demonstrate not only the breadth of the Bible's treatment of such matters but also its depth, we shall take a look at two case study texts that serve to confirm and illustrate our findings: the letter to the Hebrews and the Sermon on the Mount.

Hebrews

The letter to the Hebrews is a case study of how the theme of believers as children of God flows from the truth that Jesus is God's Son. The letter reminds us of the significance of the Son of God for our identity as children of God. As Amy L. B. Peeler puts it, in Hebrews "God's paternal relationship with Jesus grants to the audience members *their identity* and hope as children of God."[40]

Hebrews opens by focusing on God's relationship to his Son: "In the past God spoke to our ancestors through the prophets at many times and in various ways, but in these last days he has spoken to us by his Son" (Heb 1:1–2a). The first time that God speaks in the letter it is to his Son: "You are my Son; today I have become your Father" (1:5a). And as Peeler notes, "in God's first explicit address to the author and his audience, God declares their status as his *huioi* [sons] (Heb 12:5–6)."[41] Peeler also observes that there is a close similarity between God's initial declaration of Jesus's sonship in 1:5b ("I will be his Father, and he will be my Son") and the new covenant promise issued to the

39. Trebilco, *Self-Designations and Group Identity in the New Testament*, 308.

40. Amy L. B. Peeler, *You Are My Son: The Family of God in the Epistle to the Hebrews*, The Library of New Testament Studies 486 (London: T&T Clark, 2014), 6, emphasis added.

41. Ibid., 3.

community in Hebrews 8:10c ("I will be their God, and they will be my people"), which suggests their new identity as God's children is based on God's relationship to his Son.[42]

The letter in fact is infused with familial language. God as "Father" appears at two pivotal points. The first is in Hebrews 1:5 (quoting Ps 2:7) in reference to Jesus: "You are my Son; today I have become your Father." The second is in Hebrews 12:9 (alluding to Isa 38:16) with reference to believers: "Moreover, we have all had human fathers who disciplined us and we respected them for it. How much more should we submit to the Father of spirits and live!" Correspondingly, Jesus in Hebrews is regularly referred to as the "Son" (Heb 1:2, 5, 8; 3:6; 4:14; 5:5, 8; 6:6; 7:3, 28; 10:29) and as God's heir at his Father's right hand (1:2, 4; 8:1; 10:12; 12:2) awaiting his inheritance (1:13). Likewise, the readers are described as God's sons (Greek *huioi*, 2:10; 12:5–8) and God's children (*paidia*; 2:13–14), and as members of God's house (*oikos*; 3:6). They are also brothers and sisters (2:11–12; 3:1, 12; 10:19; 13:22) who endure training (*paideia*; 12:5–11) as they look forward to their own eternal inheritance (1:14; 6:17; 9:15; 11:40; 12:22–24, 28).

> "God's paternal relationship with Jesus his Son shapes the theology and Christology of the letter [of Hebrews], and, in so doing, constructs *the identity of the audience*, legitimizes their present experience, and supports them in their endurance. Because God is Father and Jesus is Son, the author argues, the audience can be confident in their status as God's children and in the promised future that status entails."
>
> *Amy L. B. Peeler*[43]

What does Hebrews do with the familial metaphor as applied to believers in Christ? It offers a thoroughly theological account of all believers, both male and female, as children of God in connection with Jesus as the Son of God. Just as God perfected his Son through suffering and death and gave him an eternal inheritance, so too God's children may endure hardship in the knowledge that they have a stake in that inheritance. The identification of believers with God's Son shows us how to live since God disciplines us as his children. It also gives us a vibrant hope and confident assurance in times of difficulty.

The Sermon on the Mount

If part of the answer to the question of personal identity concerns our conduct and character, the Sermon on the Mount has much to say about what it means to be a follower of Jesus Christ.

In the Bible it is a truism that identity informs behavior. Who we are is meant to flow through to how we behave: the righteous behave righteously; the wicked, wickedly; the humble, humbly; the proud, haughtily; and so on. We must be careful not to read the Sermon simply as a list of commands. Its ethics grow out of character rooted in identity.

So what is the identity that is meant to fulfill the weighty commands and undertake the radical lifestyle enjoined in the Sermon on the Mount? Who is supposed to put away anger, violence, lust, hypocrisy, pride, greed, self-assertion, and self-preservation and to love their enemies, keep their promises, and to forgive freely?

42. Ibid., 143.

43. Ibid., 8, emphasis added.

Matthew 5:43–48 provides the answer:

> You have heard that it was said, Love your neighbor and hate your enemy. But I tell you, love your enemies and pray for those who persecute you, so that you may be *sons of your Father in heaven*. For He causes His sun to rise on the evil and the good, and sends rain on the righteous and the unrighteous. For if you love those who love you, what reward will you have? Don't even the tax collectors do the same? And if you greet only your brothers, what are you doing out of the ordinary? Don't even the Gentiles do the same? Be perfect, therefore, as *your heavenly Father* is perfect. (HCSB)[44]

The Sermon on the Mount is a description of what it means to be a child of God and behave accordingly.[45]

Matthew stands out among the Synoptic Gospels for its interest in the fatherhood of God, with God as Father mentioned forty-four times, compared to just four times in Mark and eighteen times in Luke. John's Gospel, on the other hand, with its focus on the Father and the Son in God's mission to save the world, refers to God as Father around one hundred and twenty times.

However, Matthew is unique among all four Gospels in its keen interest in God as the Father of believers. God as our Father occurs just once in Mark and John and four times in Luke, but it appears twenty-one times in Matthew. And what is significant for our purposes is the fact that as many as sixteen references to God as the Father of believers appear in the Sermon on the Mount.[47] The Sermon on the Mount is about the disciples as children of God.

> The Sermon on the Mount declares "what life is like when you belong to the new aeon of God. This is what sonship is like."
> *Joachim Jeremias*[46]

The final reference to God as Father in the Sermon on the Mount differs from the rest in that it is not about God as the Father of the disciples, but God as the Father of Jesus:

> Not everyone who says to me, "Lord, Lord," will enter the kingdom of heaven, but only the one who does the will of *my Father* who is in heaven. (Matt 7:21)

In the Sermon, Jesus refers to God as "your Father" fifteen times before telling us that the same God is his Father also.

A comparison of John and Matthew on this score is intriguing. In John's Gospel, many references to God as the Father of Jesus throughout the Gospel are followed by one climactic reference to God as the Father of believers also (John 20:17).[48] In the Sermon

44. NIV translates Matt 5:45 as "children of your Father in heaven," taking *huioi* (sons) to refer to both genders.

45. This section is indebted to Stephen George's excellent unpublished Moore Theological College fourth-year BD project, "The Contribution of the Sermon on the Mount to the Christology of the Gospel of Matthew" (2009).

46. Joachim Jeremias, *The Sermon on the Mount* (Philadelphia: Fortress, 1963), 161.

47. See Matt 5:16, 45, 48; 6:1, 4, 6 (2x), 8, 9, 14, 15, 18 (2x), 26, 32; 7:11. The six in the other three Gospels are Mark 11:25; Luke 6:36; 11:2; 12:30, 32; John 20:17. The five references outside the Sermon of the Mount in Matthew are in 10:20, 29; 13:43; 18:14; 23:9.

48. See the section on "Jesus and Mary Magdalene" in chapter seven.

on the Mount, many references to God as the Father of believers are followed by one climactic reference to God as the Father of Jesus (Matt 7:21). The point is the same in both Gospels, even if the narrative artistry moves in opposite directions: there is a close connection between God as the Father of Jesus and God as the Father of Jesus's disciples.

Jesus is identified in Matthew 1:1 as "the son of David, the Son of Abraham," and "Matthew devotes the first main part of his Gospel to the theme of the person of Jesus the Messiah."[49] Subsequently in the Gospel, Jesus is identified as Emmanuel, Messiah, King, Son of Man, and so on. But as Jack Dean Kingsbury observes, in Matthew "preeminently, Jesus is the Son of God."[50] Stephen George summarizes this focus in Matthew's Gospel:

> Matthew's placement of the title "Son of God" in the Gospel reveals its significance for his understanding of Jesus. It occurs at key moments of conflict: in Jesus's battle against evil forces (4:3, 6; 8:29); and in Jesus's confrontation with the leaders of Israel (26:63; 27:43). Its use is concentrated in key episodes in the Gospel's narrative. It is used three times in the baptismal pericope and temptation narrative (3:17; 4:3, 6), and four times in the Gospel's climax, the passion narrative (26:63; 27:40, 43, 54), where it is laden with irony. It is used at a major crux in the plot at 6:16, where God reveals to Peter the true identity of Jesus (16:17). Of the Synoptic writers, who all relate Peter's profession, Matthew uniquely includes the "Son of God" title. All this points to the significance of the title "Son of God" for understanding Matthew's Christology and the Gospel as a whole.[51]

Space forbids a full investigation of Jesus as the Son of God in Matthew. Suffice to say that it goes well beyond noticing titles. But for our purposes, we should note in particular the fact that Jesus's sonship is connected to Israel's sonship. Matthew 2:14–15, for example, quotes Hosea 11:1 to explain the significance of Jesus's escape from Herod's wrath and sets up the theme that Jesus is the true Israel and embodies Israel's calling:

> So he got up, took the child and his mother during the night and left for Egypt, where he stayed until the death of Herod. And so was fulfilled what the Lord had said through the prophet: "Out of Egypt I called my son." (Matt 2:14–15)

All of this is vital to understanding the identity of Jesus's disciples as children of God in the Sermon on the Mount. The close connection between the Son of God and his disciples as children of God extends to the lifestyle that the Sermon commends. Jesus embodies his own teaching in the Sermon on the Mount. This is underlined subtly at numerous points.

49. Jack Dean Kingsbury, *Matthew: Structure, Christology, Kingdom* (Minneapolis: Fortress, 1975), 162.

50. Jack Dean Kingsbury, *Matthew as Story*, 2nd ed. (Philadelphia: Fortress, 1988), 57.

51. George, "The Contribution of the Sermon on the Mount to the Christology of the Gospel of Matthew," 40–41. Note too the diverse characters in Matthew who profess Jesus as the Son of God. Opponents include: the tempter (4:3, 6); the demon-possessed man (8:29); the high priest (26:63); and those passing by (27:40). Supporters include: the heavenly voice (3:17; 17:5); disciples in the boat (14:33); Peter on behalf of the disciples (16:16); and the centurion (27:54).

Jesus the Son of God is his own example when it comes to expounding the conduct and character of his disciples as children of God:

- If they are to mourn (Matt 5:4), we see Jesus mourning in 26:38.
- If they are to be meek (5:5), Jesus says, "I am meek" in 11:29.[52]
- If they are to "hunger and thirst for righteousness" (5:6; see also 5:10, 20; 6:1, 33), Jesus is a model of righteousness and fulfills all righteousness (3:15).
- If they are to show mercy (5:7), Jesus leads the way in showing mercy in 9:27–30; 15:22–28; 17:15–18; 20:30–34.
- If as sons of God they are to be peacemakers (5:9), Jesus comes to bring peace in 12:15–21 and 26:52.[53]
- If they can expect persecution (5:10–12), Jesus is persecuted to the point of death in chs. 26–27 (see esp. 26:67–68; 27:30).
- If they are to be "the light of the world" (5:14), in 4:16 "the people living in darkness have seen a great light" in Jesus.
- If they are to let their "light shine before others, that they may see your good deeds and glorify your Father in heaven" (5:16), they glorify God because of what Jesus did in 9:5–8 and 15:31.
- If they are to pray, "Our Father in heaven . . . your will be done" (6:9–10), Jesus prays three times in the garden of Gethsemane, "My Father, if it is not possible for this cup to be taken away unless I drink it, may your will be done" (26:42; see also 26:39, 44).

As Jesus in the Sermon on the Mount states, the teacher must do what he teaches (5:19). Unlike the Pharisees, when it comes to his own teaching Jesus is no hypocrite (see also Matt 23). Indeed, if the disciples are to build their lives on the rock of Jesus's teaching (7:24–25), confession of Jesus as the Son of the living God is the rock on which the church is built (16:18), and Jesus promises to be with his disciples in their task of teaching all that he has commanded them (28:19–20).

"The entire Sermon on the Mount is a proclamation of the will of God to men and women who are children, and who are permitted to pray to their Father because he is near to them and hears them."

Ulrich Luz[54]

The impressive linguistic and conceptual correlation between the Sermon on the Mount and the presentation of Jesus in the Gospel points to the conclusion that, as Karl Barth put it, "the Commander . . . embodies the command."[55] Or as Helmut Thielicke states: The Sermon on the Mount "is inseparably bound up with Jesus Christ as the representative of the coming aeon. . . . It proclaims a love which has meaning

52. In the New Testament Greek, *praus*, "meek," only appears in Matt 5:5; 11:29 and 1 Peter 3:4. Also, Matt 11:28–30 is unique to Matthew in the Gospels.

53. However, Matt 10:34 indicates that this was not his only task: "Do not suppose that I have come to bring peace to the earth. I did not come to bring peace, but a sword."

54. Ulrich Luz, *The Theology of the Gospel of Matthew* (Cambridge: Cambridge University Press, 1993), 49.

55. Karl Barth, *Church Dogmatics: The Doctrine of God—Volume II, Part 2*, ed. G. W. Bromiley and T. F. Torrance (Edinburgh: T&T Clark, 1957), 690.

only with reference to him."[56] Jesus calls his disciples to a vocation analogous to Israel, God's children, but at the same time is himself the true Israel and perfect Son of God. And as we seek to obey the Sermon on the Mount, we do so in humble dependence upon and in imitation of him.

"Jesus Christ is the perfect image of God, and the image of God is being restored as we grow into our adopted identity."
J. Todd Billings[57]

DIVINE ADOPTION AND PERSONAL IDENTITY

Who am I? Who are we? As believers in Christ we are children of God, loved by God and given full rights of inheritance as heirs of God and co-heirs with Christ. We are brothers and sisters in God's family, with our big brother Jesus being the model to whom we conform, thereby taking on the family likeness. This identity leads to a host of implications for our conduct. We imitate our heavenly Father by walking in love, light, and wisdom, and we imitate his Son Jesus Christ by living lives of loving sacrifice and service to others. As brothers and sisters, we are to live in harmony and with care for and support of our spiritual siblings. And we expect God our Father's loving discipline.

Our identity as God's children and the character that goes along with it has a long backstory. It's not as though divine adoption comes out of the blue. To recap from the earlier chapters of this book, if Adam was a rebellious son of God and suffered "death" as a result,[58] Israel proved to be God's wandering children, and David and his dynasty of kings were God's often-disobedient sons. Only Jesus Christ was God's perfect and well-pleasing Son; and all believers in Christ are children of God in him. Our new identity as God's children by union with God's Son is our true identity, since, being made in the image of God, we were made to be God's children from the very beginning. In Christ, as those known by God as his children, we regain our true selves.

RELEVANT QUESTIONS

1. Do you experience "brotherly and sisterly" love rather than friendship at the church you belong to? If not, why not?
2. Is it easy for you to relate to the idea of sonship? Why does this chapter argue for its importance?
3. As believers we are adopted into a new family, as sons and daughters of God the Father. How do you feel about the fact that God as your Father knows you intimately and loves you deeply?
4. The Sermon on the Mount shows that ethics grow out of character rooted in identity, so who you are flows through to how you behave. Discuss.

56. Helmut Thielicke, *Theological Ethics, Volume 1: Foundations* (Grand Rapids: Eerdmans, 1969), 354.

57. J. Todd Billings, *Union with Christ: Reframing Theology and Ministry for the Church* (Grand Rapids: Baker, 2011), 33.

58. Cf. Deut 21:18–21 where a rebellious and disobedient son receives the most severe punishment.

CHAPTER 10

SHARED MEMORY AND DEFINING DESTINY

When you first meet people, along with noticing their gender and race, guessing their age and learning their name, you might ask about their cultural background, occupation, significant relationships, and where they live. Going deeper, a more penetrating question is to ask them about their story: What is their family background? What in their past has made them who they are today? Where are they heading in life? What defines them? Human beings tell stories about themselves that matter.

Indeed, our stories play a vital role in expressing who we are. We each have what Timothy Keller calls a narrative identity: "Everyone lives and operates out of some narrative identity, whether it is thought out and reflected upon or not."[1] Such narratives give meaning to our lives, sketch our character in outline, and tell us what is important in life.

Often a person's story begins before that person was born. My father was born in Vienna in a Jewish family. He was an only child, and when he was a young teenager, he and his parents fled Europe soon after Hitler took over Austria in 1938. They headed for Shanghai where there was an international settlement that accepted stateless refugees. They spent ten years there, in the "waiting room," as the settlement has since been called. All three became Christians there. In 1949, after the war was over, they immigrated to Australia. My father met my mother, an Australian, in Sydney, and they married in 1953. Seeing I didn't come along until 1959, how can all of this be part of my story?

It is in fact quite common for family histories to have an impact on a person's identity. In my case, my father's history affects a number of things about me, including my attitude to education (which my father missed out on), to refugees, to Jews and Judaism, to European history and culture, to playing chess, to food, music, and so on. Of course my life has had many other influences. But my experience is not unusual. Such "second hand" memories, in which we were not present or the primary actor, are testimony to the formative power of larger narratives for personal identity, stories of which we find ourselves a part and which we share with others.

National identities are another illustration of the role of shared memories in forming identity. National identity is all about past events that shape national

1. Timothy Keller, *The Reason for God: Belief in an Age of Skepticism* (New York: Penguin: 2008), 15.

character today. For example, the high value Americans place on freedom and personal rights derives significantly from the story of the Revolution and national formation in the 1770s and 1780s. Foundational figures such as George Washington and Thomas Jefferson and documents such as the Declaration of Independence and the Constitution of the United States remain a part of public discourse and imagination. With these stories and symbols, Americans have woven together an ongoing cultural narrative of their society as a land of opportunity and as a "melting pot" of peoples from diverse ethnic backgrounds.

The Bible, in fact, has much to say about the impact of shared memories on what makes you, you. It also highlights the significance of future destiny for your identity. As Bruce Waltke puts it, in the Bible "identity is formed by two factors: memory and destiny."[2] And as we'll see in this chapter in both the Old and New Testaments, *shared memory* and a *defining destiny* play a major role in the stories God's people tell about themselves.

"We are grass, no doubt of it. But with a sense of history we can have a perspective that lifts us out of our very brief moment here. Certainly this is one purpose of biblical narrative."

Marilynne Robinson[3]

To some degree, tracing your history is easily done. But knowing where your life is heading can be more difficult to ascertain. According to literary critic Gary Saul Morson:

> *Closure and structure* mark the difference between life as it is lived and as it is read about; and real people live without the benefit of an outside perspective on which both closure and structure depend.[4]

Viewed from "under the sun," the vast majority of people's lives do not seem to build towards a satisfying ending or any sense of resolution. Our lives appear to be driven in large part by random events, and, as much as we try, they do not proceed in any predictable direction over the long course. Indeed, an atheist worldview has often led to pessimistic nihilism and the conclusion that human existence is meaningless.

Yet Christians believe that God provides the necessary "outside perspective" of which Morson speaks. In other words, being known by God gives our lives both structure and closure. As the psalmist prays: "You have searched me, Lord, and you know me. . . . all the days ordained for me were written in your book before one of them came to be" (Ps 139:1, 16). While it is true, as Ecclesiastes puts it, that living "under the sun" means that our lives are dogged by harsh adversity and constraining limitations, we can still know that the genre of our life stories is set and the ending has already been written.

As those who are known by God as his children, the defining moment of our lives was long before we were born, namely the death of Jesus Christ, a death with

2. Bruce K. Waltke, *An Old Testament Theology: An Exegetical, Canonical, and Thematic Approach* (Grand Rapids: Zondervan, 2007), 13.

3. Marilynne Robinson, *The Givenness of Things: Essays* (New York: Farrar, Straus and Giroux, 2015), 154.

4. Gary Saul Morson, *Narrative and Freedom: The Shadows of Time* (New Haven: Yale University Press, 1994), 38, emphasis added.

which we so closely identify that it can be called our own. And our destiny is likewise tied up with him inextricably, for when Christ returns and is publicly made known as the risen Son of God, our true identity as children of God will also be revealed:

> You died [our shared memory], and your life is now hidden with Christ in God. When Christ, who is your life, appears, then you also will appear with him in glory [our defining destiny]. (Col 3:3–4)

To say that Christ is your life (Col 3:4) is one of the most profound and yet puzzling claims in Scripture. What does it mean? Comparable statements elsewhere in Paul's letters include Philippians 1:21, where he writes that for him, "to live is Christ." Here Paul is saying that his life is filled with the joy of knowing Christ and the task of proclaiming Christ. Closer to Paul's meaning in Colossians 3:4 perhaps are those passages where he says that Christ is "in" him (Gal 1:16) or "lives in" him (Gal 2:20), or where he affirms that Christ is "in" believers (Col 1:27) and dwells in their hearts (Eph 3:17). In Galatians 4:19, Paul declares that he wants Christ to be formed in the Christians to whom he writes. The thrust of these passages is that the one in whom Christ dwells "should become like Christ in character."[5] Having Christ "in you" is to become like Christ.

Richard Bauckham suggests that personal identity can be viewed from two angles, both of which relate directly to finding your identity in Christ: "The self is a unique and particular center of personal identity that can be characterized as relational and narratival. It is relational in that it is formed in personal and non-personal relationships. . . . It is narratival in that it is formed in and through time and finds its unique identity in a story with a past, present and expected future. The human self has no independent being, outside of relationships, and no timeless existence outside of the temporal reality that we can only describe in narrative."[6] The self is relational; we are known by God, and the narratival self is known in Christ in connection with his death, resurrection, and return.

However, Paul's assertion that Christ is your life (Col 3:4) seems to be saying something slightly different. In context, Paul is claiming in Colossians 3 that our lives have the shape of Christ's life; *the life of Christ is our narratival identity*. We share his death, and we will share his resurrection. Being in Christ (see chapter eight) means that when he died, we died, and when he is vindicated as the Son of God, our own secret but true identity will be revealed.[7]

"You have a 'true life,' the hidden life of your real self, your new self."

N. T. Wright[8]

There are many passages in the New Testament, especially in Paul's letters, that speak of our identity in terms of a shared memory and a defining destiny. We will consider eight that are especially clear with regard to the critical importance of a common past and a momentous future for the personal identity of believers in Christ:

5. James D. G. Dunn, *The Epistle to the Galatians*, BNTC (London: Continuum, 1993), 241.

6. Richard Bauckham, *The Bible in the Contemporary World: Hermeneutical Ventures* (Grand Rapids: Eerdmans, 2015), 138–39.

7. The notion that Christ is our life has profound implications for our character and conduct, which the following verse in Colossians 3 makes clear: "Put to death, therefore, whatever belongs to your earthly nature: sexual immorality, impurity, lust, evil desires and greed, which is idolatry" (Col 3:5). See chapter fourteen, "Direction."

8. N. T. Wright, *The Early Christian Letters for Everyone: James, Peter, John, and Judah* (London: SPCK, 2011), 65.

Shared Memory

- We Were Bought at a Price—1 Corinthians 7:21–24
- We Died with Christ—Romans 6:3–10
- We Carry Around the Death of Jesus—2 Corinthians 4:10–12

Defining Destiny

- We Are Hard Pressed for Time—1 Corinthians 7:29–31
- We Have Been Sealed for the Day of Redemption—Ephesians 1:13–14
- We Belong to the Day—Romans 13:11–14
- We Shall Be Like Him—1 John 3:1–3
- We Await Our Resurrection Bodies—1 Corinthians 15

Note that these eight summary statements are not phrased in the singular—"I was bought at a price" and so on—but rather in the plural: "We were bought at a price" (1 Cor 7:23). While the Bible does not collapse personal identity into some notion of corporate identity, our individual lives nonetheless fit into God's bigger plans for all of his people. Along with exploring the narrative identity of believers in Christ, this chapter continues the Bible's emphasis on corporate identity; who I am derives from and sits underneath who we are. We begin with a brief consideration of the analogous role of memory and destiny in the identity of God's ancient people in the Old Testament.

MEMORY AND DESTINY IN ISRAEL

The fact that a shared memory and a common destiny leads to a new identity for God's people is well and truly established in the Old Testament. When God redeemed his people from slavery in Egypt, that saving event was commemorated in Israel with the annual Passover celebration (Exod 12:12–16). In some Old Testament texts, recollections of the event of the exodus are recounted at "arm's length." For example Numbers 33:3 states that "*the Israelites* set out. . . . *They* marched out defiantly in full view of the Egyptians," and so on. Commands to, "Remember the former things, those of long ago" (Isa 46:9) and to "remember the wonders he [the Lord] has done" (1 Chr 16:12) are scattered throughout the Old Testament.[9]

These events happened to other people. Yet remembering is strikingly personalized when later generations of Israelites are included in references to the saving events, as if they had experienced them personally. For example, the generation who followed those who died in the wilderness following the exodus are told: "Remember that *you* were slaves in Egypt and that the Lord your God brought *you* out of there

9. See also Deut 4:9: "Only be careful, and watch yourselves closely so that you do not forget the things your eyes have seen or let them fade from your heart as long as you live. Teach them to your children and to their children after them."

with a mighty hand and an outstretched arm" (Deut 5:15). Likewise, "be careful that you do not forget the LORD, who brought *you* out of Egypt, out of the land of slavery" (Deut 6:12; see also 8:10–18). Technically, the Lord brought their parents and grandparents out of Egypt, not most of them. But that shared memory is of such consequence for the identity of the people of God that the events in question can rightly be said to have happened to them.

Michael Horton explains the significance of such shared memories for personal identity:

> The present generation makes history their story. . . . History is not only rendered contemporary; it is internalized. One's people's history becomes one's personal history. One looks out from the self to find out who one is meant to be. One does not discover one's identity, and one certainly does not forge it oneself. . . . Instead, it is the consequence of what are presented as the acts of God. . . . Israel began to infer and to affirm her identity by telling a story.[10]

Just as importantly, the Israelites are also defined by the prospect of entering and inheriting the promised land of Canaan, their common and defining destiny. If their redemption from slavery in Egypt, the exodus, formed them as a people, the promise of God is always before them that they would "enter and possess the land I swore to their ancestors to give them" (Deut 10:11).

Who are you, and what is your story? What might an Israelite living in the wilderness following the rescue of God's people from Egypt have said in response to these two questions? Alec Motyer's suggested answer underscores the role of shared memory and defining destiny:

> I was in a foreign land under the sentence of death, in bondage, but I took shelter under the blood of the lamb. Our mediator let us out, and we crossed over, and now we're on our way to the Promised Land. We're not there yet, but he's given us his law to make us a community. And he's given us the Tabernacle because you have to live by grace and forgiveness. And his presence is in our midst, and he's going to stay with us until we get home.[11]

MEMORY AND IDENTITY

What then of our identity as those who are known by God as his children through faith in Jesus Christ? What shared memories relate to that identity? Of what story do we find ourselves a part?

10. Michael Horton, *The Christian Faith: A Systematic Theology for Pilgrims on the Way* (Grand Rapids: Zondervan, 2011), 86–87.

11. Cited by Timothy Keller in the forward of J. Alec Motyer, *A Christian's Pocket Guide to Loving the Old Testament* (Fearn, Scotland: Christian Focus, 2015), x.

Backstory is a literary term used in discussions of novels, films, and television dramas. It refers to those events previous to the start of the plot which are essential to understanding present circumstances and characters. The backstory of volume four of the Harry Potter stories is volumes one, two, and three. Some television series briefly bring viewers up to date with the essentials of the backstory before the new episode begins: "Previously on . . ."

> "I can only answer the question 'What am I to do?' if I can answer the prior question 'Of what story or stories do I find myself a part.'"
>
> *Alasdair MacIntyre*[12]

The main point in the backstory of Christians is the death and resurrection of Jesus Christ. Just as the people of Israel were instructed to remember their deliverance in the exodus with the Passover, so Christians "remember" Jesus "until he comes" (1 Cor 11:26) by celebrating the Lord's Supper. And remembering Jesus is an identity-confirming act, as Miroslav Volf explains:

> In remembering Christ [at Communion], Christians remember themselves as part of a community of people who have died and risen together with Christ and whose core identity consists in this spiritual union with Christ. They remember Christ's story not just as his story but also as their story.[13]

We will deal further with the role of the Lord's Supper in the final chapter of this book and the way in which the Supper, along with baptism and other Christian practices, reinforces our identity as children of God in union with Christ. For now, three passages from 1 and 2 Corinthians and Romans underscore the significance of remembering Christ's death for knowing who we are.

> "Paul argues for a new identity in Christ, one defined historically in relation to Christ's death and resurrection and eschatologically in relation to believers' ultimate and completed destiny."
>
> *Craig S. Keener*[14]

We Were Bought at a Price—1 Corinthians 7:21–24

In 1 Corinthians 7:21–24, Paul addresses slaves in the church of God in Corinth:

> Were you a slave when you were called? Don't let it trouble you—although if you can gain your freedom, do so. For the one who was a slave when called to faith in the Lord is the Lord's freed person; similarly, the one who was free when called is Christ's slave. *You were bought at a price*; do not become slaves of human beings. Brothers and sisters, each person, as responsible to God, should remain in the situation they were in when God called them.

"Were you a slave when God called you to faith in Christ?" Paul says, "Don't let it trouble you." The Greek verb "to trouble [someone]"[15] is translated elsewhere in the New

12. Alasdair MacIntyre, *After Virtue: A Study in Moral Theory* (Notre Dame, IN: Notre Dame University Press, 1981), 216.

13. Miroslav Volf, *The End of Memory: Remembering Rightly in a Violent World* (Grand Rapids: Eerdmans, 2006), 98–99.

14. Craig S. Keener, *The Mind of the Spirit: Paul's Approach to Transformed Thinking* (Grand Rapids: Baker, 2016), 53.

15. Greek *melei*, "be a source of concern" (BDAG 626–27).

Testament as "pay no attention to" (Matt 22:16), "don't you care" (Mark 4:38; Luke 10:40; John 10:13), and "show no concern" (Acts 18:17; 1 Cor 9:9). The Corinthian Christian slaves are not to worry about their lowly status and unenviable social identity.

Paul does not say that "slavery is nothing," as he does of circumcision back in 1 Corinthians 7:19. And he encourages the Christian slaves to take the opportunity for freedom if it presents itself: "if you can gain your freedom, do so" (1 Cor 7:21).[16] It is not that God is unmoved by the distress of his people. The God of all comfort comforts us in all our troubles (2 Cor 1:3–4). But our circumstances do not determine who we are before God. Even the lowest social status and the most menial and unrewarding of jobs do not define us.

In 1 Corinthians 7:22, Paul gives a reason to the slaves not to despair. He points to an identity that trumps being a slave and contains a clue as to how a believer in Christ can cope with a low social status: "For the one who was a slave when called to faith in the Lord is the Lord's freed person; similarly, the one who was free when called is Christ's slave." God sees things differently than we see things, upside down in fact. Apparently, our place in society and how society regards us is the not the way he sees us. Whether slave or free, high social status or low—all believers in Christ belong to the Lord and live with him as our Lord and Master. As Richard Hays puts it, "all, regardless of worldly social status, are now under the authority of Christ."[17]

However, the new identity as the Lord's freed person/Christ's slave is not based on something the individuals in question have done. On the contrary, it is something that the Lord Jesus Christ did for them that gives them their identity: "You were bought at a price" (1 Cor 7:23a). As a slave owner purchases a slave, Christ's death has paid a ransom for their redemption. And on that basis, they belong to God. The implication is that *to embrace one's identity as the Lord Jesus Christ's freed person and slave requires remembering something.*

"Bought at a price" would have been especially poignant for slaves. Before God called them, the defining moment of their lives would have been becoming a slave and being bought by a human master. Or if they came from a family of slaves, they would have the shared memory of their father or mother or other ancestor becoming a slave. Paul says God gives them a new identity and a new memory that they share with all believers. They are Christ's freed people, and they are to recall the costly death of Christ as having paid the price for their redemption.

As it turns out, the same memory is decisive for the identity of all believers and not just Christian slaves. In 1 Corinthians 6:19b–20a, Paul writes to all of the Christians in Corinth: "You are not your own; you were bought at a price." And we see the same call to remember the death of Christ as paying the price of our

16. Roy E. Ciampa and Brian S. Rosner, *The First Letter to the Corinthians*, PNTC (Grand Rapids: Eerdmans, 2010), 320.

17. Richard B. Hays, *First Corinthians*, Interpretation (Louisville: Westminster John Knox, 1997), 125.

redemption in other parts of the New Testament. The apostle Peter, for example, also reminds those to whom he writes of the shared memory of Christ's death. Note too his reference to the defining destiny of Christian hope:

> You know that it was not with perishable things such as silver or gold that you were redeemed from the empty way of life handed down to you from your ancestors, but with *the precious blood of Christ, a lamb without blemish or defect.* He was chosen before the creation of the world, but was revealed in these last times for your sake. Through him you believe in God, who raised him from the dead and glorified him, and so *your faith and hope are in God.* (1 Pet 1:18–21)

We are to remember not only the death of Christ as securing our status as God's people but also his forgiveness of our sins. The cross means that we are not prisoners of our past. The defining moment of many people's lives is something they regret and of which they are deeply ashamed. The good news of the gospel is that our failures in life do not define us. Having been bought at a price, we remember Christ's death as that which makes us who we are and gives us our new identity as those who belong to Christ.

We Died with Christ—Romans 6:3–10

However, not only do we remember Christ's death as paying the price of our ransom from sin, Paul also insists that we remember Christ's death as signifying our own death to sin:

> Don't you know that all of us who were baptized into Christ Jesus were baptized into his death? *We were therefore buried with him* through baptism into death in order that, just as Christ was raised from the dead through the glory of the Father, we too may live a new life.
>
> For if we have been united with him in a death like his, we will certainly also be united with him in a resurrection like his. For we know that our old self was crucified with him so that the body ruled by sin might be done away with, that we should no longer be slaves to sin—because anyone who has died has been set free from sin.
>
> Now if *we died with Christ,* we believe that we will also live with him. For we know that since Christ was raised from the dead, he cannot die again; death no longer has mastery over him. The death he died, he died to sin once for all; but the life he lives, he lives to God. (Rom 6:3–10)

All believers are included as participants in the story of Christ's death and resurrection. And by dying with Christ, we regard ourselves as dead to living for pure self-interest. The selfishness of sin no longer has mastery over us. And the new life we live in Christ is one where we are set free to love God and others as we were intended to from the beginning.

We Carry Around the Death of Jesus—2 Corinthians 4:11–12

A third text from Paul's letters again shows the relevance to our lives in the present of remembering Christ's suffering and death in the past:

> *We always carry around in our body the death of Jesus*, so that the life of Jesus may also be revealed in our body. For we who are alive are always being given over to death for Jesus' sake, so that his life may also be revealed in our mortal body. (2 Cor 4:10–11)

The notion of "carrying around in our body the death of Jesus" is among Paul's most unpalatable teachings. I doubt if it is anyone's favorite memory verse, in anyone's "promise box," or on anyone's refrigerator. Certainly "to carry" something in English can denote a constant and unpleasant experience: someone "carries" a burden, a virus, an injury, and so on. According to Paul, we carry around in our body the death of Jesus.

> "As Christians, we locate and interpret our suffering within the narrative of the life, death and resurrection of Jesus."
> *John Swinton*[18]

What could he mean? Paul seems to be referring to the meaning he attaches to the painful hardships of his life: He understands his experience of being "hard pressed on every side," "perplexed," and "struck down" (2 Cor 4:8) as sharing in Jesus's sufferings.[19] When we suffer, as the Phillips paraphrase of 2 Corinthians 4:10 says, "we experience something of the death of Jesus." And that identification with Jesus's death is necessary "so that his life may also be revealed in our mortal body" (2 Cor 4:11).

To remember the death of Jesus when we suffer can be of some assistance when our lives don't go according to plan. There are many layers to suffering, one of which is its seeming meaninglessness. It is common for Christian people who experience loneliness, pain, shame, exclusion, and any form of unjust suffering to find comfort and hope in the shame and pain of Jesus's unjust crucifixion.

When my wife left me in the late 1990s, it helped me greatly to deal with feelings of rejection and abandonment to remember that on the cross Jesus had been rejected and abandoned by God, no less. It would be easy to respond that my suffering should not be compared to the suffering of Jesus. But that is exactly what Paul recommends.

We share the past suffering of Christ so that we have a part in the future glory of Christ. It is not that we earn our salvation by suffering. But in our suffering we have hope because Christ suffered and rose to life to give us life. By thinking of our

18. John Swinton, *Raging with Compassion: Pastoral Responses to the Problem of Evil* (Grand Rapids: Eerdmans, 2007), 112.

19. Several features of the passage underscore the connection between the sufferings of Paul and Christ. For example, the Greek verb to "be given over," *paradidōmi*, is used for the "giving over" of Jesus to death (see Rom 4:25; 8:32; 1 Cor 11:23). Paul says that he is "always being given over to death for Jesus' sake" (2 Cor 4:11) just as Jesus was "delivered over to death for our sins" (Rom 4:25). Also, the three uses of the simple name "Jesus" in 2 Cor 4:10–11 draws attention to the earthly life of Christ.

own suffering in the light of the suffering of Jesus, we identify with him, and our life story follows the shape of his life story.

When we remember the suffering of Jesus in the midst of our own troubles, and carry around in our bodies the death of Jesus, some beneficial results ensue: "For just as we share abundantly in the sufferings of Christ, so also our comfort abounds through Christ" (2 Cor 1:5). As Paul states in Romans 5:3–4, rightly understood, our "suffering produces perseverance; perseverance, character; and character, hope" (see also Jas 1:2–4). Our shared memory of the death of Jesus gives meaning to our suffering and instills in us a measure of comfort and hope.

DESTINY AND IDENTITY

It may sound odd, but destiny can be memory too. Not only can you remember the past, you can also remember the future. At the mundane level, you can remember that the sun will rise tomorrow morning at 6:30 am. More profoundly, our experiences in the past can color what we anticipate in the future. Miroslav Volf explains:

> Traumatic memories are in part so disturbing because they project themselves into the future in an unwelcome way; they become a "prememory" of what will happen. Careful consideration reveals that the same is often true of experiences of reliability and love; trustworthiness and love experienced are trustworthiness and love anticipated.[20]

As believers in Christ, we remember our past deliverance at the cross and our future deliverance by the same faithful God. And this destiny shapes our identity.

Central to our status as God's children is the fact that we are heirs of God and co-heirs with Christ (see chapter nine). Being known by God as his children puts us in line for an "inheritance in the kingdom of Christ and of God" (Eph 5:5): "Now if we are children, then we are heirs—heirs of God and co-heirs with Christ" (Rom 8:17a). And this expectation of a great inheritance impacts how we live today. If our destiny is "light," we are, in Paul's words, to "put aside the deeds of darkness and put on the armor of light" (Rom 13:12). If our destiny is to live in the presence of the God of love, we are to be loving in the present.

What does a defining destiny look like?

Prince Charles was born at Buckingham Palace on November 14, 1948, the first child of Princess Elizabeth, Duchess of Edinburgh, and Philip, Duke of Edinburgh. When Charles was three, his mother's accession as Queen Elizabeth II immediately made him the heir apparent to the seven countries over which she reigned. His whole life has been lived in anticipation of being crowned King Charles III.

Charles' destiny has defined him. It has affected everything from his education, his involvement in the military, his working life, his choice of marriage partners, and his religious affiliation to his tastes in architecture, hobbies, and sports. Obviously other factors play into the mix, including his personality, life experiences, opportunities, and the choices he has made. But there is no doubt that Charles would have led a very different life had he not been the Prince of Wales, the heir apparent.

20. Volf, *End of Memory*, 100.

My daughter Elizabeth was born in Dallas, Texas, when I was a student there. She was granted American citizenship by birth and Australian citizenship by descent. The same goes for my daughter Emily, who was born in Cambridge, England, and is a citizen of both the United Kingdom and Australia. Elizabeth and Emily live in one place, but belong to two places.

Believers in Christ also enjoy the benefits and responsibilities of dual citizenship. We belong to this world and the next. It is not just that we believe we will belong to heaven; we do so now. In that sense our destiny has already taken hold. And if this is true, it clearly has implications for who we are now and how we are to live. As citizens of heaven, we are to "conduct [ourselves] in a manner worthy of the gospel of Christ" (Phil 1:27).

"Christians believe the lifespan of each of us is not the full running length; it is a kind of preview. They believe that the human injustice that infects everything in the world will find an ultimate answer in God's justice. They believe that the groanings of an afflicted creation will be answered when God recreates the world in glory. These beliefs change what a person thinks, the way they live, *who they are.*"

John Dickson[21]

A *story arc* is the overall narrative in episodic storytelling media such as television or comic books. On a television series, for example, the story arc is the governing trajectory that unfolds over many episodes. All the episodes are moving towards a death, or a wedding, or a car crash, or some other climax that has been in the mind of the scriptwriters from the beginning. And when you watch one episode, even if in one sense it can stand on its own, it forms part of a larger narrative that is told over the whole series. The things that happen in the individual episodes take on full significance only when you know the story arc to which they contribute. Remembering your story arc is key to the new identity of Christians as children of God known by him.

"In Christian thinking generally, present and future overlap and interlock in various confusing ways."

N. T. Wright[22]

The most unexpected twist in the story of Christian hope is the idea that the Christian's story arc is the same as that of the rest of creation. In Romans 8:19–21, Paul believes that not only are Christians looking forward to the final consummation, but also "the creation waits in eager expectation." What is it waiting for? The creation is waiting for the same thing believers are waiting for: "for the children of God to be revealed." Paul explains, as best he can:

> For the creation was subjected to frustration, not by its own choice, but by the will of the one who subjected it, in hope that the creation itself will be liberated from its bondage to decay and brought into the freedom and glory of the children of God. (Rom 8:20–21)

21. John Dickson, *A Doubter's Guide to the Bible: Inside History's Bestseller for Believers and Skeptics* (Grand Rapids: Zondervan, 2014), 210. Emphasis added.

22. N. T. Wright, *Revelation for Everyone* (Louisville: Westminster John Knox, 2011), 75.

Things are not the way they're supposed to be. This is true of each of us, in all our well-intentioned and sometimes ill-intentioned and messy lives. It's also true of all of us together in the communities in which we live and work. And it's true of whole countries. Even the world itself, Paul reckons, feels like it has been "subjected to frustration . . . [and wants to be] liberated from its bondage." Disobedience to God has brought death to us all. The good news is that God intends to reverse this tragedy. Raising Jesus from the dead was the first step in the process.

Biblical Theology = Backstory + Story Arc

The identity of believers in Christ is bound not only to a shared memory of Christ's death but also to a defining destiny with the risen Christ. The glorious day of his appearing will not only be a revelation of who he is as the Son of God, but also of who we are as God's children. The following subsections explore five passages that make this point and show what difference it makes to who we are in the present.

We Are Hard Pressed for Time—1 Corinthians 7:29–31

Some of the members of the church of God in Corinth would have answered the question of personal identity in terms of their marital status: I am married; I am single; I am engaged; I am widowed; I am divorced. Others might have pointed to their personality or temperament: I am sad; I am happy. Still others might have thought of their possessions: I am wealthy; I am poor. In a startling passage, complete with poetic rhythm and puzzling paradoxical content, Paul urges believers in Christ not to define themselves in these ways:

> What I mean, brothers and sisters, is that the time is short. From now on those who have wives should live as if they do not; those who mourn, as if they did not; those who are happy, as if they were not; those who buy something, as if it were not theirs to keep; those who use the things of the world, as if not engrossed in them. For this world in its present form is passing away. (1 Cor 7:29–31)

What does Paul mean by "the time is short" (v. 29)? What "time" is he referring to? The time until what? The last part of verse 31 provides the answer: "this world in its present form is passing away." Evidently, Paul is referring to the time remaining until the return of Christ and the end of all things (see also 1 Cor 1:7–8).

Paul is not just talking about the quantity of time left but also about the quality of time.[23] The fact that the end is coming affects the character of the time we have left. Time is subjectively perceived. Since time cannot be directly perceived, it must

23. In other parts of 1 Corinthians, Paul talks to the Corinthians about his own future plans to visit them (4:19; 11:34; 16:5–8) and their part in Paul's relief work among churches in Judea (16:1–4; see also 2 Cor 8–9), plans which could take a couple of years to complete.

be reconstructed by the brain. Our perception of time differs from other senses by virtue of having no clear raw input, such as photons in the case of visual perception or sound waves in the case of hearing. The way we talk about time reflects this: Time flies when you're having fun, and time drags in the dentist's chair. "The time is short" refers to a certain type of time.

How does an exciting future event take the edge off the disappointment of missing out on something good in the present?

Some years ago I visited the US to teach an intensive course at a seminary in Boston. I stayed with my good friends Roy and Marcelle Ciampa, and after a long day in the classroom I was keen to eat at the Agawam Diner, a Ciampa family tradition. Clam chowder and coconut cream pie were two Bostonian specialties I was eagerly anticipating. The Diner was an American experience I did not want to miss out on.

But when Roy picked me up, he said to me that the time was short, and we had to miss the meal at the Agawam as he had secured tickets to the baseball game at Boston's famous Fenway Park. The Red Sox were playing to a packed house, as they had been at every game for seven years in a row.

The future had squashed the present. We were hard pressed for time. In the light of that future, our priorities in the present had changed. The meal at the Agawam Diner would not happen. But my disappointment was overshadowed by the joy of the prospect of attending the game. (The Red Sox won in the bottom of the ninth.)

So what sort of time is Paul referring to? The key phrase literally reads, "the time has been compressed" or "gathered in."[24] The idea is that the future is pressing in on the present. To use our idiom, Paul is saying that, in view of the end of the world, Christians are "*hard pressed for time.*" This shortness of time radically affects the way believers are to think about their lives in the here and now; knowing we are in the end times and that this world will be brought to a conclusion ought to condition how we think about all of our activities in the meantime.

How should we live in the light of the fact that the time is short? The most important example in the context of 1 Corinthians 7 that Paul considers is being married rather than single: "From now on those who have wives should live as if they do not" (1 Cor 7:29b). Paul is not suggesting that those who are married should literally live as if they are not. In 1 Corinthians 7:2–6, he tells those who are married in no uncertain terms to have sex: "The husband should fulfill his marital duty to his wife, and likewise the wife to her husband. . . . Do not deprive each other" (7:3, 5)! Instead, Paul downgrades the significance of being married in the light of something of much greater significance.

Paul reasons that since believers know where the world is headed, we are not to allow the world to dictate our existence. The primary purpose of 1 Corinthians 7:29–31 is to set the question of whether to marry or not in proper proportion and perspective. The prospect of a new heaven and new earth takes the edge off prevailing troubles on this earth and may even enable a believer to endure a marital or social status they consider unsatisfying or undesirable and still glorify God within it. According to Paul, being married or not is not central to our identity as Christians. Neither is being sad or happy or having certain possessions. Paul is not disparaging

24. Greek perfect passive participle of *sustellō*.

a full-blooded engagement with the world (see also 1 Cor 5:10b), but wants it to be tempered by a sober assessment of life's ups and downs in the light of something that eclipses them.

What is critical in Paul's radical reappraisal of marital status, personality, and possessions in 1 Corinthians 7:29–31 as markers of personal identity is that he points to the future rather than the past: our *defining destiny* relativizes the various identity markers in question. We are *hard pressed for time* as the glorious climax of world history and of our lives approaches, which makes other things in the present seem less important.

We Were Sealed for the Day of Redemption—Ephesians 1:13–14

Ephesians 1:13–14 contains several descriptions of Christian identity:

> And you also were included in Christ when you heard the message of truth, the gospel of your salvation. When you believed, you were marked in him with a seal, the promised Holy Spirit, who is a deposit guaranteeing our inheritance until the redemption of those who are God's possession—to the praise of his glory.

Some of the ways in which Christians are described in this text look back to the past, namely, the believers' conversion: they are those who are now in Christ, having heard and believed the gospel. Other ways indicate a look to the future, but still with some sense of who Christians are in the present: they are also those who are sealed by the promised Holy Spirit, a sign that they belong to God and are guaranteed an inheritance as his children. It is to this future-oriented identity that we are concerned in this section.

The description of the Holy Spirit as one who was "promised" is a reference to the coming of the Spirit as the fulfillment of prophecy. Joel 2:28, a text quoted in Acts 2 and alluded to in 1 Corinthians 12, contains the promise of God: "And afterward, I will pour out my Spirit on all people. Your sons and daughters will prophecy."[25]

The Holy Spirit is also called "a deposit guaranteeing our inheritance" in Ephesians 1:14. The Greek word "deposit," *arrabōn*, signifies a "down payment" (HCSB) or "pledge (NRSV) and refers to a mark denoting ownership. It was a commercial term for the purchase of something by paying a first installment. Being indwelt by the Spirit indicates that we belong to God, which means we have an inheritance in the age to come and that we are also God's inheritance in the age to come.[26] Peter O'Brien states: "The Spirit received is the first installment and

25. See "the promised Holy Spirit" in Acts 2:33.

26. The NLT of Eph 1:14 states: "The Spirit is God's guarantee that he will give us the inheritance he promised and that he has purchased us to be his own people."

guarantee of the inheritance in the age to come that awaits God's sons and daughters" (Eph 1:5).[27]

The Spirit is also a "seal," marking us out for a glorious future. Paul's statements elsewhere identify the Spirit as the first course, so to speak, of the heavenly banquet that awaits us:

> And do not grieve the Holy Spirit of God, with whom you were sealed for the day of redemption. (Eph 4:30)
>
> He anointed us, set his seal of ownership on us, and put his Spirit in our hearts as a deposit, guaranteeing what is to come. (2 Cor 1:21–22)

Two points arise from Ephesians 1:13–14 for a biblical theology of personal identity. First, it is not just that we look forward to a glorious future with God; we have a taste and guarantee of it now. And that aspect of our identity comes from "outwith" us, to use a word from Scottish English; but at the same time it comes to reside within us—the promised Holy Spirit indwells us. Second, as those whose future is sealed and inheritance guaranteed, our glorious future impacts who we are now and how we live in the present.

We Belong to the Day—Romans 13:11–14

Another passage in Paul's letters that connects our identity to our destiny as those connected to Jesus Christ is Romans 13:11–14:

> And do this, understanding the present time: The hour has already come for you to wake up from your slumber, because our salvation is nearer now than when we first believed. The night is nearly over; the day is almost here. So let us put aside the deeds of darkness and put on the armor of light. Let us behave decently, as in the daytime, not in carousing and drunkenness, not in sexual immorality and debauchery, not in dissension and jealousy. Rather, clothe yourselves with the Lord Jesus Christ, and do not think about how to gratify the desires of the flesh.

Paul urges believers in Rome to behave in ways that are consistent with their new identity as those who belong to the age to come. Using the familiar biblical imagery of light and darkness, "the present time" in which we live is compared to nighttime, and the time of future salvation is likened to "the daytime." The NLT renders v. 13: "Because *we belong to the day*, we must live decent lives for all to see."

A fundamental question for a biblical approach to personal identity is this: *What time is it?* According to Paul, it is close to dawn: "The night is nearly over;

27. Peter T. O'Brien, *The Letter to the Ephesians*, PNTC (Grand Rapids: Eerdmans, 1999), 120.

the day is almost here" (Rom 13:12). As Paul says in 1 Corinthians 7:29–31 (see above), we are hard pressed for time. Colin Kruse explains the significance of "the present time" in Romans:

> The "present time" for Paul is the time ushered in by the first advent of Jesus Christ. So in 3:25–26, speaking of God presenting Christ as the sacrifice of atonement, he declares, "he did it to demonstrate his righteousness *at the present time*, so as to be just and the one who justifies those who have faith in Jesus". Similarly, in 5:6 he asserts, "You see, *at just the right time*, when we were still powerless, Christ died for the ungodly". In 2 Corinthians 6:2 he adds that the present time is the day of salvation: "For he says, 'In the time of my favor I heard you, and in the day of salvation I helped you'. I tell you, now is the time of God's favor, *now is the day of salvation*."[28]

We belong to the day
To the day that is to come
When the night falls away
And our Saviour will return
For the glory of the King is in our hearts
On that day we will be seen for what we are
We belong to the day
Let us journey in the light
Put on faith, put on love
As our armour for the fight
And the promise of salvation in our eyes
On that day the proud will fall, the faithful rise
We belong to the day
We were bought with Jesus's blood
Soon he comes as the judge
In the power of his word
We must tell of his salvation while we wait
For the day when Jesus comes will be too late
Michael Morrow[29]

But as decisive as the present time is for God's plan of salvation, the coming day of salvation is meant to shape our behavior in the present: "Believers, even though for the present they still live in the 'night,' must live as people of the 'day.'"[30] Consistent with the metaphor, four of the shameful deeds of the darkness which are unsuitable to daytime people—carousing, drunkenness, sexual immorality, debauchery (Rom 13:13)—are typically done in the nighttime. The next two vices, dissension and jealousy, are concerns that Paul has in particular for the house churches in Rome.[31]

The Bible uses a number of strategies to encourage believers to resist temptation to sin and to motivate them to godliness. These include threats and warnings, appeals to God's character, and the work of the Spirit in our lives. The Bible also reminds us that we live under the lordship of Christ and must therefore imitate both God and Christ. Here in Romans 13:11–14, the appeal is to our new identity based on our defining destiny. We are to behave, "as in the daytime,"[32] as those who belong

28. Colin G. Kruse, *Paul's Letter to the Romans*, PNTC (Grand Rapids: Eerdmans, 2012), 503. Emphasis original.

29. Garage Hymnal, "We Belong to the Day," *Bring on the Day* (Sydney: Michael Morrow, 2006). Lyrics used with permission.

30. Kruse, *Paul's Letter to the Romans*, 505.

31. See Brian Rosner, "What to Do When Christians Differ: Disputable Matters in Romans 14:1–15:7," in *Mending a Fractured Church*, ed. Michael F. Bird and Brian S. Rosner (Bellingham, WA: Lexham Press, 2015), 56–77.

32. Ben Witherington III and Darlene Hyatt state, "Christians are to walk properly as in the day. Thus, in some sense, the eschatological day or its light is already at hand, for Christians can walk in it. *Hōs* here means 'as is actually the case.' Believers are already standing under the sign of a new day" (*Paul's Letter to the Romans: A Socio-rhetorical Commentary* [Grand Rapids: Eerdmans, 2004], 317).

Trade apprentices are defined by their future and are expected increasingly to conform to that identity in the present. A carpentry apprenticeship can take up to four years to complete, and you cannot claim the title of "carpenter" until you have finished the entire course and gained the requisite experience. But you are meant to start, however imperfectly, behaving like a carpenter from the beginning. When my son William began his carpentry apprenticeship, the goal of completing the course and gaining the qualification defined him as he learnt his trade. His boss modeled best practices in the industry, and slowly but surely William became like him until he graduated as a fully qualified carpenter. William's anticipated future shaped his behavior and gave him an identity in the present.

to the day, and to dress appropriately: "clothe yourselves with the Lord Jesus Christ." Once again, Jesus Christ is critical for Christian identity and conduct.

We Shall Be Like Him—1 John 3:1–3

With 1 John 3:1–3, we venture beyond Paul's letters and yet find the same themes unmistakably on display: our identity as God's children, our likeness to Christ, the decisive nature of Christ's appearing for our own identity, and the practical implications for our lives here and now:

> See what great love the Father has lavished on us, that we should be called children of God! And that is what we are! The reason the world does not know us is that it did not know him. Dear friends, now we are children of God, and what we will be has not yet been made known. But we know that when Christ appears, we shall be like him, for we shall see him as he is. All who have this hope in him purify themselves, just as he is pure. (1 John 3:1–3)

The passage puts great emphasis on the identity of those who believe in Jesus as God's children. Numerous elements make this clear:

1. The great love lavished on us is from "the Father"—a description of God that is underlined by its delay in the Greek until the end of the clause; we might translate literally: "See what great love he has given us—the Father!"
2. We are called "children of God" twice (vv. 1 and 2);
3. We are called children of God *by the Father.*[33]
4. The Greek word translated "Dear friends" (v. 2), *agapētos*, means "one who is dearly loved, *dear, beloved, prized, valued* . . . indicating a close relationship, esp. that between parent and child."[34]
5. Being like Christ (v. 2) is to share the family likeness; 1 John calls Jesus God's Son several times (e.g., 3:8; 4:15), and this is the letter's favorite way of referring to Jesus.

The identity as "God's children" is our true identity: "And that is what we are!" (1 John 3:1). It is who we are presently: "*Now* we are the children of God" (v. 2).

33. "The implied agent of the passive form [of the Greek verb "to call" in v. 1] is 'the Father'" (C. Haas, Marinus de Jonge, and J. L. Swellengrebel, *A Translator's Handbook on the Letters of John* [New York: United Bible Societies, 1994], 81).

34. BDAG 7 (emphasis original).

However, it is also our destiny: "What we will be has not yet been made known. But we know that when Christ appears, we shall be like him" (v. 2).

Our status as God's children is a reality in the present, but we will be blown away when it is fully revealed. John Calvin is right to compare the sentiment here with Colossians 3:3–4 (see at the beginning of this chapter): "John teaches the same thing with Paul, in Col 3:3, 4, where he says, 'Your life is hid with Christ in God: when Christ, who is your life, shall appear, then shall ye also appear with him in glory.'"[35] The present implications for conduct which fits with our identity as God's children is also made explicit in 1 John 3:3: "All who have this hope in him purify themselves, just as he is pure."

How will our final transformation into God's children come about? John says that "we shall be like him, for *we shall see him as he is*" (1 John 3:2). Seeing the Son of God face to face results in becoming like Christ; we will be mature children of God like our older brother.

Significantly, the apostle John's explanation here summons to mind the apostle Paul's words in 1 Corinthians 13:12[36] : "For now we see only a reflection as in a mirror; then we shall see face to face. Now I know in part; then I shall know fully, even as I am fully known." We will see, or know, the Son of God as he really is, his essential character, just as he has always seen and known us.

We Await Our Resurrection Bodies—1 Corinthians 15

Who am I if death is my ultimate destiny? What would life look like if it were? In Isaiah 22:13, the prophet depicts the reaction of the inhabitants of Jerusalem when the city is under siege. With the ruthless Assyrians at the door, they are facing the grim prospect of their annihilation. With such a destiny, they decide to "party like there is no tomorrow": "Let us eat and drink . . . for tomorrow we die!" Paul quotes this text in 1 Corinthians 15:32 to point to the futility of life without the direction and motivation given by the resurrection of Jesus.

There are, of course, exceptions. Unbelievers can live lives that are not wasteful and self-indulgent. But it is not just Christians who think life without the hope of resurrection lacks purpose. Some philosophers agree. Existentialism, for instance, stresses human individuality and freedom and is deeply

Christians around the world affirm their faith on a regular basis using the ancient Apostles' Creed. It begins: "I believe in God, the Father almighty, Creator of heaven and earth. I believe in Jesus Christ, his only Son, our Lord." It closes with the words: "I believe in the Holy Spirit . . . the forgiveness of sins, *the resurrection of the body*, and the life everlasting. Amen."[37] Most Christians today are more at home thinking about eternal life than the resurrection of the body.

35. John Calvin and John Owen, *Commentaries on the Catholic Epistles* (Bellingham, WA: Logos Bible Software, 2010), 205.

36. Noted in Haas, de Jonge, and Swellengrebel, *A Translator's Handbook on the Letters of John*, 81.

37. *A Prayer Book for Australia* (Sydney: Broughton, 1999), 12, emphasis added.

"Materialist atheism says we are just a collection of chemicals. It has no answer whatsoever to the question of how we should be capable of love or heroism or poetry if we are simply animated pieces of meat. The Resurrection, which proclaims that matter and spirit are mysteriously conjoined, is *the ultimate key to who we are*. It confronts us with an extraordinarily haunting story. J. S. Bach believed the story, and set it to music. Most of the greatest writers and thinkers of the past 1,500 years have believed it. But an even stronger argument is the way that Christian faith transforms individual lives—the lives of the men and women with whom you mingle on a daily basis, the man, woman or child next to you in church tomorrow morning."

A. N. Wilson[38]

There are three types of cars on display at a motor show: (1) Concept cars—peculiar vehicles that will never be built that are used to trial innovative features; (2) Cars for sale; and (3) Prototypes—new models, not yet for sale, but soon to be produced in large numbers. Jesus Christ is the prototype of a new humanity, the first cab off the rack. He is the last Adam, a new and vastly superior model to end all models. He is the first one off the production line with the promise of many more to come.

pessimistic about life in a meaningless world. Life under the shadow of death can seem pointless.

At the heart of the Christian's hope is the resurrection from the dead. The New Testament connects this destiny inextricably to that of Jesus Christ who was raised from the dead: "For if we have been united with [Christ] in a death like his, we will certainly also be united with him in a resurrection like his" (Rom 6:5). It is this anticipated resurrection life, our defining destiny, that gives our lives an identity in the present.

So how does the resurrection of Christ relate to the future of believers in Christ? Paul's great exposition of the meaning of the resurrection of Christ in 1 Corinthians 15 climaxes with the words: "Death has been swallowed up in victory." "Where, O death, is your victory? Where, O death, is your sting?" (1 Cor 15:54b–55). Through the resurrection of Jesus Christ, death has lost its sting. By his resurrection Jesus destroyed death and brought "life and immortality to light" (2 Tim 1:10).

Kevin Vanhoozer explains the significance of the resurrection of Jesus for human identity:

> Human destiny—the full flowering of the image of God—has already been realized in Jesus's resurrection. Only through Jesus Christ do the general concepts of human nature and destiny, as well as of God and the Logos, acquire their true content. In the historical life of Jesus, the eternal relation of the Son to the Father takes human shape. *Theological anthropology understands the human creature neither from its past nor its present, but above all from the perspective of its future destiny*—fellowship with God—manifested by Christ. Jesus is the eschatological man who, as the last Adam, reveals the true nature and meaning of the first.[39]

38. A. N. Wilson, "Religion of Hatred," *Mail Online*, April 10, 2009, http://www.dailymail.co.uk/news/article-1169145/Religion-hatred-Why-longer-cowed-secular-zealots.html. Emphasis added. Wilson is an English author. Among his biographies are books about Leo Tolstoy, C. S. Lewis, John Milton, and Sir Walter Scott. For much of his adult life, Wilson was not a believer. In fact in his biography of Jesus, Wilson tried to show that Jesus was no more than a failed messianic prophet. However in recent years, he changed his mind. At the heart of his new-found faith is the resurrection of Jesus from the dead, which he believes is "the ultimate key to who we are."

39. Kevin Vanhoozer, "Human Being, Individual and Social," in *The Cambridge Companion to Christian Doctrine*, ed. Colin E. Gunton (Cambridge: Cambridge University Press, 1997), 173. Emphasis added.

MEMORY, DESTINY, AND PERSONAL IDENTITY

According to the Bible, memory is critical for personal identity. Our memories form us, and remembering our destiny defines us. People remember significant life events and their hopes for the future, and such memories play a big part in shaping who they are. But such formative memories go beyond the personal and individual, reaching back to family and even national histories.

All of this is especially true for the identity of Christians. It is not that our personal experiences and memories don't matter. But they appear in an entirely different light when we remember that our lives are part of a much bigger story. Michael Horton puts it well:

> The "self"—understood as an autonomous individual—does not exist, but is already bound up with tradition, history, and community. . . . In the process of summoning us, *the covenant Lord renarrates our lives, calling us away from our dead-end plots and casting us in his unfolding drama.*[40]

Believers in Christ look back and internalize the death and resurrection of Jesus Christ, remembering them as events that change who we are today and who we will be in the future. Christians see their life story fitting into and mirroring the life story of Jesus Christ. This is certainly what Dietrich Bonhoeffer believed:

> It is in fact more important for us to know what God did to Israel and in God's Son Jesus Christ, than to discover what God intends for us today. The fact that Jesus Christ died is more important than the fact that I will die. . . . I find salvation not in my life story, but only in the story of Jesus Christ.[41]

Paul said something similar when he claimed that "I have been crucified with Christ and I no longer live, but Christ lives in me" (Gal 2:20a). The story of Jesus Christ forms the template of our own life stories by supplying the essential backstory and critical story arc.

This chapter opened with the questions: *Who are you, and what is your story?* How might a Christian answer?[42] Note the role of memory and destiny in the formation of personal identity in the following answer:

> *I was in slavery to sin under the sentence of death, but God redeemed me and set me free through the death of his Son Jesus Christ. When Christ died, I also died and was buried along with him, putting an end to a futile life of self-centered living. I rose from the dead with Christ to a new life in him. I now carry around in my*

40. Horton, *The Christian Faith*, 86. Emphasis added.

41. Dietrich Bonhoeffer, *Life Together* (Minneapolis: Fortress, 1996), 62.

42. See Alec Motyer's suggested answer to this question on behalf of an Israelite at the beginning of this chapter.

> *body the death of Jesus, which brings me comfort during my afflictions in the present and bright hope for the future. I am now hard pressed for time in the light of the glorious return of Christ, which puts my present circumstances, both my successes and disappointments, in the shade. I am sealed for the day of final redemption. In fact, I belong to that day. Along with all of creation, I groan awaiting the gift of my resurrection body and the moment when my true identity as God's child will be revealed when the Son of God appears.*

To conclude part two, it is worth noting that this narrative identity relates directly to the major theme of this book, that of being known by God. Colossians 3:3–4, which we quoted near the beginning of this chapter, is Paul's most profound explanation of the notion that Christ is our life story and his most direct assertion that memory and destiny define identity. In these verses, Paul also declares that our life is hidden with Christ in God.

> For you died [our shared memory], and your life is now hidden with Christ in God [we are known by God]. When Christ, who is your life, appears, then you also will appear with him in glory [our defining destiny]. (Col 3:3–4)

The Christian's personal identity follows the pattern of Christ's representative life because we are known by God.

RELEVANT QUESTIONS

1. How does your family and your family's history influence your sense of identity? Are there any "second hand memories" which affect your personal narrative? Are these good or bad memories?
2. Have you allowed a difficult past to become a "prememory" that negatively influences your expectations of the future? Does defining your narrative identity in terms of the life of Christ help you to have a different perspective on both your life and destiny?
3. Our circumstances do not determine who we are before God. How might this change your perspective on your current social status or the material possessions you own?
4. How does remembering the death of Jesus when we suffer help us when our lives don't go according to plan?

PART 3

REFLECTING ON RELEVANCE

CHAPTER 11

SIGNIFICANCE

Who am I? In part two of this book, I argued that believers in Christ have a secret identity. We are those who are known by God as his children, and our identity is tied up with the identity of Jesus Christ, God's Son. We died and rose with Christ, and when he is revealed as the Son of God in glory, we too will be revealed as God's children.

In part three, we explore the practical implications of this new identity. What difference does it make to our lives here and now? I have found that being known by God makes a world of difference. There are four main benefits. The first, which is the focus of this chapter, is that being known by God gives our fragile, feeble, and fleeting lives significance.[1]

Sometimes a building might seem strong and stable, yet it turns out in reality to be flimsy and structurally unsound. That was certainly my experience with reference to my personal identity in the late 1990s when my wife of thirteen years left me. The underpinnings of my identity in terms of my relationships, occupation, and financial security appeared to be in place, but they each fell away one by one, and my self-esteem fell with them. At around the halfway point of my life, it felt as if I was starting again. The progress I had made in what I expected from my life proved to be illusory. Worse still, I felt worthless and dejected and fell into a depression that lasted six months. We generally discard only those things that are of no value. Seeing that I fell into that category, it was hard not to think about myself in negative terms. What meaning did my life have when the things I had worked for came crashing down?

Two of the Wisdom books of the Old Testament in fact pronounce a pessimistic verdict on the meaningfulness of human lives in general. The difficulties of building and maintaining a substantial personal identity are on full display in the *book of Job*'s "in-your-face" case study, in which righteous behavior does not lead to a successful life. Job is introduced in chapter one of the book as having a prominent social position, a thriving family, and considerable wealth. But in one fell swoop, he loses it all. If your social standing, possessions, and relationships make up your personal identity, Job's extreme example shows us that everything can change in an instant. As we saw in chapter three, our occupation, possessions, and even relationships are insufficient and insecure foundations upon which to build a personal identity.

1. Being known by God also provokes humility (see chapter twelve), supplies cheering comfort (see chapter thirteen), and offers clear direction for living (see chapter fourteen).

Job's responses to his losses reflect on the fragility of human life and also its brevity: "My days are swifter than a weaver's shuttle, and they come to an end without hope" (Job 7:6); "Mortals, born of woman, are of few days and full of trouble" (14:1). Job's so-called friend Eliphaz had similarly said: "Man is born to trouble as surely as sparks fly upward" (5:7). Disturbingly, Job's experience demonstrates that you can build a successful life and identity only to have it crumble and collapse through no fault of your own.[2]

The *book of Ecclesiastes* is even more glum. The teacher asks, "What do people get for all the toil and anxious striving with which they labor under the sun? All their days their work is grief and pain" (2:22–23). Indeed, Ecclesiastes opens and closes with the verdict "everything is meaningless" (1:2; 12:8). Just as Adam after his transgression had to labor by the sweat of his brow (Gen 3:19), so humanity ever since labors "under the sun," an expression emphasizing the adverse conditions in which we conduct our lives.[3] The word "meaningless" here translates the Hebrew word *hebel*. Depending on the context, *hebel* denotes "breath, vapor, mist," that which is passing, ephemeral, pointless, without profit. To describe human lives as *hebel* judges our existence to be short, inconsequential, and without purpose.

There are in fact several ways to feel that your life lacks significance. If Job lost much of his identity with the removal of certain crucial things, some feel that they have never achieved their life goals and fall well short of becoming who they wanted to be, while others believe that their lives are so restricted in one way or another that they will never reach their potential.

A final blow to having an identity of lasting significance is the reality of death. As the teacher in Ecclesiastes puts it, you can work and accumulate wealth all your life, but in the end your possessions do not define you because coffins have no pockets!

> A person may labor with wisdom, knowledge and skill, and then they must leave all they own to another who has not toiled for it. This too is meaningless and a great misfortune. (Eccl 2:21)
>
> I have seen a grievous evil under the sun:
> wealth hoarded to the harm of its owners,
>   or wealth lost through some misfortune,
> so that when they have children
>   there is nothing left for them to inherit.
> Everyone comes naked from their mother's womb,
>   and as everyone comes, so they depart. (5:13–15)

---

2. While Job concedes that he may have sinned (e.g., Job 10:14), he is pictured as utterly righteous (1:1; 2:3) and not to blame for his losses.

3. The New Testament does not dispute the verdict of Ecclesiastes that life is, in Hebrew, *hebel*. In fact, in Rom 8:19–24 Paul tells of the same frustrating character of life in the present. The Old Testament's characterization of life in a fallen world as pointless, passing, and without profit (*hebel*), is matched by the New Testament's depiction of a world subject to "frustration" (Greek *mataiotēs*).

Three things in particular pose threats to having a personal identity that has true and lasting significance: *life's unfulfilled hopes*, *life's limitations*, and *the end of life*. It is to these three that we now turn. My aim is to show that being known by God personally and intimately goes a long way to relieving life's disappointments and compensating for life's limitations, and it offers eternal significance in the face of death.

As we saw in part two of this book, numerous texts in both the Old and New Testaments affirm that God knows us by name and remembers us when we are in trouble. In chapter six, I concluded that there is something reassuring and beautiful about God really knowing you. In this chapter, we begin to put flesh on the bones of this assertion.

Along with considering further relevant biblical teaching, we will look at some case studies that illustrate how being known by God gives our lives significance. These include the striking example of Dietrich Bonhoeffer and his own crushing disappointments, the diminished existence of two friends of mine (one disabled from birth, the other suffering a terminal illness), and the troubling category of the unidentified fallen in war. Each of these is an extreme case of a life losing or lacking significance. Sometimes examples with "the volume turned up" can serve as points of reference with which those of us who are hopefully more fortunate can identify. How about you?

- Have you had or do you have major disappointments in your life, and have these affected your sense of identity?
- Have you faced or do you face limitations in your life? What is the impact of these limitations on your personal identity?
- Many of us don't think about our own death. Might that hint at the fact that death is the ultimate threat to personal identity?

A DISAPPOINTING LIFE

Despite what celebrities and music and sports stars might tell us, having your dreams come true is not simply a function of bravely following your heart; most people's lives fall well short of their hopes and aspirations. Disappointment with one's lot in life is in fact most people's experience. And not living up to your own expectations can make you feel small and insignificant.

For many people, the self is constructed in terms of their expectations, and living in the present is in large measure about *anticipation*. "Who I am" is mostly about "who I intend to be." This applies not just to young people anticipating adulthood or adults working towards various qualifications, as in "I plan to be a teacher or a carpenter." At no point in our lives do we stop hoping for better things.

Do you have hopes for the future that are core to the person you see yourself being? Such aspirations could relate to getting married and having children, or owning a home, or having a particular job. What if such hopes are never realized? Envy of one's peers, many of whom may seem to be achieving the desired changes in their identities, can make the situation all the more distressing. The disappointments associated with not having your hopes come to fruition, and not becoming the person you hope to be, are dispiriting and can cause some to think that their lives lack significance.

Golf was once described as a long walk punctuated by disappointments. Somewhat histrionically, Anne of Green Gables complained: "My life is a perfect graveyard of buried hopes."[4] According to George Orwell in *Animal Farm*, "the unalterable law of life [is] . . . hunger, hardship and disappointment."[5] It seems that no one is immune from the displeasure caused by having their hopes or expectations unfulfilled.

As a case study in coping with profound disappointment, we may again consider Dietrich Bonhoeffer, the pastor, author, and church leader in 1930s and 1940s Germany.[6] We looked at Bonhoeffer in chapter one in connection with his famous poem, "Who Am I?"

Bonhoeffer's life story is a mixed genre. It started out like a *fairy tale*. He was born in 1906, along with his twin sister Sabine, the sixth of eight children. His family had been prominent in German society for centuries, with many doctors, lawyers, judges, and professors among his ancestors. He was a tall man with an athletic physique and a round, boyish face. With his mother's blue eyes and blond hair, he fitted perfectly Adolf Hitler's Aryan stereotype. However, any affinity between Dietrich and the Third Reich stopped there.

Bonhoeffer's fairy tale took a dangerous turn and transformed into a *spy thriller*. His opposition to the Nazis commenced a few days after Hitler first took power in 1933. Bonhoeffer gave a radio broadcast on the dangers of charismatic leadership that was abruptly ended by governmental censure. For the next ten years, he worked for the good of his nation, eventually operating as a double agent. Employed by the *Abwehr*, a division of German intelligence, Bonhoeffer used his contacts outside of Germany to support the insurgency. In particular, he briefed a member of the English House of Lords and convinced him to seek favorable terms of peace in the event of the Führer being removed. A man of impeccable integrity, Bonhoeffer also functioned as the conscience of the conspirators, commending their moral courage and bolstering their resolve.

Along with the spy thriller, Bonhoeffer's life was a *tragic love story*. In June 1942, Dietrich met Maria von Wedemeyer. Maria was beautiful, poised, fresh, cultured, and filled with vitality, but only eighteen years of age, fully seventeen years younger than Dietrich! But Dietrich and Maria fell in love. Maria's father had been killed on the Russian front, and her mother insisted on a year's separation to test the couple's

4. L. M. Montgomery, *Anne of Green Gables* (London: L. C. Page and Company, 1908), 36.

5. George Orwell, *Animal Farm* (London: Penguin, 2000), 128.

6. For a full treatment, see Brian S. Rosner, "Bonhoeffer on

feelings. Maria convinced her mother otherwise, and in January 1943, with some restrictions in place, they were engaged to be married. Unfortunately, "happily ever after" is not the way the story ended.

Two aspirations dominated Bonhoeffer's life, one national, the other personal: (1) he worked for the renewal of the German church and people; and (2) he planned to marry his fiancée, Maria von Wedemeyer. Both desires were cruelly thwarted in 1943 when he was arrested by the Gestapo, incarcerated for two years, and finally executed at the order of Adolf Hitler.

How did Dietrich Bonhoeffer handle his disappointments? How did he maintain a healthy and secure sense of self when his life had come up so far short of his own expectations? Bonhoeffer's response to his struggles illustrates and reinforces central themes from our biblical theology of personal identity in part two and draws out their practical value.

Bonhoeffer located his identity in his union with Christ and believed that suffering must be endured in solidarity with Christ if we are to live with integrity in this world. The day after a major plot to kill Hitler failed, Bonhoeffer wrote to console his friend and fellow conspirator, Eberhard Bethge: "By this-worldliness I mean living unreservedly in life's duties, problems, successes and failures, experiences and perplexities. In so doing we throw ourselves completely into the arms of God, taking seriously, not our own sufferings, but those of God in the world—*watching with Christ in Gethsemene*."[7] Bonhoeffer knew what it meant to carry around in his body the death of Jesus and to reckon himself to have died with Christ.

Bonhoeffer also exhibited an unflinching trust in the goodness and sovereignty of God—the God he knew as "Father," and who knew him as his "child." He was convinced in the face of his heart-breaking setbacks that "such things come from God and from him alone."[8] In relation to his fiancée's well-being, Bonhoeffer was encouraged that Maria too had "learnt very early to recognize a stronger and more gracious hand in what men inflict upon us."[9] He wrote to Maria concerning the German poet Adalbert Stifter's description of pain as "the holiest angel," that "there is an even holier angel than pain, and that is joy in God."[10] He encouraged her to believe that "God is forever upsetting our plans, but only in order to fulfill his own, better plans through us."[11]

To Maria's mother Bonhoeffer wrote: "We want to receive what God bestows on us with open, outstretched hands and delight in it with all our heart, and with a quiet heart we will sacrifice what God does not yet grant us or takes away from us."[12]

Disappointment," in *The Consolations of Theology*, ed. Brian S. Rosner (Grand Rapids: Eerdmans, 2008), 107–28.

7. Dietrich Bonhoeffer, *Letters and Papers from Prison* (London: Collins, 1964), 370. Emphasis added.

8. Ibid., 32.

9. Ibid., 180.

10. Dietrich Bonhoeffer and Maria von Wedemeyer, *Love Letters from Cell 92: The Correspondence between Dietrich Bonhoeffer and Maria Von Wedemeyer*, ed. Ruth Alice von Bismarck (Nashville: Abingdon, 1995), 118.

11. Ibid., 221.

12. Bonhoeffer, *Letters and Papers from Prison*, 247.

Bonhoeffer asks all those experiencing disappointment whether they have sacrificed to God what he has not yet granted. This God-centered view of life's unfulfilled desires was the bedrock of Bonhoeffer's resilience.

As observers, we may understandably be appalled at the apparent futility of Bonhoeffer's tragic story and conclude that his life, given its untimely end, lacked meaning and significance. If so, we need to hear Bonhoeffer's own interpretation of his plight: "I believe that nothing that happens to me is meaningless, and that it is good for us all that it should be so, even if it runs counter to our wishes. As I see it, I'm here for some real purpose, and I only hope to fulfill it. In the light of the great purpose all our privations and disappointments are trivial."[13]

Bonhoeffer's experience illustrates how the shared memory of Christ's death and the defining destiny of Christian hope powerfully transform our present and give our lives lasting significance even in the face of bitter disappointments. Ultimately Bonhoeffer found his sense of self not in himself but in God and in being known by him, as we noted in chapter one with reference to his poem "Who Am I?" While the bulk of the poem expresses Bonhoeffer's anguish and bewilderment, the last lines run:

> Who am I? Lonely questions mock me.
> Who I really am, *you know me*, I am yours, O God![14]

The answer to Bonhoeffer's question about his own identity was that in the midst of the desperation and confusion of his imprisonment and impending execution, *God knew him.*

Bonhoeffer ponders the question of the self at other points in his writings. In a letter from prison written about the same time as the poem, he comes to similar conclusions. His thoughts form an admirable commentary on his poem: "One must completely abandon any attempt to make something of oneself. . . . [instead] we throw ourselves completely into the arms of God."[15] In another letter, Bonhoeffer wrote: "In short, I know less than ever about myself, and I'm no longer attaching any importance to it."[16]

Who are you if the aspirations that are key to your identity never come to fruition? Bonhoeffer calls those of us who find ourselves living a disappointed life—which is the vast majority of us, to some extent—to affirm that Christ is our life and to rest in the sure knowledge that God knows us and has our lives in his hands.

---

13. Ibid., 289.

14. My translation from the German found in Dietrich Bonhoeffer, *Widerstand und Ergebung: Briefe und Aufzeichnungen aus der Haft*, ed. E. Bethge (Muenchen: Christian Kaiser, 1964), 243, emphasis added.

15. Bonhoeffer, *Letters and Papers from Prison*, 370.

16. Dietrich Bonhoeffer, *The Prison Poems of Dietrich Bonhoeffer: A New Translation with Commentary*, ed. Edwin H. Robertson (Grand Rapids: Zondervan, 1999), 41.

A DIMINISHED LIFE

Limitations on our lives come in all shapes and sizes and can range from mildly irritating to profound and permanent. Such restrictions might have to do with our physical or mental capacity. Others relate to our circumstances. Some people feel constrained by responsibilities for children or aging parents, lack of money or opportunity, oppressive relationships, physical incapacity, chronic illness, or loneliness. Who are you if your life is severely limited in certain key respects?

Country singer Kasey Chambers's song "The Captain" is a kind of anthem for many women in bad relationships: "And you be the Captain, and *I'll be no one.*"[17]

Two extreme examples illustrate the importance of being known for the identity of those whose lives are diminished.

Friends of mine had a profoundly disabled son who was deaf and blind. Michael was twelve years old when I knew him. If measured by his capacity for knowledge, someone might think that there was only a marginal case for his status as a person. But to those who met him, it was obvious that his identity depended not on what he knew, but rather on the fact that he was known by his parents. Their loving interactions with him, attending to his needs and drawing out his responses, gave him a secure and meaningful identity. They dressed him and cared for him, called him by name, read his moods, understood his needs, drew out his playful responses, and so on. In short, they knew him and gave his life significance and a secure identity. In a similar way, God gives all his children a significant identity by knowing them, regardless of the limitations they might bear.[18]

Those with dementia or diminishing capacities for other reasons provide another example. My sixty-five-year-old friend Soullis Tavrou was diagnosed with a terminal brain tumor. Eight months later, I took him to a doctor's appointment because he had lost the ability to tell the time. His speech was erratic, and he had trouble finishing a sentence. The doctor did not know him, and, frustratingly, his records were not available. Later at the pharmacy, he was too confused to pay for his medication. Both the doctor and the pharmacist looked at him with impatience and pity. Neither had any idea who he was. However, his identity was maintained by those who knew him and loved him—his wife, six children, colleagues, and friends:

> Dr. Soullis Tavrou: Loving husband, proud father, doting papou, caring son, dependable brother, loyal friend, scholar, coach, soldier, champion. We will never forget you.[19]

---

17. http://songmeanings.com/songs/view/50823/; emphasis added.

18. The notion of being known, ultimately by God, may have something to contribute to modern debates about the status of a person in various conditions. If being human means having the capacity to know, then embryos, people who have severe mental disabilities, and those in a persistent vegetative state, for example, fail the test. Gilbert Meilaender (*Bioethics: A Primer for Christians* [Grand Rapids: Eerdmans, 2005], 5) is typical of a growing number of Christian ethicists who lament the modern tendency to define personhood in terms of consciousness and self-awareness. If being human is fundamentally to be known, a case for the human status of the aforementioned may be more readily mounted.

19. The epitaph at his grave. Soullis passed away at the end of 2015.

Ultimately, Soullis is known unto God.

In response to the view that to lose your memory is to lose your life, John Swinton's book on dementia, subtitled *Living in the Memories of God*, locates personal identity in being known and loved by God. He argues that "if our identity is held in and by the memory of God, then we can be certain that dementia does not destroy us now or in the future."[20] Put another way, according to Swinton "we are not what we remember; [rather] we are remembered."[21] "To be remembered is to exist and to be sustained by God. . . . Our identity is safe in the memory of God."[22]

Swinton suggests a revision of Descartes's "I think, therefore I am" along the lines of, "We are because God sustains us in his memory."[23] He counsels that those caring for dementia sufferers and those suffering dementia can take heart in knowing that "the deep fear of forgetting is overcome by the deeper promise of being remembered."[24]

Who are you if you struggle with serious limitations in your life? Does your life seem to lack value and significance? A biblical theology of personal identity reminds you that your identity does not depend on your capacity, circumstances, or achievements. Instead, your true self is hidden and kept safe with Christ in God, and he knows you intimately as his child.

THE END OF LIFE

The Bible speaks about death with depressing bluntness. Death is "the way of all the earth" (Josh 23:14) and "the place appointed for all the living" (Job 30:23). Death is inevitable: "Who can live and not see death, or who can escape the power of the grave?" (Ps 89:48).

Death also strikes at the heart of human identity and significance. It is no respecter of persons, and it brings us all down to the same miserable level:

> One person dies in full vigor,
>   completely secure and at ease,
> well nourished in body,
>   bones rich with marrow.
> Another dies in bitterness of soul,
>   never having enjoyed anything good.
> Side by side they lie in the dust,
>   and worms cover them both. (Job 21:23–26)

---

20. John Swinton, *Dementia: Living in the Memories of God* (Grand Rapids: Eerdmans, 2012), 214.
21. Ibid., 198.
22. Ibid., 221.
23. Ibid., 197.
24. Ibid., 197.

> Surely the fate of human beings is like that of the animals; the same fate awaits them both: As one dies, so dies the other. All have the same breath; humans have no advantage over animals. Everything is meaningless. (Eccl 3:19)

> Like water spilled on the ground, which cannot be recovered, so we must die. (2 Sam 14:14a)

According to the books of Job and Ecclesiastes, death erases every trace of our achievements and we have no advantage over animals because we share their miserable fate. As James puts it: "What is your life? You are a mist that appears for a little while and then vanishes" (Jas 4:14b). Death is the greatest threat to personal identity if we think in terms of the lasting significance of our lives.

Psalm 39 repeats many of the same themes but also points to the solution in its closing question and answer:

> Show me, Lord, my life's end
> and the number of my days;
> let me know how fleeting my life is.
> You have made my days a mere handbreadth;
> the span of my years is as nothing before you.
> Everyone is but a breath,
> even those who seem secure.
> Surely everyone goes around like a mere phantom;
> in vain they rush about, heaping up wealth
> without knowing whose it will finally be.
> But now, Lord, what do I look for?
> My hope is in you. (Ps 39:4–7)

I've sometimes asked students in my lectures whether or not they know the first name of their great grandparents. Disturbingly, few people do. With the passing of two or three generations, no one will remember you. Of what value is your life when, "All people are like grass, and all their glory is like the flowers of the field" (1 Pet 1:24, quoting Isa 40:6–8)?

"For the wise, like the fool, will not be long remembered; the days have already come when both have been forgotten." (Eccl 2:16)

When it comes to matters of life and death, putting your hope in God makes good sense. The psalmist believes that "all the days ordained for me were written in your book before one of them came to be" (Ps 139:16). Job likewise confesses: "A person's days are determined; you [Lord God] have decreed the number of his months" (Job 14:5). God himself declares in Deuteronomy 32:39: "See now that I myself am he! There is no god besides me. I put to death and I bring to life."

God does two things to give our life significance in spite of its depressing transience. First, even if we will not be long remembered on earth, God remembers us. Our lives are kept safe in him. If we "honor his name," our lives are recorded in his "scroll of remembrance" (Mal 3:16). And our names are in the book of life, which is appropriately named for those destined for eternal life. Death does not mean oblivion for the children of the living God.

As an extreme example of losing one's identity in death, consider a certain class of casualties in war. In the First World War, Britain was faced with the dilemma of how to mark the remains of soldiers whose identity had been lost. At the suggestion of Rudyard Kipling, who was a member of the Imperial War Graves Commission, every grave of an unidentified British Empire soldier was marked with the words, "Known unto God."[25] This poignant inscription gave the person buried therein a significance and identity he would otherwise have been denied.

At the west end of the nave of Westminster Abbey is the grave of the Unknown Warrior, whose body was brought from France to be buried there on 11 November 1920. The grave, which contains soil from France, is covered by a slab of black Belgian marble from a quarry near Namur. On it there is an inscription which begins: "Beneath this stone rests the body of a British Warrior unknown by name or rank." Around the main inscription are four texts from the Bible, the first and third of which relate to being known by God: *"The Lord knoweth them that are his"* (2 Tim 2:19); "Greater love hath no man than this" (John 15:16); *"Unknown and yet well known"* (2 Cor 6:9); and "In Christ shall all be made alive" (1 Cor 15:22). The four texts together supply an identity to the unknown soldier based on God's personal knowledge and love and a defining destiny in connection with Jesus Christ.

The second thing that God does to protect our identity from the scourge of death is the promise of resurrection and eternal life. The New Testament answer to the question of James 4:14, "What is your life?" is found in Colossians 3:4: Christ is your life. And having Christ as your life means that you share his destiny. According to 2 Timothy 1:10, "our Savior, Christ Jesus . . . has destroyed death and has brought life and immortality to light through the gospel." And in his own words in Revelation 1:18, Jesus Christ says: "I am the Living One; I was dead, and now look, I am alive forever and ever! And I hold the keys of death and Hades."

Many Jews in Jesus's day believed in a general resurrection of all people at the end of time ushering in the new age.[26] We see this belief in Martha's response to Jesus when he tells her that her dead brother, Lazarus, will live again: "I know he will rise again in the resurrection at the last day" (John 11:24). When Jesus tells Lazarus to come out of the tomb then and there, it certainly wasn't what Martha was expecting.

But as remarkable as the resurrection of Lazarus was, it does not compare with the resurrection of Jesus. Lazarus needed someone to take off his grave clothes. He rose to return to life as it was before he died. And he could expect to die again. In fact, death threats against Lazarus appear as soon as the next chapter in John (12:10)! The resurrection of Jesus is of an entirely different order. Jesus leaves his grave clothes behind. He arises to a new life beyond death—a new dimension of living. He will never die again. His resurrection was the beginning of the new age.

It is not that the Jews were wrong about the great resurrection at "the last day." What took everyone by surprise is that God did for Jesus in the middle of history

25. Officially adopted in World War One, this practice has also been used in subsequent conflicts. I wish to thank Dr. Colin Bale for alerting me to its origin.

26. See Dan 12:1–2: "At that time Michael, the great prince who protects your people, will arise. There will be a time of distress such as has not happened from the beginning of nations until then. But at that time your people—everyone whose name is found written in the book—will be delivered. Multitudes who sleep in the dust of the earth will awake: some to everlasting life, others to shame and everlasting contempt."

what most Jews believed he would do at the end of history. And the resurrection of Jesus is the harbinger of that great day for which we still wait in confident hope. Christ's resurrection, as we noted in chapter ten, was the "firstfruits" of the future resurrection (1 Cor 15:20, 23). Jesus is the "firstborn" of the new creation (Rom 8:29).

But we must not think of the coming, general resurrection as producing a completely new "me" with no connection to "my life." There is an organic relationship between your resurrection body and your present bodily existence. The new "you" is the old "you" rebooted and fitted out perfectly for life in the age of the Spirit.

Who are you, and what will come of your identity if you are destined to die? Those who are known by God can rest assured that their identity is kept safe in him. And those who are in Christ will share his destiny and be raised from the dead.

"In proclaiming the resurrection of Christ, the apostles proclaimed also the resurrection of mankind in Christ; and in proclaiming the resurrection of mankind, they proclaimed the renewal of all creation with him. The resurrection of Christ in isolation from mankind would not be a gospel message. The resurrection of mankind apart from creation would be a gospel of a sort, but of a purely Gnostic and world-denying sort which is far from the gospel that the apostles actually preached."

Oliver O'Donovan[27]

TRUE AND LASTING SIGNIFICANCE

There are two ways to communicate to someone that you value them. One is to tell them; the other is by doing something. And as the old saying goes, actions speak louder than words.[28] The father who insists that his child is important to him but never does anything to prove it leaves his child confused and uncertain at best. In the case of God, our heavenly Father, both his words and actions reassure us that our lives have significance.

"Because you're worth it"

L'Oréal Paris Advertisement

The costliness of our redemption is the firm ground for our confidence that we are valuable to God. When we feel uncertain whether God truly knows and loves us, and whether our feeble and fleeting lives have significance and value, we should look to the cross:

> God demonstrates his own love for us in this: While we were still sinners, Christ died for us. (Rom 5:8)

> For you know that it was not with perishable things such as silver or gold that you were redeemed . . . but with the precious blood of Christ, a lamb without blemish or defect. (1 Pet 1:18–19)

27. Oliver O'Donovan, *Resurrection and Moral Order: An Outline for Evangelical Ethics* (Leicester, UK: Inter-Varsity Press, 1986), 31.

28. See 1 John 3:18: "Dear children, let us not love with words or speech but with actions and in truth."

> You were bought at a price. (1 Cor 6:20; 7:23)

Being known by God gives our lives true and lasting significance, no matter how disappointing or diminished they may be. God reassures us of our significance and worth by reminding us that our names are written in heaven, that he remembers us constantly, and that he knows us intimately and personally. And he backs up his words with a deed that confirms the truth of his words once and for all.

RELEVANT QUESTIONS

1. What unfulfilled hopes, disappointments, or limitations are you living with?
2. For many people, the self is constructed in terms of their expectations, and living in the present is in large measure about anticipation. Are you content with your life now, or are you living in anticipation of who you intend to be?
3. What help does Dietrich Bonhoeffer's reflections on his life give to those living "a disappointed life"?
4. How does John Swinton's statement, "We are because God sustains us in his memory," elevate the status of a person with diminished capacities?
5. What does Jesus's death on the cross and the promise of resurrection mean for our identity?

CHAPTER 12

HUMILITY

Many jobs have occupational hazards: Carpenters need to watch their thumbs when hammering nails; office workers can suffer from RSI (repetitive strain injury); school teachers catch colds from their pupils. Those of us in the higher education industry have something more sinister to worry about; namely, the sin of *pride.*

How so? It comes down to the nature of Western education, which is built on the regular assessment of students and their comparison and ranking against each other. If you come out on top, such evaluation can lead to feeling superior to those "beneath you." Academics, by definition, are those who have excelled in their educational pursuits, often having as many as two or three degrees. And it doesn't stop there. In many institutions where academics work, in order to maintain job security and get promoted, you have to publish articles and books. These are also ranked not only in terms of quantity but according to the prestige of the journals and publishers who print them. Scholarly conferences likewise reflect a hierarchy, with so-called "big names" being given the most prominent speaking platforms. In such an environment, there is a constant temptation—and I speak from personal experience—to treat people as means to an end and to focus exclusively on personal advancement. If the essence of academia is the pecking order, there are numerous subtle reminders of where you sit on the ladder of advancement.

Does your occupation foster a culture of competition and encourage you to compare yourself with others? How do you interact with colleagues who enjoy a better reputation? Do you treat those below you as if they are "below you"? Is pride a problem for you?

What is pride, anyway, and what is wrong with it? How can you know if you are proud? Is there such a thing as legitimate pride in your work and achievements? Does pride rule out ambition? On the other hand, what is humility? Is humility thinking poorly of yourself? How, if at all, does being known by God help to combat the sin of pride and promote humility?

In part two of this book, we saw repeatedly that God knows us better than we know ourselves. We know him in part; he knows us fully. We know him because he first knew us. And we know ourselves in large measure due to his complete knowledge of us. The task of this chapter is to tease out the implications of God's perfect knowledge of us for how we think about ourselves.

THE PROBLEMS WITH PRIDE

There are three problems with pride. The first is that it does serious damage to our relationships and is the death of community. Pride leads us to look down on others and to insist on our own superiority. In fact, the proud hold others in contempt (Ps 123:4), are prone to quarreling (Prov 13:10) and violence (Ps 73:6), and are guilty of injustice (Ps 119:78) and oppression (Ps 10:2). Because of excessive self-love, the proud are in no position to love others. As Paul states, love is the solution to the two sins of comparison, pride and envy: "Love is patient and kind. It does not envy, it does not boast, it is not proud" (1 Cor 13:4).

The second problem with pride is that God is opposed to the proud (Prov 3:34; Jas 4:6). The proud do not obey God's commands (Neh 9:16) and stubbornly turn their backs on him (Neh 9:29). "*In their own eyes* they flatter themselves too much to detect or hate their sin" (Ps 36:2). God sees them differently than others: "Why do you boast all day long, you who are a disgrace *in the eyes of God*?" (Ps 52:1). "The LORD detests all the proud of heart. Be sure of this, they will not go unpunished" (Prov 16:5).

The third problem, and most pertinent for our interests, is that pride produces a distorted view of the self. The Bible faults the proud on this very point. Paul states, "If anyone thinks they are something when they are not, *they deceive themselves*" (Gal 6:3). The prophet Jeremiah writes that "The terror you inspire and the pride of your heart have deceived you" (Jer 49:16, see also Obad 3). And Isaiah states that the problem with "Moab's pride" is that "her boasts are empty" (Isa 16:6). The dreadful irony is that even though the proud spend a lot of time thinking about themselves, they don't know who they are.

> "Humility is fundamentally a form of self-forgetfulness as opposed to pride's self-fixation."
>
> Jason Meyer[1]

However, contrary to much popular thinking, humility is not about thinking poorly of yourself. In fact, when Paul warns against pride, he does not say to think little of yourself: "Do not think of yourself more highly than you ought, but rather *think of yourself with sober judgment*" (Rom 12:3). We are to have an accurate and realistic sense of who we are, which is one of the goals of this book. The Bible nowhere recommends thinking about yourself in some exaggeratedly low way or ignoring your achievements. If pride involves self-promotion and elevation, humility is not about self-degradation and demotion.

Rather than thinking *less of yourself*, humility leads to thinking *less about yourself*: "In humility consider others as more important than yourselves. Everyone should look out not only for his own interests, but also for the interests of others" (Phil 2:3–4 HCSB). The truth is that the humble, although thinking less about themselves, know themselves more accurately than do those who are proud.

---

1. Jason Meyer, "Pride," in *Killjoys: The Seven Deadly Sins*, ed. Marshall Segal (Minneapolis: Desiring God, 2015), 12.

In this chapter, we will explore how being known by God is one of the ways in which God helps his children avoid the sin of pride and embrace humility and thus to have a healthier and more accurate sense of self. To these ends, we shall do three things:

1. Take a look at the story of the tower of Babel, the archetypal sin of pride in the Bible, in order to understand the essence of pride;
2. Reflect on the awesome and humbling privilege of being known by the Lord of the Universe; and
3. Notice the primacy of God's initiative in all our dealings with him and recognize how this leads us to give him humble thanks.

The goal of this chapter is to show that, along with giving our fragile lives significance, being known by God provokes needed humility.

"There is one vice of which no man in the world is free; which everyone in the world loathes when he sees it in someone else and of which hardly any people, except Christians, ever imagine that they are guilty themselves. I have heard people admit that they are bad tempered, or that they cannot keep their heads about girls or drink, or even that they are cowards. I do not think I have ever heard anyone who was not a Christian accuse himself of this vice. And at the same time I have very seldom met anyone, who was not a Christian, who showed the slightest mercy to it in others. There is no fault which makes a man more unpopular, and no fault which we are more unconscious of in ourselves. And the more we have it ourselves, the more we dislike it in others."

C. S. Lewis on pride[2]

THE TOWER OF BABEL

What is pride? The story of the tower of Babel in Genesis 11:1–9 gives us some clues:

> Now the whole world had one language and a common speech. As people moved eastward, they found a plain in Shinar and settled there.
>
> They said to each other, "Come, let's make bricks and bake them thoroughly." They used brick instead of stone, and tar for mortar. Then they said, "*Come, let us build ourselves a city, with a tower that reaches to the heavens, so that we may make a name for ourselves*; otherwise we will be scattered over the face of the whole earth."
>
> But the LORD came down to see the city and the tower the people were building. The LORD said, "If as one people speaking the same language they have begun to do this, then nothing they plan to do will be impossible for them. Come, let us go down and confuse their language so they will not understand each other."
>
> So the LORD scattered them from there over all the earth, and they stopped

"The tower of Babel was intended to be a monument to human effort: instead it became a reminder of divine judgment on human pride and folly."

Gordon Wenham[3]

2. C. S. Lewis, *Mere Christianity* (London: HarperCollins, 2012), 121.

3. Gordon Wenham, *Genesis 1–15*, ed. David A. Hubbard, Glenn W. Barker, and John D. W. Watts, Word Bible Commentary 1 (Dallas: Word, 1987), 241–42.

> building the city. That is why it was called Babel—because there the LORD confused the language of the whole world. From there the LORD scattered them over the face of the whole earth.

Verse 4 is especially helpful in defining the sin of pride. Pride is described as: (1) seeking to make a name for yourself; and (2) reaching to the heavens. In both cases, being known by God is an effective antidote to human pride.

Pride as Making a Name for Yourself

Intriguingly, making a name for yourself is uncannily current, with everyone in our day seemingly looking to have, as Andy Warhol put it, their "fifteen minutes of fame." The builders of the city and tower of Babel were hoping to become famous for their achievement. Ironically, they did make a name for themselves, but it was not one of which they would have been proud. Instead of gaining notoriety, as a more literal translation of the Hebrew of Genesis 11:4 indicates, God said of their city and tower that "its name was called Babel" (v. 9 ESV); in Hebrew, "Babel" sounds like the word for "confused." He might as well have called it, "the tower of Babble." The "name" they made for themselves (v. 4) was one of derision. Gordon Wenham comments:

> The people's express purpose in building, "to make a name, lest we are scattered over the face of the whole earth," is precisely what they fail to achieve. For ultimately the Lord does scatter them (vv. 8, 9), and the name given to their construction commemorates their failure, not their success.[4]

It was not the first time in Genesis that sin was associated with making a name for yourself. The first city in Genesis was also a place where someone hoped to immortalize a name: in Genesis 4:17 when Cain built a city, "he named it after his son Enoch."[5] Hidden from God's presence (4:14), like the builders of the tower in Genesis 11, Cain sought to create a society "that boasted of its power and its technological developments."[6] If Cain the murderer wanted fame for his family, the end result was that Cain's descendant Lamech made a name for himself in terms of exceedingly violent behavior: "I have killed a man for wounding me, a young man for injuring me. If Cain is avenged seven times, then Lamech seventy-seven times" (Gen 4:23b–24).

In Genesis 6:1–4, the "sons of God" also seek to make a name for themselves by marrying "the daughters of humans." Verse 4 describes the children of these sons of God as "heroes of old, men of renown," or literally, "men of name."[7] As Kenneth Mathews explains:

4. Wenham, *Genesis 1–15*, 239.

5. See also Ps 49:11: "Their tombs will remain their houses forever, their dwellings for endless generations, though they had named lands after themselves."

6. Noel D. Osborn and Howard A. Hatton, *A Handbook on Exodus* (New York: United Bible Societies, 1999), 75.

7. The LXX of Gen 6:4 uses *onomastos*, which means "having one's name used widely, illustrious, famous" (BDAG 714).

> As men of "renown" (*šēm* [name]) they seek reputation by their wicked deeds in the way the people of Babel will seek fame through their building enterprise (see also 11:4). The allusion in 6:2 to Eve's vain desires (3:6) and the inclusion of "name" here contribute to the motif of prideful autonomy, which characterizes the sins of prepatriarchal times (chaps. 1–11).[8]

To use our idiom, the sons of God were intent on making a "big name" for themselves. Is making a name for yourself something that you find attractive? Do you dream of standing out above the crowd in some way? Do you long to be noticed?

In Genesis 11, God sees the aspiration of the builders of the tower of "Babble" to make a name for themselves, like Cain in Genesis 4 and the sons of God in Genesis 6, as an act of *rebellion*. In the Bible, to make a name for someone is God's sole prerogative. Wenham explains:

> God promised to make Abram's name great (12:2) and also David's (2 Sam 7:9, fulfilled in 2 Sam 8:13). But elsewhere in Scripture it is God alone who makes a name for himself (e.g., Isa 63:12, 14; Jer 32:20; Neh 9:10). Mankind is attempting to usurp divine prerogatives [with the tower of Babel].[9]

We may add from the New Testament that Paul believed Jesus Christ's humiliation in death on a cross led to him being given "the name above every name" by God (Phil 2:6–11).

The aim of the tower builders was not merely to excel or to make some outstanding contribution to society, something that Scripture does not condemn. Their motives were more malign. They sought fame and independence from God. In modern terms we might describe them as egotistical and narcissistic. The truth is that most of the time our motives are mixed. But there is a problem if the main reason we are doing something is to be noticed and to impress. The Bible equates such motivations with pride. And as the tower of Babel demonstrates, "Pride goes before destruction" (Prov 16:18a).

Ultimately, seeking fame, the sin of pride, is folly. If we set out to make a name for ourselves, in the long run, as an ancient Jewish text observes, "our name will be forgotten in time" (Wis 2:4). Seeking to make a name for ourselves ignores our mortality and limitations as finite creatures.

How does being known by God help with the desire to make a name for yourself? In short, it takes care of that desire without inflating our destructive pride. As we saw in chapter

> The tower-makers' desire to make a name for themselves is "nothing other than man's proud contempt for God. . . . To erect a citadel was not in itself so great a crime. But to raise an eternal monument to themselves that might endure throughout all ages showed head-strong pride as well as contempt for God."
>
> *John Calvin*[10]

8. Kenneth A. Mathews, *Genesis 1–11:26*, NAC 1A (Nashville: Broadman & Holman, 1996), 339.

9. Wenham, *Genesis 1–15*, 240.

10. John Calvin, *Genesis* (Wheaton, IL: Crossway, 2001), 103.

six in the section "Naming as Knowing," throughout the Bible God knows his people by name and keeps a permanent list of our names. Our names are written in the Lamb's "book of life from the creation of the world" (Rev 17:8). I have no need to make a name for myself—my name is already known in "high places."

With respect to builders seeking to make a name for themselves, the books of Ezra and Nehemiah form a telling contrast to Genesis 11. The central focus of Ezra and Nehemiah are the people returning from exile who will build the city wall and house of God in Jerusalem. If the builders of the tower of Babel in Genesis 11 are unnamed, despite their stated intention, the names of the builders of God's temple and the city walls are listed with great specificity in Ezra 2 and 8 and in Nehemiah 3, 7, and 10–12.

Nehemiah 3, to take one example, makes it clear that the names of those who work in God's building projects have their names recorded. Their identities are known, and their significance is preserved for posterity. Note the opening verses:

> Eliashib the high priest and his fellow priests went to work and rebuilt the Sheep Gate. They dedicated it and set its doors in place, building as far as the Tower of the Hundred, which they dedicated, and as far as the Tower of Hananel. The men of Jericho built the adjoining section, and Zakkur son of Imri built next to them.
>
> The Fish Gate was rebuilt by the sons of Hassenaah. They laid its beams and put its doors and bolts and bars in place. Meremoth son of Uriah, the son of Hakkoz, repaired the next section. Next to him Meshullam son of Berekiah, the son of Meshezabel, made repairs, and next to him Zadok son of Baana also made repairs. The next section was repaired by the men of Tekoa, but their nobles would not put their shoulders to the work under their supervisors. (Neh 3:1–5)

Pride as Thinking "the Sky is the Limit"

The tower of Babel was built with a second express purpose, that of reaching "to the heavens" (Gen 11:4). It might be possible to regard building a tower as high as the sky simply as an exercise in human ambition. However, "it seems likely that Genesis views it as a sacrilege. For the sky is also heaven, the home of God, and this ancient skyscraper may be another human effort to become like God."[11]

> "However triumphant our achievements may seem to us, to an all-competent observer we might appear entangled in a small dense web of our own weaving."
> *Marilynne Robinson*[12]

God's response to the building project in 11:5–7 is dripping with irony. If the tower was meant to reach to heaven, God has to come down from heaven even to see it! As Isaiah 40:22a says, the Lord "sits enthroned above the

11. Wenham, *Genesis 1–15*, 240.

12. Marilynne Robinson, *The Givenness of Things: Essays* (New York: Farrar, Straus and Giroux, 2015), 84.

circle of the earth, and its people are like grasshoppers." God regards even our most outrageous ambitions as puny.

In Genesis 11:6, God's concern is that if they build the city and tower, "nothing they plan to do will be impossible for them." Apparently planning without limit is God's exclusive prerogative. To bring out its nefarious connotations in this context, the Hebrew verb "to plan" might be better translated "to plot." It tends to be used in the Old Testament either of God's own plans (e.g., Jer 4:28; 51:12) or of sinful human scheming (Deut 19:19; Ps 31:13; 37:12).[13] Osborn writes:

> The language of Genesis 11:6 clearly indicates God's concern about the actions of the builders in terms that suggest an act of hubris: an attempt to challenge divine prerogatives. . . . the Hebrew verbs used there of the builders' actions are used elsewhere in the OT of actions reserved for God.[14]

As it turns out, the Hebrew root of the word for "pride" means "lofty" or "high." And in the Old Testament, "pride (*gevah*, *ga'on*, *gbh*) with its associated words" also carry this sense of vaunting oneself above others and are "translated 'loftiness', 'height', 'majesty', 'exaltation', *etc.*"[15] In Isaiah 2:12–16, the proud are compared to tall trees and tall ships. Similarly, in the New Testament pride is to "have an exaggerated self-conception, to be puffed up" (*phusioō*),[16] as in for example 1 Corinthians 8:1: "Knowledge inflates with pride" (HCSB).

English has the same understanding of pride reflected in idioms such as looking down your nose at someone and with terms like "arrogance" and "haughtiness." Pride is thus a sin of comparison whereby people see themselves as superior to others.[17] The proud want to be "looked up to" and inevitably look down on others.

It is thus no coincidence that in the Old Testament God's resolve to punish the proud is often expressed in terms of bringing them low:

> You save the humble, but your eyes are on the haughty *to bring them low.* (2 Sam 22:28; see also Job 40:11–12; Ps 18:27)
>
> The eyes of *the arrogant will be humbled and human pride brought low.* (Isa 2:11)

The judgment of Isaiah 26:5 is an echo of the demise of the tower of Babel: "[God] humbles those who dwell on high, he lays the lofty city low; he levels it to the ground and casts it down to the dust." (See also Prov 15:25; 29:23.)

Pride seeks the ultimate supremacy not only over other human beings but also over God. At worst such "reaching for the sky" is enacted in deliberate defiance of

13. See Wenham, *Genesis 1–15*, 241.

14. Osborn and Hatton, *Handbook on Exodus*, 75.

15. D. C. Searle, "Humility, Pride," in *New Dictionary of Biblical Theology*, ed. T. D. Alexander and B. S. Rosner (Downers Grove, IL: InterVarsity Press, 2000), 567.

16. BDAG 1069.

17. The other sin of comparison is envy, when people think of themselves as lacking or inferior in some sense. As noted earlier, in 1 Cor 13:4 love is the solution to both: "Love is patient, love is kind. It does not envy, it does not boast, it is not proud."

God, or it is simply a matter of ignoring God. The proud act as if God did not exist or at least will not hold them to account. They are too busy seeking elevation so they can look down on others to look up and notice God.

When you and I make plans, do we acknowledge that they are always provisional and ultimately depend on the will of God? I am frequently struck by how often "successful" people attribute their success to hard work, when the truth is that luck and timing (providentially governed), both fully outside of our control, play a major part in most successful ventures. If your plans succeed, do you take full credit and think how hard-working or shrewd you have been? Or do you say, along with Paul, what do we have that we did not receive (1 Cor 4:7)?

Does the Bible then oppose attempts to make ambitious plans for the future? The answer is no, but planning must take place in recognition of God's sovereignty and in dependence on him. Notice that in his advice to those making plans, James refers both to human limitations—"What is your life?"—and the temptation to pride—"All such boasting is evil."

> Now listen, you who say, "Today or tomorrow we will go to this or that city, spend a year there, carry on business and make money." Why, you do not even know what will happen tomorrow. What is your life? You are a mist that appears for a little while and then vanishes. Instead, you ought to say, "If it is the Lord's will, we will live and do this or that." As it is, you boast in your arrogant schemes. All such boasting is evil (Jas 4:13–16).[18]

Such sentiments are widespread in the Bible. Proverbs 27:1 says: "Do not boast about tomorrow, for you do not know what a day may bring." Douglas Moo notes that "Paul frequently expressed his submission to the Lord's will in his plans for missionary work (Acts 18:21; Rom 1:10; 1 Cor 4:19; 16:7; see also Heb 6:3)."[19] Pride is the foolish attempt to usurp the prerogatives of God.

How does being known by God help with the urge to elevate myself and to think that the sky is the limit when it comes to my plans and ambitions? The solution is to know and be known by the Most High God. The way to stop looking down on others is to look up in worship and praise of the One who names you. It is to boast in God (Jer 9:24; Rom 5:11) rather than in ourselves. Being known and loved by God frees us to think of the needs of others before ourselves because we know that ultimately our needs will be taken care of by our heavenly Father who knows what we need before we even ask him. The recognition that God has me marked

18. I-Jin Loh and Howard A. Hatton state, "James identifies *arrogance* as the cause of the failure to take God into account in making plans" (*A Handbook on the Letter from James* [New York: United Bible Societies, 1997], 162 [emphasis added]).

19. Douglas J. Moo, *The Letter of James*, PNTC (Grand Rapids: Eerdmans, 2000), 205. We may add Acts 18:21; Phil 2:19, 24.

out means that I feel less concerned about making my own mark. Being known by God reminds me of my limitations and mortality without that knowledge leading me to despair.

There are two foolish responses to the fact that my life is "a mist that appears for a little while and then vanishes" (Jas 4:14). One is to say, "Let us eat and drink, for tomorrow we die" (1 Cor 15:32/Isa 22:13).[20] The other is to ignore my mortality and in pride seek to establish my own identity apart from God.

In Luke 10, Jesus sends out seventy-two disciples to preach about the kingdom of God and to heal the sick. These were no easy tasks. Jesus sends them out like "lambs among wolves" (10:3). When they return, they are elated and report to Jesus with joy: "Lord, even the demons submit to us in your name" (v. 17). Jesus does not dispute their achievements. He responds: "I saw Satan fall like lightning from heaven" (v. 18); he judges their work to be a "sky-high" achievement! But then Jesus offers a gentle but firm correction: "However, do not rejoice that the spirits submit to you, but rejoice that your names are written in heaven" (v. 20). Apparently being known by God in heaven is worth more than the impressive achievement of causing Satan to fall from heaven.

Is Jesus recommending that we take no pleasure in our achievements? We must be careful not to take Jesus's rebuke of his disciples too absolutely. He is not denying his disciples any joy in being used so mightily in God's work. The "don't do this, but rather that" construction is a Jewish way of speaking that seemingly negates something in order to stress the importance of something else.[21]

Nonetheless, Luke 10:20 offers a salutary lesson for "high achievers." Jesus says not to seek your significance in your achievements, no matter how impressive they are. We are worth more than our greatest accomplishments, which in the grand scheme of things are of little significance. Those who look to such things to secure their identity and boost their self-esteem will be let down in the long run. God's esteem is of much greater value.

Jesus tells us that even if your achievements reach to heaven, instead "rejoice that your names are written in heaven" (Luke 10:20). As we saw in chapter six in the section "Naming as Knowing," God knowing your name is a synonym for being known by God. Once again it is helpful to spell out the agent of the action in the

---

20. See also Jesus's parable of the rich fool: "I'll say to myself, 'You have plenty of grain laid up for many years. Take life easy; eat, drink and be merry'" (Luke 12:19).

21. See Maximilian Zerwick, *Biblical Greek: Illustrated by Examples*, English ed., adapted from the fourth Latin ed., vol. 114 (Rome: Pontifical Biblical Institute, 1963), 150. Other examples make it clear that we are not meant to take the "do not" command as complete negation. In Matt 6:19–20, Jesus says: "Do not store up for yourselves treasures on earth, where moths and vermin destroy. . . . But store up for yourselves treasures in heaven, where moths and vermin do not destroy." This verse is not a prohibition against saving money. The surrounding context makes it clear that Jesus is calling for a radical change of priorities: "For where your treasure is, there you heart will be also" (6:21). Disciples are to "seek *first* [God's] kingdom and his righteousness" (6:33).

"The metaphorical expression, *your names are written in heaven*, means, that they were acknowledged by God as His children and heirs, as if they had been inscribed in a register."

John Calvin[23]

passive Greek verb, in this case the verb "to write": it is God who has written our names in heaven and who knows us.[22]

Your work matters to you and to God. But finding your identity in your achievements is unwise. Having your name known to God and inscribed permanently in heaven represents genuine and lasting significance and should lead to a healthy and realistic humility, enabling you to put the interests of others ahead of yourself and to serve them in love.

THE WONDER OF BEING KNOWN BY GOD

One of the dimensions of humanness that we explored in chapter three was our predilection to worship. Human beings inevitably ascribe greatness to one thing or another, be it traditional religion or some substitute. People trust, love and serve, and assign ultimate significance to all sorts of things. Along with worshipping a deity, we are prone to make money or family or sex or nation the big thing in our lives. Pride is the most convenient form of idolatry in elevating our very selves to the place of honor.

Not everyone who fails to look up becomes proud and self-absorbed. But the chances are increased. And even from a secular perspective, the benefits of looking beyond yourself are acknowledged by positive psychology. Positive psychology argues that one of the keys to human flourishing and a meaningful life is being committed to something bigger than yourself.

If one of the causes of pride is looking down on others, one of the keys to humility is to practice looking up and seeing ourselves from a bigger perspective. Psalm 8 is a good example:

> LORD, our Lord,
> how majestic is your name in all the earth!
> You have set your glory
> in the heavens. . . .
> When I consider your heavens,
> the work of your fingers,
> the moon and the stars,
> which you have set in place
> what is mankind that you are mindful of them,
> human beings that you care for them? (vv. 1, 3–4)

22. Robert H. Stein writes, "'Are written' is a divine passive meaning *God has written your names in heaven*" (*Luke: An Exegetical and Theological Exposition of Holy Scripture*, NAC 24 [Nashville: Broadman & Holman, 1992], 310, emphasis original).

23. John Calvin and William Pringle, *Commentary on a Harmony of the Evangelists Matthew, Mark, and Luke*, vol. 2 (Bellingham, WA: Logos Bible Software, 2010), 35, emphasis original.

However, simply adoring the awesome majesty of God does not provoke a wholesome humility. It may make you feel small, but on its own it does not give us the secure sense of significance that frees us to put the interests of others ahead of ourselves, which is how Paul defines humility in Philippians 2:3. For true humility, *you need the far-away God to come near.*

We see this in action with the God of the Bible in Psalm 113. In verses 4–6, it is the majesty of God that turns the psalmist to praise:

> The LORD is exalted over all the nations,
> his glory above the heavens.
> Who is like the LORD our God,
> the One who sits enthroned on high,
> who stoops down to look
> on the heavens and the earth? (Ps 113:4–6)

But in verses 7–9, the psalmist moves from the greatness of God to the grace of God as cause for praise:

> He raises the poor from the dust
> and lifts the needy from the ash heap;
> he seats them with princes,
> with the princes of his people.
> He settles the childless woman in her home
> as a happy mother of children. (Ps 113:7–9)

The psalmist testifies that the far away God has come close. And the movement of condescension is from unimaginable heights—above the heavens—to the lowest points in society, the poor in the dust and on the ash heap. But note it is not just a breathtakingly steep descent that God undertakes. At the very bottom, he takes the poor and elevates them to a new identity, seated with princes; and he takes the barren woman and settles her "as a happy mother of children."

The same V-shaped pattern is repeated in the gospel:

> For you know the grace of our Lord Jesus Christ, that though he was rich, yet for your sake he became poor, so that you through his poverty might become rich. (2 Cor 8:9)

Jesus's descent from spiritual riches to poverty elevates the spiritually poor to a new identity, that of being rich towards God. And that new identity, by satisfying our inclination to worship and our longing for significance, gives us a firm basis for true humility. We are freed to be who we are meant to be and to serve others in love.

To grasp the wonder of being known intimately and personally by God, it is useful to reflect on the uniqueness of the God of the Bible in the Greco-Roman world of the first century. Sometimes we need a point of comparison to appreciate the scale and stature of something.[24] Eckhard Schnabel concludes his survey of the concepts of knowing the divine and divine knowledge in Greek and Roman religion in the ancient world as follows:

> Our survey has shown that Greeks and Romans were very much aware of the fact, which was often stated and even more often implied, that it is difficult to know the gods. . . . The essential self-absorption of the gods focuses their attention on themselves rather than on human beings. If a god is deemed omnipotent, as for example Zeus, his power is regarded as arbitrary. The omniscience of the gods, when it is claimed, does not mean that a particular god is interested in or knows human beings. Omniscience is general, not personal.[25]

Generally speaking, the Greek and Roman gods are best described as self-absorbed and uninterested in human beings. Cicero has Velleius present the Epicurean view of "the mode of the life of the gods and how they pass their days" as follows:

> Their life is the happiest conceivable, and the one most bountifully furnished with all good things. God is entirely inactive and free from all ties of occupation. Neither does he labor, but he takes delight in his own wisdom and virtue, and knows with absolute certainty that he will always enjoy pleasures at once consummate and everlasting.[26]

Furthermore, in the Greco-Roman world humans did not have personal relationships with their gods. In Homer, it is only the gods who address each other as "dear." And while some Greeks had the name *philotheos* (lover of god), as Aristotle bluntly states, "It would be absurd if someone were to say that he loves Zeus."[27] It was also beneath the dignity of Zeus to be described as loving human beings. As Cicero said of the Stoic view of the nature of the gods, "the gods attend to great matters; they neglect small ones."[28]

The contrast with the God of the Bible could not be more stark: the God who made us and the universe knows us as intimately and personally as a father knows his child.

24. In literary terms, we need a "foil." An example from the Bible is the function of Orpah in Ruth 1 as a foil to the character of Ruth. Ruth's loyal love towards Naomi is best seen in comparison with Orpah's willingness to leave Naomi.

25. Eckhard Schnabel, "Knowing the Divine and Divine Knowledge in Greco-Roman Religion," (Unpublished paper; Ridley College Theology Conference: Known by God, 29–30 May 2015), 20.

26. Quoted in Schnabel, "Knowing the Divine and Divine Knowledge in Greco-Roman Religion," 5. The quotation is from Cicero, *De natura deorum* 1.51.

27. Aristotle, *Magna moralia* 1208b30.

HUMBLE GRATITUDE

Several times in the Bible, being known by God is a reason for humility. These texts typically combine the affirmation that certain people know God with the admission that God knowing them is what really counts. To prevent a sort of perverted spiritual pride in knowing God, the primacy of God's grace is underscored with the reminder that, adapting 1 John 4:19,[29] we know God because he first knew us.

We see this knowing in Exodus 33:12b–13a, where Moses admits that God knowing his name precedes and is the precondition for him knowing God:

> You have said, "*I know you by name* and you have found favor with me." If you are pleased with me, teach me your ways *so I may know you* and continue to find favor with you.

The priority of being known by God is also evident in Hosea 13:4–5, where God's knowledge of the nation is temporally prior to their knowledge of him:

> I am the LORD your God [who brought you out]
> from the land of Egypt;
> *you know no God but me,*
> and besides me there is no savior.
> *It was I who knew you in the wilderness,*
> in the land of drought. (RSV)[30]

It is true that there is a mutual knowing in our relationship with God. We know God as he really is, especially in Jesus Christ, who "is himself God and is in closest relationship with the Father" and who "has made him known" (John 1:18). But there is also an asymmetry in the relationship. He knows us much better than we know him.

In 1 Corinthians 13:12, Paul reminds believers of the incomplete nature of our knowledge of God compared with his knowledge of us with reference to the age to come. Paul confesses: "Then [and only then] I shall know just as fully as I am myself known" (NJB). As C. K. Barrett puts it, "Then, not now, there will be complete mutuality of knowledge."[31] Not only does God know us better than we know him, he knows us better than we know ourselves; he already knows us "fully."[32]

Paul uses the theme of being known by God specifically to puncture pride and promote humility on two occasions in his letters. In Galatians 4:8–9, Paul reminds

28. Cicero, *De natura deorum* 2.167.

29. "We love because he first loved us."

30. See Gen 16:13, where Hagar acknowledges that her apprehension of the Lord is made possible by his apprehension of her: "She gave this name to the LORD who spoke to her: 'You are the God who sees me,' for she said, 'I have now seen the One who sees me.'"

31. C. K. Barrett, *The First Epistle to the Corinthians*, BNTC (London: Black, 1971), 307.

32. See David's "who am I?"—"you know your servant" (2 Sam. 7:18, 20; see also John 21:17; 1 John 3:20).

the gentile Christians of their previous plight before affirming their current blessed status: "Formerly, when you did not know God, you were slaves to those who by nature are not gods. But now that you know God—or rather are known by God."

Another clear use of the theme of being known by God to promote humility is in 1 Corinthians 8:1–3. Apparently certain Corinthians felt that knowing God and knowing that idols do not exist qualified them to consume food sacrificed to idols. Paul warns them about the dangers of becoming proud in such circumstances: "'Knowledge' puffs up, but love builds up. If anyone imagines that he knows something, he does not yet know as he ought to know" (1 Cor 8:1–2 RSV). He recommends love, which "builds up" others as the alternative to pride, which builds up (inflates) one's self. A number of commentators have noticed that the next verse contains a surprising twist: Conzelmann explains: "We expect: 'The man who loves God, knows him rightly.' But the thought is deliberately given a different turn"[33] : "But if one loves God, *one is known by him*" (8:3 RSV). Whereas we anticipate the active voice, Paul uses the passive voice to express the critical nature of God knowing them as a way of deflating the pride of the Corinthian "know-it-alls." Paul reasons that while it is true that "all of us possess knowledge" (8:1a RSV), the knowledge that really counts is a knowledge we do not possess. God knowing us is more critical than us knowing God.

The fragility of human knowledge of God is in fact frequently underscored in the Bible: "No one knows the thoughts of God except the Spirit of God" (1 Cor 2:11b), for God "lives in unapproachable light" (1 Tim 6:16). Thinking in grammatical terms, in biblical thought generally the passive voice takes precedence over the active when describing how humans relate to God. We know God truly, but not fully. As Richard Hays puts it, "what counts is not so much our knowledge of God as God's knowledge of us. That is the syntax of salvation."[34] This observation applies not only to the Hebrew and Greek verbs "to know," but also to the verbs "to choose," "to call," "to love," and so on; we choose, see, call, and love God because he first chose, saw, called, and loved us. Such constructions highlight the grace of God and promote the appropriate human response of humble gratitude.

Being known by God personally and intimately means that we are released from the futile drive to establish our own significance and to assert our superiority over other people, which is the essence of pride. It provides the security we need to rise above our anti-social need to be noticed. Instead of obsessing about ourselves, we are free to focus on serving others in love. As believers in Christ, we have no need to make a name for ourselves and to reach for the sky—our names have already been permanently inscribed by God in heaven!

33. See Hans Conzelmann, *1 Corinthians: A Commentary on the First Epistle to the Corinthians*, ed. George W. MacRae, trans. James W. Leitch, Hermeneia (Philadelphia: Fortress, 1975), 141. See also Richard B. Hays, *First Corinthians*, Interpretation (Louisville: Westminster John Knox, 1997), 139.

34. Hays, *First Corinthians*, 138, on 1 Cor 8:3.

RELEVANT QUESTIONS

1. Many of us are driven by a need to be noticed or a desire to make a name for ourselves. How does the fact that our name is already known in high places release us from this drive?
2. Our needs are taken care of by our heavenly Father who knows what we need before we even ask him. How can this idea free you, especially in terms of showing love and generosity to those around you?
3. This chapter contrasts the self-absorbed and uninterested Greek and Roman gods with the God of the Bible—the "far away God" who has "come near" and knows us intimately and personally. Does this comparison move you?
4. God knowing us is more critical than us knowing God. Why is this?

CHAPTER 13

COMFORT

To be human is to experience sorrow. People go hungry, children die, the wicked prosper, and good people suffer.[1] Jesus said, "The poor you will always have with you" (Matt 26:11), so too are the ill, the heartbroken, the grief-stricken, and the lonely. As someone in his late fifties, I can report that all of my peers have experienced things that they did not expect which have proven to be major burdens. As the book of Job states: "Man is born to trouble as surely as sparks fly upward" (Job 5:7).

Should we expect comfort from God when we find ourselves in trouble? Paul certainly believed so and goes as far as to describe God as "the Father of all compassion and the God of all comfort, who comforts us in all our troubles" (2 Cor 1:3b–4a). He wrote these words from personal experience, recalling a grave situation in the province of Asia:

> We do not want you to be uninformed, brothers and sisters, about the troubles we experienced in the province of Asia. We were under great pressure, far beyond our ability to endure, so that we despaired of life itself. (2 Cor 1:8)

We don't know the details of Paul's troubles, but two things are clear. We are right to look to God for comfort when we are suffering—he is "the God of all comfort." And secondly, once we have received comfort, God expects us to pass that comfort on to others: Paul writes that God comforts us "*so that* we can comfort those in any trouble with the comfort we ourselves receive from God" (2 Cor 1:4b). Reading this passage motivated me to write this book. At a time in my life when I felt dejected and lost, pondering the biblical theme of being known by God was of great comfort to me. Having received comfort from God, I write in the hope of passing that comfort on to others.

One of the things people need when facing serious hardship is the encouragement that others know what they are going through. As Hugh Mackay puts it: "We place a high value on the people who are prepared to listen attentively and sympathetically to us. Being truly, seriously listened to feels like a welcome and precious gift."[2]

This was certainly my experience when things went off the rails for me in

1. See Eccl 8:14: "Here is another enigma that occurs on earth: Sometimes there are righteous people who get what the wicked deserve, and sometimes there are wicked people who get what the righteous deserve" (NET).

2. Hugh Mackay, *What Makes Us Tick: The Ten Desires that Drive Us* (Sydney: Hachette Australia, 2010), 29.

Scotland. Fortunately I had a group of close friends who willingly spent time helping me to process what had happened, where things had gone wrong, how they saw my past, and how I might think about the future. It took months, and I imagine that such time-consuming interaction was not without some cost to them. They all had busy lives themselves. At a particularly low point one friend, Richard, took me camping on the west coast for a couple of nights. Peter and Sheana had me and my children over for dinner once a week on Tuesday nights. To be treated as a person worthy of attention was indeed a precious gift.

Similarly, knowing that I was known by God brought real and lasting comfort. It meant that I did not lose hope. God had not abandoned or forgotten me. Being known in my distress gave me a sense of safety and security—a fixed point when everything else was shaky. The comfort I received from God was not the sort that had me leaping out of bed in the mornings or whistling a happy tune. But it did douse a destructive pessimism that was threatening to engulf me. If I felt unsure about who I was any more, at least God knew me.

In part two, we noticed the profound sense in which in the Old Testament God knew his people intimately and personally (see chapter six). He remembered them when they were in strife, and he knew their names. There we saw that the identity of God's people as the children of God was grounded and sustained by his constant attentiveness. Similarly, in the New Testament (see chapter seven) the people of God belong to him as his dearly loved children, and he knows our names. And believers in Christ are known by Jesus just as intimately as the Father knows the Son. Such teaching reminds us of God's tenderness and compassion towards us and the fact that each one of us is of supreme value to him.

Indeed, the most common pastoral function of being known by God in the Bible is in fact bringing comfort to those in distress. According to the prophet Nahum, "The Lord is good, a stronghold in the day of trouble; *he knows those who take refuge in him*" (Nah 1:7 ESV).

J. I. Packer, author of the best-selling book *Knowing God*, claims that there is "unspeakable comfort" in being known by God.[3] In this chapter, we will attempt to speak about this comfort by looking at:

1. How being known by God brings comfort;
2. Three specific examples from the history of ancient Israel of the nation in distress being known by God; and
3. The tension between complaining to God, being known by God, and taking refuge in God.

3. J. I. Packer, *Knowing God*, 20th Anniversary ed. (Downers Grove, IL: InterVarsity Press, 1993), 37.

THE COMFORT OF BEING KNOWN BY GOD

In the seventeenth century, Richard Baxter called being known by God "the full and final comfort of a believer."[4] But how does this comfort work? And what difference does being known by God make when you are in trouble?

The comfort of being known when in distress ranges from God's specific and active care in which he meets the need in question to a more general notion of consolation simply in being known by him as a parent knows their child. In terms of the latter, it seems that being known by God within a secure and loving relationship can help provide a stable and secure identity, not unlike that which parents hope to give to their young children, which is cheering and comforting in and of itself. This can be the case irrespective of practical assistance. Being known by God meets our deepest need to be acknowledged and valued when such things are most needed.

With respect to the comfort of being known by God, psychologist Maureen Miner likens God to the ideal parent who offers his children his loving attention and a secure attachment that provides "a safe haven and a secure base from which to engage the world."[5]

When a young child stubs their toe, they might need some medical attention. But they also need the reassuring embrace of a caregiver. When confronted with uncertainty and hardship, being known by God offers this sort of comfort. In Isaiah 66:13, God says: "As a mother comforts her child, so will I comfort you." In psychological terms, according to Loyola McLean:

> The benefits of such consolation also extend psychologically to the affirmation of one's lovability, one's value and one's belonging to someone that can be internalized in a positive schema of self and potentially then accessed at times of challenge.[6]

On one occasion I was playing with Toby, my youngest child, in the front yard of our house. Toby chased a ball into the garden bed among the rose bushes. He emerged with a few minor scratches. Before having his wounds cleaned and dressed, what he wanted was a reassuring embrace from his imperfect earthly father. He needed the comfort of knowing that he was known in the midst of his distress.

In times of distress, we often feel worthless and unloved, as if no one cares or even notices. Being known by God puts the lie to these destructive thoughts.

THE EXPERIENCE OF ISRAEL

The three lowest points in the history of ancient Israel were slavery in Egypt, wandering in the wilderness, and exile in a foreign land. All three shape the historical

4. Richard Baxter, *The Practical Works of Rev Richard Baxter: Volume 15* (London: James Duncan, 1830), 285.

5. Maureen Miner, "Back to the Basics in Attachment to God: Revisiting Theory in Light of Theology," *Journal of Psychology and Theology* 35.2 (2007): 117.

6. Loyola McLean and Brian S. Rosner, "Theology and Human Flourishing: The Benefits of Being Known by God," in *Beyond Well-Being: Spirituality and Human Flourishing*, ed. Maureen Miner, Martin Dowson, and Stuart Devenish (Charlotte, NC: Information Age Publishing, 2012), 77.

consciousness of Jews to this day. And even though the vast majority of us will never be literally enslaved, lost in a desert, or sent into exile, all three are highly suggestive of a range of distressing experiences that are still very common today. Such experiences threaten not only your happiness but also your very identity. A shaken self-perception is among the most painful side effects of adversity. Significantly, in each case God comforted the Israelites by reassuring them that he knew them in their distress.

Oppressed and Enslaved

Early in the life of the nation, the Israelites suffered considerable hardship in bondage in Egypt. They performed "hard labor" making bricks and had a maniacal taskmaster in the person of the pharaoh. Exodus 2:23 states baldly: "The Israelites groaned in their slavery."

Whereas most parts of the Western world today thankfully are free of slavery, it is fair to say many people can identify to some degree with the distress of feeling trapped. These experiences may include the confinement of overwhelming debts, dead-end jobs, chronic illnesses, or oppressive relationships. Feelings of helplessness combined with a sense that there is no end in sight can make life a misery.

Do you ever feel like you are imprisoned by your circumstances and unable to free yourself? Who are you if you feel like a slave? Does God know you when you feel trapped and helpless?

What did the Israelites do in their distress? They "cried out, and their cry for help because of their slavery went up to God" (Exod 2:23). What did God do in response? "God heard their groaning and he remembered his covenant with Abraham, with Isaac and with Jacob" (Exod 2:24). The promise of blessing to the nation that God gave to these three men put their slavery in perspective. God would eventually come to their rescue.

Exodus 2:24 confirms that the Israelites were not left forgotten and unnoticed: God looked on the Israelites and *knew them*. God had not turned away, and he was not unaware. Even if the alleviation of their suffering was some way off, knowing that God had taken notice of their anguish was the first step in its alleviation. It affirmed their identity as those who belonged to him. Their plight had not escaped his notice.

Wandering Aimlessly

Following their rescue from Egypt, the Israelites sojourned in difficult conditions in the wilderness for some forty years. They knew of the promised land and looked forward to taking possession of it, but year after year they languished. Where was the promise of blessing the nation?

For some of us, life feels like we are in an interminable "holding pattern" and are never going to arrive at our desired destination. Things seem like they are going nowhere. The same problems dog us year after year, with things getting worse rather than better. While "a journey" can be a positive image for human existence, it is decidedly unpleasant if the endpoint seems further away as the years go by.

Most modern English versions of the Old Testament translate the Hebrew verb *yadah* in ways other than "to know" in contexts that speak of the comfort of being known by God:

- In Exodus 2:25 instead of "God knew the Israelites," the NIV has, "So God looked on the Israelites and *was concerned about them.*"
- In Hosea 13:5, instead of "It was I who knew you in the wilderness" (ESV), the NIV has, "*I cared for* you in the wilderness, in the land of burning heat."
- In Nahum 1:7, instead of "he knows those who take refuge in him," the NET Bible has, "*he protects* those who seek refuge in him."

Bible translation always involves a trade off between the priorities of accuracy and intelligibility. In my view, the concept of "being known" is a sufficiently comprehensible idiom in modern English to be retained in translation. The cost of not doing so is to obscure a major biblical theme.

Do you ever feel aimless in life? Who are you if you feel lost? Does God know you when things seem to be going nowhere?

God comforts the Israelites with the reassurance that he knew them in the wilderness too: "It was *I who knew you* in the wilderness, in the land of drought" (Hosea 13:5 ESV). In the wilderness, God knew of their distress and had provided for them in spite of their disobedience. The hopes of the nation would not prove empty.

Longing for Home

In the ancient world, exile was an extreme form of punishment. In 587/6 BC, for example, Nebuchadnezzar of Babylon captured the city of Jerusalem, destroyed its temple, and sent into exile a large number of its inhabitants. The psalmist wrote: "By the rivers of Babylon we sat and wept when we remembered Zion [i.e., Jerusalem]" (Ps 137:1). The book of Lamentations records the devastating effect on the people of God: "Remember, Lord, what has happened to us; look, and see our disgrace" (Lam 5:1).

Isaiah 49 contains a famous passage promising the restoration of Israel from exile in Babylon. The passage includes words of comfort: "This is what the Lord says: 'In the time of my favor I will answer you, and in the day of salvation I will help you'" (Isa 49:8). However, despair is also reported, as the nation (represented by Zion) cries out: "The Lord has forsaken me, the Lord has forgotten me" (Isa 49:14). Suffering often evokes a concern that God has forgotten us and has not seen our plight.

The idea of "home" has a meaning beyond the literal sense of the place where you live or grew up. Simon Smart explains:

> The concept of home is a powerful motif in human experience. It can evoke feelings of nostalgia, joy, love, or alternatively loss, sadness and heartbreak. . . . Home is where you have connections. Where you have relationships, community,

> rituals, memories. It's familiarity and warmth, nurture and love. Home is where you are known.[7]

Missing home is a powerful and unpleasant emotion, and it can be an aching loss. Do you ever feel that you don't belong? Who are you if you have that gnawing sense of feeling out of place? Does God know you when your life seems to be missing the warmth, nurture, and love of home?

God promises not to forget his people Israel in exile. Describing his relationship to them as that of a devoted mother to her child, he insists that there is less chance of him forgetting them than of a mother forgetting her child:

> Can a mother forget the baby at her breast
> and have no compassion on the child she has borne?
> Though she may forget,
> *I will not forget you*!" (Isa 49:15)

Humanity knows no closer bond than a mother to her newborn child. Yet God's attachment to us and his attentive and nurturing concern is even greater.

TAKING REFUGE IN GOD

The most frequent type of psalm in the book of Psalms is lament. "A lament is a repeatable cry of pain, rage, sorrow, and grief that emerges in the midst of suffering and alienation."[8] A good example is Psalm 13, which opens with a fourfold complaint to God of "how long?"

> How long, LORD? Will you forget me forever?
> How long will you hide your face from me?
> How long must I wrestle with my thoughts
> and day after day have sorrow in my heart? (Ps 13:1–2)

The phenomenon of lament in the Bible presents a potential problem for the idea that being known by God brings comfort. Several laments complain that God has forgotten or abandoned the psalmist, the very opposite of affirming God's reassuring personal knowledge. Take Psalm 10 as an example, which opens with two anguished questions:

> Why, LORD, do you stand far off?
> Why do you hide yourself in times of trouble? (Ps 10:1).

7. Simon Smart, "Finding the Way Home," ABC Online, September 8, 2010, http://www.abc.net.au/religion/articles/2010/09/08/3005930.htm. Book review of *Home Truth*, ed. Carmel Bird (Sydney: HarperCollins, 2010).

8. John Swinton, *Raging with Compassion: Pastoral Responses to the Problem of Evil* (Grand Rapids: Eerdmans, 2007), 104.

"Everyone has moments when they question things, and one sees that in the Psalms. The psalmist in Psalm 44 asks God if he is asleep, and challenges him in the most direct terms about his failure to deliver Israel. It is a psalm of protest. . . . When friends suffer, when evil seems to cover the face of the Earth, then we should be like the psalmist. But that is not the same as a settled belief that God does not exist, or even any serious questioning about his reality. It's a moment of protest and arguing. It's very much part of my normal prayer life, together with praise and wonder, with delight and awe, with petition and lament, with celebration and rejoicing."
Justin Welby[9]

Far from experiencing God's loving attention and gaze, the psalmist protests that God stands aloof and pays him no attention. Do such laments undermine the idea that God comforts his people by knowing them in their distress?

The answer is, no. It is a mistake to read the lament psalms as expressing unbelief in the goodness of God. In one sense the opposite is the case. The psalmists complain to God because they expect better of him. And as it turns out, almost all the lament psalms end in trust and praise, and many take comfort specifically from being known by God. John Swinton cites the end of Psalm 13 to make this point:

> Lament provides us with a language of outrage that speaks against the way things are, but always in the hope that the way things are just now is not the way they will always be. . . . [Psalm 13 ends,] "But I trust in your unfailing love; my heart rejoices in your salvation. I will sing to the Lord, for he has been good to me."[10]

Psalm 10 also closes on a more confident note, affirming that God does know of the psalmist's plight and responds with fatherly care:

> But you, God, see the trouble of the afflicted;
> you consider their grief and take it in hand.
> The victims commit themselves to you;
> you are the helper of the fatherless. (Ps 10:14)

Such psalms of lament are only apparent exceptions to the observation that God knowing us in our distress brings comfort. The cry that God has forgotten the psalmist is in effect a petition to be remembered by him. And the Psalter is dotted not only with complaints that God pays no attention but also reassurances that he has by no means forgotten his people.

Still, the psalms of lament set an example and offer the opportunity for those in genuine distress to voice their frustrations and pain in the context of their faith in God. In his own dark night, Jesus prays the first verse of Psalm 22 on the cross:

> My God, my God, why have you forsaken me?
> Why are you so far from saving me,

9. Justin Welby, "Why Arguing with God Is Not the Same as Not Believing in Him," The Archbishop of Canterbury, November 23, 2015, http://www.archbishopofcanterbury.org/blog.php/25/why-arguing-with-god-is-not-the-same-as-not-believing-in-him.

10. Swinton, *Raging with Compassion*, 105.

so far from my cries of anguish?
My God, I cry out by day, but you do not answer,
by night, but I find no rest. (Ps 22:1–2; see Mark 15:34)

If being known by someone is to carry any comfort, it helps if they know what you are feeling. As we saw in 2 Corinthians 1:3–4, those best placed to pass on comfort are those who have been comforted. In Jesus Christ, "We do not have a high priest who is unable to empathize with our weaknesses" (Heb 4:15). In my case, when I was in pain from rejection and abandonment, I vividly recall discovering the comfort that Jesus knew what I was experiencing.

Along with many laments, the book of Psalms also reassures the people of faith that God has not forgotten or forsaken them. The theme of the righteous being known by God in the Psalms is announced in Psalm 1:6 in general terms: "The Lord knows the way of the righteous, but the way of the wicked will perish" (ESV). Then throughout the Psalter, the same note is struck not only in psalms of lament but also in psalms of thanksgiving: "I will be glad and rejoice in your love, for you saw my affliction and knew the anguish of my soul" (Ps 31:7). Or as the HCSB translates this verse, "You have known the troubles of my life."

Psalm 9 combines taking refuge in God, being known by God, and knowing God:

The Lord is a refuge for the oppressed,
a stronghold in times of trouble.
Those who know your name trust in you,
for you, Lord, have never forsaken those who seek you. (Ps 9:9–10)

Finding refuge in God is the other side of the coin of being assured that God knows you and has not forsaken you.

There are three things you may do as a child of God when you find yourself in trouble and distress:

1. Complain to God;
2. Be reassured that you are known by God in your distress; and
3. Take refuge in God.

To complain to God should not be equated with unbelief. Lament in the Bible is not a crisis of *faith* so much as a crisis of *understanding*. As John Swinton states, "Lament has a purpose and an endpoint beyond the simple expression of pain: reconciliation with and a deeper love for God."[11] Lament expresses both disappointment with but also trust in God. And it leads to a renewed confidence in God's care and provision. But learning afresh that you are known by God is not the end of the process. Passive reception of God's loving concern must lead to an active faith in

11. Swinton, *Raging with Compassion*, 111.

God. Knowing that you are known by God is an invitation to trust and take refuge in God.

Indeed, Psalm 37:18 connects being known by God to a renewed confidence about the future: "The Lord knows the days of the blameless, and their heritage will abide forever" (NRSV). Reflecting on this psalm, John Calvin underscores how being known by God is a source of comfort in any circumstance:

> David now says, that *God knows the days of the righteous*; that is to say, he is not ignorant of the dangers to which they are exposed, and the help which they need. This doctrine we ought to approve as a source of consolation under every vicissitude which may seem to threaten us with destruction. We may be harassed in various ways, and distracted by many dangers, which every moment threaten us with death, but this consideration ought to prove to us a sufficient ground of comfort, that not only are our days numbered by God, but that he also knows all the vicissitudes of our lot on earth.[12]

In Psalm 31:19, the psalmist testifies to the goodness of God and introduces the critical notion of taking refuge in God:

> How abundant are the good things
> that you have stored up for those who fear you,
> that you bestow in the sight of all,
> on those who take refuge in you.

The comfort of being known by God is best experienced when we seek refuge in him: "Come near to God and he will come near to you. . . . The Lord is full of compassion and mercy" (Jas 4:8; 5:11).

THE PROOF OF GOD'S LOVE

When Paul wrote to the Christians in Rome, he made it clear that being a Christian does not exempt us from pain and adversity. In Romans 8:35 he lists seven negative experiences that might come our way: trouble, hardship, persecution, famine, nakedness, danger, and sword.[13] Paul asks whether such things will "separate us from the love of Christ."

His answer is that the Christian can be certain of God's love despite life's difficulties. Paul's confidence is based on the fact that "God is for us" (Rom 8:31). For God to be "for us" is another way of saying that we are the objects of God's love. Indeed, Paul says as much at the end of the unit:

12. John Calvin and James Anderson, *Commentary on the Book of Psalms*, vol. 2 (Bellingham, WA: Logos Bible Software, 2010), 33, emphasis original.

13. "Nakedness" following "famine" should probably be understood in general terms as another way of referring to "poverty" (GNT) or "destitution" (Goodspeed).

> For I am convinced that neither death nor life, neither angels nor demons, neither the present nor the future, nor any powers, neither height nor depth, nor anything else in all creation, will be able to separate us from the love of God that is in Christ Jesus our Lord. (Rom 8:38–39)

But can you be sure that you are known and loved by God and that he has not forgotten you when life goes badly? How can you be sure that your heavenly Father will pay you the loving attention you need when things go wrong?

The proof of God's loving concern for his people is given in Romans 8:32:

> He who did not spare his own Son, but gave him up for us all—how will he not also, along with him, graciously give us all things?

At great cost God sent his Son to die for you and me. The logic is clear. Big gifts demonstrate the generosity of the giver and signify that they can be counted on to be generous in the future. If God gave his Son, he will also along with him give us "all things." The "all things" that we can count on because of the cross include being known and loved by God under any and every circumstance. The fact that God "did not spare his own Son" convinces us that God is paying us loving attention. Nothing is more important for us when we are in distress than to remember the cross. The cross convinces us that God knows the troubles of our lives (Ps 31:7 HCSB).

RELEVANT QUESTIONS

1. Have you been able to bring comfort to others because of the hard times you've experienced in your own life?
2. Correspondingly in the midst of disappointment or even despair, have you had people in your life who have treated you as a person worthy of attention?
3. Are you feeling trapped, helpless, lost, or a long way from home? Even during the low points of Israel's history, God did not turn away from his people. How could this reminder of God's character and being known by God help you in times of distress?
4. The psalmist's cry that God has forsaken him is in effect a petition to remember him. What is the role of lament in the book of Psalms?

CHAPTER 14

DIRECTION

Significance, humility, comfort. A fourth benefit of being known by God is moral direction for living.

My crisis of identity back in the 1990s left the door open to major changes in my life. If you don't know who you are, how you live is an open question. I had been a Christian since I was a young man. And even though I was no angel, I had sought to live a Christian life for some twenty years. But then I was left wondering about all sorts of behaviors that had previously seemed out of bounds: dishonesty, greed, malice, anger, pornography, casual sex. For me, being known by God as his child confirmed the shape of my life and steadied its course.

The idea that an identity carries with it a certain character or set of behaviors is widely accepted. Nationality, gender, and social class all form the basis of who we are and, at one level, how we are expected to behave. Americans typically behave one way. The English, another. Australians, yet another. Men behave one way. Women, another. And so on. The point can be exaggerated, as if no individual differences exist. But naïve stereotypes aside, ethicists of almost every stripe will tell you that *who you are will have a big impact on your conduct.*

In chapter nine, we considered in depth the identity of believers as children of God and how imitating God our Father and Christ his Son is meant to flow from that identity. As children of our heavenly Father, we are to love our enemies (Matt 5:44) and to follow God's example as dearly loved children by walking in the way of love (Eph 5:1–2). And we are to be conformed to the image of God's Son (Rom 8:29). As brothers and sisters in God's family, we are to live in harmony with each other and express mutual care and support. The identity of those known by God as his children carries with it a distinctive lifestyle.

This chapter builds on chapter ten where we looked at the role of memory and destiny in forming identity. There we saw that, as important as our own individual life stories might be, there is a bigger narrative in which we find our true selves. We are part of a bigger story. And our shared memory of Christ's death and resurrection, and remembering our share in his glorious destiny, defines who we are in the present. Specifically, we remember that we were in slavery to sin, but God has set us free through the death of his Son. We remember that we died with Christ and to living purely for self-interest. We remember that we rose to new life in him. And we remember that we belong to the day of final redemption and the glorious unveiling of the Son of God and of us as God's children.

Here we focus directly on the relationship between identity and conduct. How does our new identity in Christ, as someone known by God as his child, affect our behavior? How does our shared memory and common destiny teach us to live in the present? To answer these questions, we look at three key ideas, each of which regularly appear in current discussions of identity and character: (1) *authenticity*, and the question of whether you should be true to yourself; (2) the way in which someone's identity is formed by a *defining moment* in that person's life; and (3) the way in which someone's identity is expressed in a person's *signature move*. In addition, we focus on Colossians 3 as a major case study of how being known by God gives moral direction to our lives.

THE SEARCH FOR AUTHENTICITY

How important is authenticity for a person's identity and conduct according to the Bible? As noted in chapter one (see "Be True to Yourself"), our world puts a premium on being true to yourself and following your heart. Charles Taylor states it well: "Modern freedom and autonomy centres us on ourselves, and the ideal of authenticity requires that we discover and articulate our own identity."[1] What are we to make of this major cultural shift?

On the one hand, psychologists generally regard authenticity as a basic requirement of mental health:

> Authenticity is correlated with many aspects of psychological well-being, including vitality, self-esteem, and coping skills. Acting in accordance with one's core self—a trait called self-determination—is ranked by some experts as one of the three basic psychological needs.[2]

> "Authenticity is one of those motherhood words—like community, family, natural, and organic—that are only ever used in their positive sense, as terms of approbation."
>
> Andrew Potter[3]

It is hard to argue with the call to live authentically if the alternative is to live disingenuously. Who wants to be a fake or a phony?! "Authenticity points towards a more self-responsible form of life. . . . at its best it allows for a richer mode of existence."[4] Authentic living can mean behaving in a way that is honest and open, not overly concerned with the impression you are making on others nor second-guessing what others make of you.

1. Charles Taylor, *The Ethics of Authenticity* (London: Harvard University Press, 1991), 81.

2. Karen Wright, "Dare to Be Yourself," *Psychology Today* (May 1, 2008): 72.

3. Andrew Potter, *The Authenticity Hoax: Why the "Real" Things We Seek Don't Make Us Happy* (New York: Harper Perennial, 2011), 6.

4. Taylor, *Ethics of Authenticity*, 74.

However, taking authenticity to be the sole or chief criterion for human behavior and the main way to direct our lives raises significant concerns. The urge to self-fulfillment can lead to a shallow and destructive narcissism. And on its own, the urge to be true to ourselves ignores the social fabric of our existence. Relationships can easily become disposable if they stand in the way of self-expression: "Our ties to others, as well as external moral demands, can easily be in conflict with our personal development."[5]

Indeed, ignoring factors outside of ourselves is both limiting and unrealistic. As Charles Taylor notes:

> I can define my identity only against the background of things that matter. But to bracket out history, nature, society, the demands of solidarity, everything but what I find within myself, would be to eliminate all candidates for what matters.[6]

Worse still for those committed to following their hearts, Jesus issues this sober word of warning: "For out of the heart come evil thoughts—murder, adultery, sexual immorality, theft, false testimony, slander" (Matt 15:19). Following our heart can lead to the terrible abuse of other people.

"The notion that each one of us has an original way of being human entails that each of us has to discover what it is to be ourselves."

Charles Taylor[7]

Ecclesiastes 11:9 tells young people to "follow the ways of your heart and whatever your eyes see," but not without adding a warning: "But know that for all these things God will bring you into judgment."

Ironically, self-deception is also a danger. Gregg A. Ten Elshof's insightful exploration of the phenomenon of deceiving ourselves, aptly entitled *I Told Me So*, explains that the rise of authenticity and being true to yourself as supreme values in today's world has meant that being self-deceived has been increasingly seen as a vice: "To the degree that we value authenticity, we will be averse to the suggestion that we are self-deceived."[8] But with only myself to measure myself against, it becomes increasingly difficult to judge my behavior as anything but admirable. As Obadiah 3 warns the Edomites, "The pride of your heart has deceived you." Paul warns the Galatians of the same delusion: "If anyone thinks they are something when they are not, they deceive themselves" (Gal 6:3).

Perhaps the greatest problem with looking to the ideal of authenticity to provide direction for our lives is its naivety. While it is true that who you are affects how you behave, it is also true that *what you do changes who you are.* The sixth-century philosopher Boethius put it well:

5. Ibid., 57.

6. Ibid., 40. The ideal of authenticity can lead to "anthropocentrism, which by abolishing all horizons of significance, threatens us with a loss of meaning and hence a trivialization of our predicament" (ibid., 68).

7. Ibid., 61.

8. Gregg A. Ten Elshof, *I Told Me So: Self Deception and the Christian Life* (Grand Rapids: Eerdmans, 2009), 12.

> Whatever loses its goodness loses its being. Thus wicked men cease to be what they were. To give oneself to evil is to lose one's human essence. Just as virtue can raise a person above human nature, vice can lower those whom it has seduced from the condition of men, beneath human nature.[9]

As well as having your identity drive your behavior, your behavior can alter your identity. As C. S. Lewis observes: "Every time you make a choice you are turning the central part of you, the part of you that chooses, into something a little different from what it was before."[10] Authenticity is a two-way street: we act out of our identity, but our repeated acts can alter that identity. Our character, which is formed by settled habits of action and feeling, is both fed by our identity and feeds that changing identity. Following our heart can turn us into a different person, and not necessarily for the better.

Does the Bible espouse the ideal of authenticity for believers in Christ? Should you aim to be who you are? How important is self-expression? If authenticity is acting in accordance with who you really are, the answer is a resounding, "Yes!" A frequent strategy for moral transformation in the Bible is the call to live in accordance with our new identity as those known by God as his children.

In Colossians 3:12, Paul calls on Christians to act in keeping with who we are in Christ: "Therefore, *as God's chosen people, holy and dearly loved*, clothe yourselves with compassion, kindness, humility, gentleness and patience." Believers in Christ are to be true to themselves, that is, their new selves in Christ. The Christian life is about knowing who you are in relation to God and "dressing appropriately."

The catalogs of virtue and vice in the New Testament offer lists of behaviors to acquire or relinquish. But these descriptions of behavior must be read in context. They are not "rules for living." Most such lists make it clear that the conduct enjoined is that which fits our new identity. Or in the case of the vice catalogs, they are behaviors that are not in keeping with who we are in Christ.

In Galatians 5, for example, the fruit of the Spirit are the behaviors appropriate to those who belong to Christ, have died with him, and are raised to new life by the Spirit:

> The fruit of the Spirit is love, joy, peace, forbearance, kindness, goodness, faithfulness, gentleness and self-control. . . . *Those who belong to Christ Jesus have crucified the flesh* with its passions and desires. Since *we live by the Spirit*, let us keep in step with the Spirit. (Gal 5:22–25)

Commentators regularly describe the fruit of the Spirit as the work of the Holy Spirit in our lives, the evidence of the Spirit's presence and activity.[11] However, this is

---

9. Cited by Peter Kreeft in "Identity," *peterkreeft.com*, June 6, 2005, http://www.peterkreeft.com/audio/30_lotr_identity/identity_transcription.htm.

10. C. S. Lewis, *Mere Christianity* (London: HarperCollins, 2012), 86–87.

11. See also Matt 7:17a: "Every good tree bears good fruit."

only part of the story. Behaviors like self-control flow out of those who carry around in their bodies the death of Jesus and have crucified the flesh. A shared memory and a new belonging work together, along with the new life of the Spirit, to give believers powerful motivations and effective resources to live in ways that befit a Spirit-indwelt person.

Similarly, the rationale for avoiding the vices in 1 Corinthians 6 is the fact that they are not in keeping with the believers' new identity:

> Or do you not know that *wrongdoers will not inherit the kingdom of God*? Do not be deceived: Neither the sexually immoral nor idolaters nor adulterers nor men who have sex with men nor thieves nor the greedy nor drunkards nor slanderers nor swindlers will inherit the kingdom of God. And that is what some of you were. But *you were washed, you were sanctified, you were justified in the name of the Lord Jesus Christ and by the Spirit of our God.* (1 Cor 6:9–11)

If in Galatians 5 the appeal to our new identity is based on the shared memory of being crucified with Christ, in 1 Corinthians 6 the appeal is to a shared memory of being washed, sanctified, and justified in Jesus's name by God's Spirit, as well as the defining destiny of inheriting the kingdom of God.

Christian teaching recommends being true to yourself, your true self, as someone known by God as his child. As children of God, we are included in God's story and tell Christ's story as our own story, reckoning ourselves as having died with him to self-interest and seeking to live in the light of sharing his glorious future in the kingdom of God. This is seen nowhere more clearly than in Paul's teaching about the Christian life in Colossians 3.

SAMPLE TEXT: COLOSSIANS 3:1–14

In chapter ten, we noted that in Colossians 3:3–4 the identity of believers in Christ is tied up with our shared memory of having died with Christ and our future hope of appearing with him in glory:

> You died [our shared memory], and your life is now hidden with Christ in God. When Christ, who is your life, appears, then you also will appear with him in glory [our defining destiny]. (Col 3:3–4)

To have our life hidden with Christ in God is synonymous with being known by God. Both refer to our personal identity as a gift from God and acknowledge that our lives are kept safe by him.

In this section, we consider how our secret identity relates to our everyday conduct in Colossians 3:1–14. A patient reading of this text will help us to answer the question: How does being known by God as his child and finding our identity in Christ provide moral direction for living?[12] The passage is worth reading in full:

> Since, then, you have been raised with Christ, set your hearts on things above, where Christ is, seated at the right hand of God. Set your minds on things above, not on earthly things. For you died, and your life is now hidden with Christ in God. When Christ, who is your life, appears, then you also will appear with him in glory.
>
> Put to death, therefore, whatever belongs to your earthly nature: sexual immorality, impurity, lust, evil desires and greed, which is idolatry. Because of these, the wrath of God is coming. You used to walk in these ways, in the life you once lived. But now you must also rid yourselves of all such things as these: anger, rage, malice, slander, and filthy language from your lips. Do not lie to each other, since you have taken off your old self with its practices and have put on the new self, which is being renewed in knowledge in the image of its Creator. Here there is no Gentile or Jew, circumcised or uncircumcised, barbarian, Scythian, slave or free, but Christ is all, and is in all.
>
> Therefore, as God's chosen people, holy and dearly loved, clothe yourselves with compassion, kindness, humility, gentleness and patience. Bear with each other and forgive one another if any of you has a grievance against someone. Forgive as the Lord forgave you. And over all these virtues put on love, which binds them all together in perfect unity.

Colossians 3 is full of both profound identity statements for believers in Christ and practical instructions about how to behave. With respect to our *identity*, believers in Christ are those who died with Christ and have been raised with him and whose destiny is tied up with his glorious appearing (vv. 1–4). We have made a break with the life we once lived and have taken off our old selves (vv. 5–9) and have put on our new selves, which involves being renewed in knowledge and in God's image (v. 10). We are God's holy, dearly loved, chosen, and forgiven people (vv. 12–14).

In terms of *conduct*, we are to live lives that are free from sexual immorality, greed, and unwholesome speech (vv. 5–9) and to act tender-heartedly and with love towards each other (vv. 12–14). Paul carries on with further directions for moral living in Colossians 3:15–4:6, with sections on gratitude and prayer and instructions for wives, husbands, children, fathers, slaves, and masters.

Several questions of interpretation must be answered in order to grasp the teaching of Colossians 3 concerning our identity in Christ and its relationship to Christian living:

---

12. The centrality of being God's children to the identity of believers in Colossians can be seen in four references to God as Father (1:2, 3, 12; 3:17) and in their description as "faithful brothers and sisters" in 1:2 (see also references to other believers as siblings in 1:1; 4:7, 9, 15).

First, what does the change of clothes language in Colossians 3:9–10, 12, and 14 signify?

The change of clothes metaphor reinforces the idea that our new identity calls for a new lifestyle. Or, to run with the metaphor, a new identity means sporting "a new look." Any identity brings with it characteristic behaviors, and a change of identity necessarily means a change of behavior. So in verse 9, believers, having "taken off your old self *with its practices*," need to put something on in its place. Having put on the new self, believers must clothe themselves (= behave consistently with that new identity) with compassion, kindness, and so on (v. 12), and "over all these virtues put on love, which binds them all together in perfect unity" (v. 14).[13]

A tradesman wears overalls, not black tie; a firefighter "turnout gear," not shorts and a t-shirt; and a judge wig and robes, not smart casual. In the same way, a child of God must take off the garb of the old self and instead put on love. "Know who you are and dress appropriately" is a good summary of the Christian life.

Second, what are the old and new selves in Colossians 3:9–10? Are they our old and new natures? Or are they some kind of corporate identity? How do they relate to Adam and Christ?

The old and new selves in verses 9 and 10 are not old and new natures, but rather the old humanity associated with Adam and the new humanity associated with Christ.[14] The key to understanding the old self (Greek *ton palaion anthrōpon*) and the new self (*ton neon* [*anthrōpon*]) is to recognize that they are corporate rather than individual concepts. Verse 11 makes this clear: "Here [in the new self] there is no Gentile or Jew, circumcised or uncircumcised, barbarian, Scythian, slave or free, but Christ is all, and is in all." In this light, it would be better to translate the expressions as "old humanity" and "new humanity," which fit the Greek *anthrōpos* (translated "self" in the NIV) and refer to the image of God in verse 11.[15]

For Paul, the old humanity is first of all a reference to Adam, and the new humanity is a reference to Christ. Hence it is no surprise that elsewhere Paul can speak of "clothe yourselves with the Lord Jesus Christ" (Rom 13:14; Gal 3:27; see also chapter eight) as another way of telling his audience to put on the new humanity. It follows too that Christ is your life (Col 3:4) if you have put on the new humanity, another way of speaking about faith in Christ. Adam and Christ, as representatives of

13. Some argue that Paul has baptism in mind in light of Gal 3:27 ("For all of you who were baptized into Christ have clothed yourselves with Christ") and the custom of putting on fresh, white clothes after being baptized. However, the Greek verbs for "taking off" (*apekduomai*) and "putting on" (*enduō*) are commonly used by Paul in a figurative sense (e.g., Rom 13:12, 14; 1 Cor 15:53–54; Eph 4:24; 6:14; Col 2:15; 1 Thess 5:8). Moo adds, "A ritual change of clothes as part of Christian baptism comes from the mid-second century" (Douglas J. Moo, *The Letters to the Colossians and to Philemon*, PNTC [Grand Rapids: Eerdmans, 2008], 266).

14. See the expression "the new man Jesus Christ" in Ignatius, *Ephesians* 20:1.

15. Moo notes that Pauline usage adds further support for this corporate sense: "The language of Colossians 3:11 strongly suggests that the 'new self' is not a part of an individual or even an individual as a whole, but some kind of corporate entity. This suspicion finds strong confirmation in Ephesians 2:15, where Paul speaks of God's intention to incorporate both Jews and gentiles in the church: 'His purpose was to create in himself one new humanity (*kainon anthrōpon*) out of the two, thus making peace' (see also Eph. 4:13). Similarly, we should recall that Romans 6:6 follows closely Paul's discussion of the corporate significance of Adam and Christ in Romans 5:12–21" (*Letters to the Colossians and to Philemon*, 267).

the old and new humanities, are associated with rebellion against God and obedience to God, respectively, and are associated with contrasting lifestyles. Moo is right that

> the contrast of "old self" and "new self" alludes to one of Paul's most fundamental theological conceptions: the contrast between a realm in opposition to God, rooted in Adam's sin and characterized by sin and death, and the new realm, rooted in Christ's death and resurrection and characterized by righteousness and life.[16]

To put on the new humanity is to enter a new sphere of existence in union with Christ.

Third, how does our ongoing renewal in Colossians 3:10 relate to knowledge and to the image of God?

In terms of ongoing behavioral transformation, the new humanity is "being renewed in knowledge and in the image of its Creator" (v. 10). As James Dunn notes:

> Here the exhortation makes more explicit use of the motif of Adam and creation, in terms both of knowledge and of the image of God, an unavoidable allusion to Gen 1:26f. For knowledge was at the heart of humanity's primal failure (Gen 2:17; 3:5, 7), and humankind's failure to act in accordance with their knowledge of God by acknowledging him in worship was the central element in Paul's earlier analysis of the human plight, of "the old self" (Rom 1:21). Renewal in knowledge of God, of the relation implied by that knowledge (see on 1:10), was therefore of first importance for Paul.[17]

The growth in knowledge that is both the goal and means of the renewal in question is knowledge of God and of Christ and also knowledge of ourselves in relation to God and Christ; we are those whose true identities are hidden with Christ in God (Col 3:3). Renewal into the image of God is the outcome of the process, and it is no accident that Paul has already said in the letter that Christ is "the image of the invisible God" (Col 1:15); "It is Christ who supplies the pattern for the renewal of the new self."[18]

Fourth, are the racial, ethnic, cultural, and social distinctions of Colossians 3:11 obliterated or just relativized by Christ?

The new humanity renders obsolete the divisions of the old humanity:

> Here [in the new humanity] there is no Gentile or Jew, circumcised or uncircumcised, barbarian, Scythian, slave or free, but Christ is all, and is in all. (v. 11)

Paul lists eight ways of categorizing human beings that are surpassed by the new humanity in Christ. Jews divided the human race into "Jews" and "gentiles,"

16. Moo, *Letters to the Colossians and to Philemon*, 268.

17. James D. G. Dunn, *The Epistles to the Colossians and to Philemon*, NIGTC (Grand Rapids: Eerdmans, 1996), 225.

18. Moo, *Letters to the Colossians and to Philemon*, 268. See also Rom 8:29a: "Those God foreknew he also predestined to be conformed to the image of his Son."

or "circumcised" and "uncircumcised." Greeks, on the other hand, tended to classify people into Greeks and "barbarians," a derogatory term referring to "a speaker of a strange, unintelligible language."[19] If these first five terms indicate racial, ethnic, and religious divisions, the last two terms in the list which are also a pair, "slave" and "free," pick up the major social or class division of Paul's day. The reason for the appearance of the term "Scythian" in the list is less obvious. It can refer simply to a person from Scythia. However, it is likely that "Scythian" is "an extreme example of a *barbarian*."[20] If barbarians were thought to be culturally inferior, Scythians even more so.[21] The list of eight groups in Colossians 3:11 makes it clear that the racial, ethnic, social, and cultural distinctions of the old humanity are not relevant for the new humanity in Christ.[22]

"Central to Paul's theology is the claim that God's ultimate gift (the gift of Christ) is given regardless of worth—the worth of ethnicity, status, knowledge, gender, or virtue. . . . Grace means not just liberation from individual guilt, but freedom also from prevailing cultural systems of value."

John Barclay[23]

However, it is not the case that such distinctions are removed entirely in the new humanity. The household code in Colossians 3:18–4:1 indicates that "the Christian community is comprised of people who maintain their gender, familial and social identities."[24] Yet such earthly identities are not all-important in the new humanity where people "bear the image of the heavenly man" (1 Cor 15:49b). As Paul concludes at the end of Colossians 3:11, "Christ is all [-important]," and Christ is "in all [believers],"[25] bringing unity to all by giving them all the same high status as God's chosen people, even "slaves," "barbarians," and "Scythians" (see v. 12).

Fifth, according to Colossians 3, how does our identity in Christ give our lives moral direction?

Colossians 3 demonstrates how the identity of believers in Christ gives moral direction to our lives. If authenticity refers to living in accordance with who you are, those whose life is hidden with Christ in God the Father are to put on their new identity and dress accordingly.

To give the Christians in Colossae moral direction, Paul could simply have said the following and no more:

19. Dunn, *Epistles to the Colossians and to Philemon*, 227.

20. Moo, *Letters to the Colossians and to Philemon*, 269. Emphasis original.

21. Dunn states: "That a note of contempt is intended is confirmed by the addition of 'Scythians,' tribes which had settled on the northern coast of the Black Sea and which in earlier centuries had terrorized parts of Asia Minor and the Middle East. Their name was synonymous with crudity, excess, and ferocity. . . . Josephus no doubt cites the common view when he refers to Scythians as 'delighting in murder of people and little different from wild beasts'" (*Contra Apionem* 2:26). GNT quite properly renders the term as 'savages' [in Col 3:11]" (*Epistles to the Colossians and to Philemon*, 226).

22. Paul makes the same point in 1 Cor 12:13 and Gal 3:28 with comparable lists.

23. John Barclay, *Paul and the Gift* (Grand Rapids: Eerdmans, 2015), 435, 567.

24. Moo, *Letters to the Colossians and to Philemon*, 271. See my discussion of the traditional identity markers in chapter three.

25. Greek *en pasin* is neuter and could mean that Christ is "in all" things. However, the context favors taking *pasin* as masculine meaning "in all" people.

> Get rid of sexual immorality, impurity, lust, evil desires, greed, idolatry, anger, rage, malice, slander, filthy language and lying. Instead, show compassion, kindness, humility, gentleness, patience, forbearance, forgiveness and love.

But to read these instructions in isolation from their context is to misread them entirely. For Paul, conduct and character are firmly anchored in our identity in Christ and in our shared memory and defining destiny. This can be seen at a number of levels.

Colossians 3 opens in verses 1–4 with a powerful description of the Christian's secret identity; believers died and rose with Christ, and when the powerful Son of God is revealed in glory, they too will be revealed as God's children. Then in verses 5–14, Paul gives instructions for Christian living. How the two sections are related is made clear by the word "therefore" at the beginning of verse 5: "Put to death, *therefore*, whatever belongs to your earthly nature: sexual immorality, impurity," and so on. Christians are to infer from their heavenly identity that they must put to death what belongs to their earthly nature.[26] The behavior that Paul enjoins in Colossians 3:5–14 is a logical inference of the identity that Paul describes in 3:1–4.[27]

In Colossians 3, our new identity as those who died and rose with Christ and whose life is now hidden with Christ in God gives moral direction to our lives. However, the focus is not merely on our present identity. Should you be true to yourself? Believers in Christ are to live out their new identity by looking in three directions:

Christian Self-Expression

1. The Future—*Be who you will be in Christ*—As one who died and rose with Christ, and will appear with Christ in glory, behave in a Christ-like manner (Col 3:1–4).
2. The Past—*Be who you were intended to be*—As a member of the new humanity, which is being renewed in the image of God, rid yourself of sexual immorality, anger, and lies (Col 3:5–11).
3. The Present—*Be who you are in Christ*—As a child of God, "holy and dearly loved," put on compassion, kindness, humility, gentleness, patience, and love (Col 3:12–14).

Should we be true to ourselves? According to Colossians 3, Christians are to live in accordance with our new identity in Christ.

26. We could translate the Greek word in question, *oun*, "so, therefore, consequently, accordingly, [or] then" (BDAG 736) to bring out the logical connection between the two sections. The same logic appears in verses 9 and 10 in connection with the memory of conversion to Christ: "Do not lie to each other, since you have taken off the old self with its practices and have put on the new self."

27. The vices and virtues that Paul lists are attached to two identities: "the life you once lived [Greek *zaō*]" (Col 3:7; see also 2:20b) and "your life [*zōē*] now hidden with Christ in God" (3:3–4). The two contrasting identities that Paul sets up both have a defining destiny that shapes their respective conduct. The conduct of believers, on the one hand, is formed by the prospect of appearing with Christ in glory (3:4). The behavior of unbelievers, on the other hand, is marked by the wrath of God that is coming upon them (3:6).

DEFINING MOMENTS AND SIGNATURE MOVES

A *defining moment* is a point at which the essential character of a person is established. It is an *identity-forming* event, something that makes someone who they are and flows through to their behavior. It can be an achievement or a failure, something you do or something done to or for you. It can also be something that happened before you were born, such as some national event or family experience.

Authenticity is living in accordance with your defining moment and performing your signature move.

A *signature move*, on the other hand, is behavior that sums up and expresses a person's identity. Its performance distills someone's character. It is a repeated action that has "your name written all over it." It is not necessarily original to you, but doing it is the purest expression of who you really are.

Both concepts regularly appear in discussions about the lives and achievements of prominent individuals. Sports stars often seek to define themselves with reference to some crowning achievement and by some move for which they have become famous and will be remembered. Both are also of relevance to understanding groups of people who have shared experiences of one sort or another:

- A defining moment of people born in the 1920s might be growing up in the Great Depression of the 1930s. Accordingly, one of their signature moves throughout their lives would be thrift and frugality.
- A defining moment for Mohandas Gandhi was his part in the 1930 "Salt March," a nonviolent protest against the British salt monopoly in India. Accordingly, his signature move became passive resistance, which against all the odds led to Indian sovereignty and self-rule.
- A defining moment for Mohammed Ali was winning the world heavyweight boxing title against George Foreman in 1974 in Zaire, the so-called "Rumble in the Jungle." Accordingly, his signature move was feats of against-the-odds athletic prowess, or to borrow a line from one of his poems, "floating like a butterfly and stinging like a bee."
- A defining moment for Nancy Reagan was her "Just Say No" speech. Accordingly, her signature move was steely determination.
- A defining moment for Margaret Thatcher was her response to the Falklands Crisis. Accordingly, her signature move became expressions of courageous fortitude.
- A defining moment for Barack Obama was his "Yes We Can" speech. Accordingly, his signature move was optimistic action on tough issues.
- A defining moment for Nelson Mandela was his unjust twenty-seven year imprisonment, principally on Robben Island. Accordingly, and perhaps surprisingly, his signature move was the posture of forgiveness and reconciliation.

- A defining moment for Marilyn Monroe was singing "Happy Birthday" to President John F. Kennedy. Accordingly, her signature move was attention-grabbing actions and performances.

What events define you? And what signature moves express your identity and character?

I could point to several defining events in my life: My upbringing in working-class Sydney, my father's Austrian heritage, becoming a father, and the opportunity of a Cambridge University education have all undoubtedly left their mark. I'm sure that all of these things have flowed through to my identity, attitudes, and behaviors. Some of the consequences of those "moments" might be my ability to relate to people of all backgrounds, my taste for wiener schnitzel and enjoyment of the odd game of chess, my fondness for "dad jokes," and my love of learning.

But in the deepest sense, the core identity of being known by God as his children and being in union with Christ brings its own defining moment and signature move. According to Colossians 3, the defining moment of all believers in Jesus Christ is something that happened two thousand years ago: we died and rose to new life in union with Christ (Col 3:1–4). It is that "moment of truth," the memory of which defines us forever. It changes everything for us. And we would not be who we are were it not for Christ's death and resurrection.

"The secure attachment of being known by God as his child fosters moral development and a direction towards others that is characterized by a propensity for forgiveness and a more humble understanding of one's own and other's frailties."

Loyola McLean and Brian Rosner[28]

And the signature move that grows out of that identity is acts of love. Our conduct is to be compassionate, kind, humble, gentle, patient, and forgiving, all of which grow out of "love, which binds them all together in perfect unity" (Col 3:14). Just as our identity as children of God was forged through an act of amazing love, so too we are to live lives of costly, selfless, other-centered love. The defining moment of believers in Christ is our identification with the death and resurrection of Jesus, the ultimate expression of God's love. Accordingly, our signature move is putting on love.

Indeed, the cross of Jesus Christ is the key not only to who we are, but also to how we must behave. If Jesus said to love God with all your heart and to love your neighbor as yourself (Luke 10:27), too often we seem to have things upside down: us first, our neighbor when convenient, and God what's left. Our new identity in Christ sets us on a different course:

> I have been crucified with Christ and I no longer live, but Christ lives in me. *The life I now live* in the body, I live by faith in the Son of God, who loved me and gave himself for me. (Gal 2:20)

28. Loyola McLean and Brian S. Rosner, "Theology and Human Flourishing: The Benefits of Being Known by God," in *Beyond Well-Being: Spirituality and Human Flourishing*, ed. Maureen Miner, Martin Dowson, and Stuart Devenish (Charlotte, NC: Information Age Publishing, 2012), 79.

Christ died not only as our substitute, to secure our forgiveness with God, but as our representative. In Christ, we died to living purely for self-interest. Jesus's death sets an unforgettable example of loving sacrifice as the pattern for our lives. But it's more than just an example that he has set. By faith we believe that we have died with him. The direction of our lives is set by that defining moment. Living authentically then becomes the task of living in accordance with our new identity and regularly performing our signature move.

> "Paul's metaphor of adoption for salvation . . . is a biblical metaphor that shows us an astonishing state of affairs: the high King, the Lord of the Universe, desires for us to be his adopted children. Thus, while God is holy and transcendent, he is not at a convenient distance. God's gracious, loving call is, in fact, a threat to our autonomy, our deep and pervasive strategies to keep hold of our lives rather than losing them for the sake of Christ."
>
> *J. Todd Billings*[29]

It is not that other identity markers and what you do with your life are of no consequence for your personal identity if you are a believer in Christ. Your race, gender, family, occupation, marital status, and so on are important, but they are not all-important (see chapter three). Obviously, life events and experiences can have a lasting impact on your identity and conduct. But at the most profound level, if you are a believer in Jesus Christ, what sets the course for your life and keeps it on track is your identification with Christ and imitation of him, and being known and loved by God as his child. Putting on that identity will determine the sort of man or woman, worker, friend, neighbor, father or mother, and son or daughter that you will become.

RELEVANT QUESTIONS

1. In terms of identity, what are both the positive and negative aspects of the current emphasis on living "authentically"?
2. As well as having your identity drive your behaviour, your behaviour can also alter your identity. Discuss this.
3. Belonging to Christ and participating in both his death and resurrection by the Spirit leads to changed behavior. Have you seen evidence of the work of the Holy Spirit—his presence and activity—in your life?
4. What is a "defining moment" in your life? Do you have a "signature move" that expresses your identity and character? Does the fact that your personal identity is a gift from God and your life is kept safe by him change your perception of these in any way?

29. J. Todd Billings, *Union with Christ: Reframing Theology and Ministry for the Church* (Grand Rapids: Baker, 2011), 21.

CHAPTER 15

KNOWN BY GOD

This book began by reflecting on the theme of personal identity in today's world. In our day, identity is a do-it-yourself project. However, despite the attractive possibilities this opens up, many factors weigh against constructing a stable and satisfying sense of self. These include relationship breakdown, the pace of modern life, the rise of social media, multiple careers, social mobility, and so on. Even the fact of living longer, with more years in retirement, makes knowing who you are more of a challenge. Ours is a day of identity angst. The frequent call to authenticity and being true to yourself seems more like a cruel taunt than a piece of realistic advice. Chapter one concludes on a pessimistic note: it is harder to know who you are today than at any point in human history.

To make matters worse, in chapter three we saw that the Bible judges the standard markers of human identity (race, gender, occupation, and so on) to be inadequate foundations upon which to build our lives. Not only are they insecure and not designed to bear too much weight, the conditions of life "under the sun" are such that these foundations crack in the heat. The world is an unjust place; the human heart is easily deceived and prone to evil; and in the end, death robs us of our accomplishments.

A BIBLICAL THEOLOGY OF PERSONAL IDENTITY

Where then should we look to answer the question of personal identity? This book's biblical theology of personal identity is built on the observation that human beings are inherently social and that we know who we are in relation to others and by being known by others. In fact, I argue that rather than knowing ourselves, ultimately being known by God is the key to personal identity. If one of the universal desires of the self is to be acknowledged and known by others, then being known by God as his children meets our deepest and lifelong need for recognition and gives us a secure identity.

In part two (chs. 2–10), we saw that the Bible's most complete answer to the question of personal identity for believers in Christ is that we are God's children. The three angles on personal identity that we explored each point to this same reality: (1) we are made in the image of God as his offspring (ch. 5); (2) we are known personally and intimately by God as his children (chs. 6 and 7); and (3) we are in union with Christ the Son of God (ch. 8) and find our identity in Christ, who is our life (chs.

9 and 10). We are defined by our memory of dying and rising with Christ, and our secret identity as children of God will be revealed when the Son of God is revealed in glory. God gives us our identity just like a parent who knows their child. As those who bear the family likeness, he calls us by name, remembers us constantly, and loves us unconditionally.

"Those who are victorious will inherit all this, and I will be their God and *they will be my children.*"
Revelation 21:7

Being known by God as his child has many practical benefits in the present. In one sense the whole of this book has been my personal testimony. At a point of crisis in my own life, discovering that God knows me gave me a sense of significance and value, provoked in me needed humility, supplied cheering comfort, and offered clear direction for how to live. In the previous four chapters in part three (chs. 11 to 14), I explored these four benefits and sought to show how the Bible promises each of them to those who are known by God.

KNOWING YOURSELF AS YOU ARE KNOWN

To close this book, I wish to give some practical advice in connection with the identity of being known by God. This is by no means a "how to" book. Having spent so many pages arguing against finding, defining, or designing yourself, it would be odd to end by telling you how to do it! If anything, it is more of a "how not to" book. If the identity of being known by God as his child and being in Christ is a gift, what is there left for us to do?

As with any gift, receiving the gift of sonship is not the end of the story. We need to take full possession of our new identity. We need to "put it on" to enjoy the significance and comfort it affords, embrace the humility it promotes, and follow the direction it provides. If we find our identity in being known by God, we need to know ourselves as we are known.

The basic disciplines of the Christian life are undertaken for a number of reasons. We pray, read the Bible, take communion, and so on to commune with God and to know him better, to align ourselves with what he is doing in the world, to please and obey him, to be built up in our faith, to serve and encourage others, and so on. However, a neglected function of such activities is self-knowledge. Establishing our identity is not the sole or main aim of these disciplines. But as it turns out, many of the regular activities of the Christian life also serve to confirm our true identity.

There are at least eight things to do if you want to know yourself as you are known by God:

1. Get baptized
2. Attend family gatherings
3. Read and hear the Bible

4. Pray to your heavenly Father
5. Sing the faith
6. Say the Creed
7. Take communion
8. Live the gospel

Known by God

= Belonging to God
= Chosen by God
= Child of God
= Known by Christ
= Remembered by God
= Your name known to God
= Your name written in heaven
= Your name written in the book of life
= Your life hidden with Christ in God
= Union with Christ

Get Baptized

Christian baptism is a rite of initiation into the body of Christ and a public recognition of a person's new identity in relation to Christ. Jesus's own baptism by John the Baptist, where God confirmed that Jesus was his beloved Son, served a similar purpose.

Notwithstanding the important debates among Christians concerning who should be baptized and how and what happens to the person being baptized, we may summarize New Testament teaching about the significance of baptism under three headings. All three relate directly to confirming our identity in Christ. Baptism speaks of a *joining*, a *journey*, and *joy*.[1]

First, baptism signifies a past *joining* to Christ. Paul states in Romans 6:3–4:

> Don't you know that all of us who were baptized into Christ Jesus were baptized into his death? We were therefore buried with him through baptism into death in order that, just as Christ was raised from the dead through the glory of the Father, we too may live a new life.

Paul teaches that the believer's identification with Christ in his death and resurrection is symbolized in the act of baptism whereby being lowered into the water signifies dying with Christ and coming up again out of the water signifies rising to new life in him. Similarly, Peter compares baptism to being incorporated into the body of Christ and joined to the risen Christ: just as the eight people entered Noah's ark and were "saved through water, [so also] this water symbolizes baptism that now saves you" (1 Pet 3:20–21). Baptism marks us out as people who are joined to Christ.

Second, baptism signifies a present *journeying* with Christ. Along with initiation into the Christian life, baptism speaks of our ongoing life in Christ. "Therefore we have been buried with him by baptism into death, so that, just as Christ was raised from the dead by the glory of the Father, so we too might walk in newness of life" (Rom 6:4 NRSV). Baptism is associated with receiving the Holy Spirit for a new life of obedience, following "the washing of rebirth and renewal by the Holy Spirit"

1. I owe this basic schema to my colleague Rhys Bezzant. The following discussion builds on his unpublished Ridley College lecture notes.

Note the connection between being baptized, being children of God, and being in union with Christ in this seventeenth-century Christian liturgy:

> "And as for you, who have now by Baptism put on Christ, it is your part and duty also, *being made the children of God* and of the light by faith in Jesus Christ, to walk answerably to your Christian calling, and as becometh the children of light; remembering always that Baptism representeth unto us our profession; which is, to follow the example of our Saviour Christ, and *to be made like unto him; that as he died, and rose again for us; so should we, who are baptized, die from sin, and rise again unto righteousness;* continually mortifying all our evil and corrupt affections, and daily proceeding in all virtue and godliness of living."
>
> *The 1662 Book of Common Prayer*[4]

(Titus 3:5). Being baptized reminds us of our need to put on Christ and to imitate him in everyday life.

And thirdly, baptism signifies future *joy* because of Christ. In baptism, we celebrate the fact that we are safe from the waters of judgment in the ark of Christ (1 Pet 3:20–22). We have escaped the coming judgment and wrath of God,[2] grateful that Jesus drank the cup of God's wrath for us and was baptized with the "baptism" unto death on a cross (Mark 10:38).[3] In being baptized, we remember our defining destiny, anticipating our own resurrection from the dead in the age to come: "If we have been united with him in a death like his, we will certainly also be united with him in a resurrection like his" (Rom 6:5).

What does being baptized say about who you are? Baptism is a symbolic action that signifies our past joining to Christ in his death and resurrection, our present journeying with Christ in a new life of obedience, and our future resurrection with Christ in his glorious kingdom. Whenever we witness a baptism, it summons us to recall our own baptism and to cherish the shared memory and defining destiny that form our identity in Christ.

Attend Family Gatherings

Irregular church attendance is nothing new, as Hebrews attests:

> Therefore, brothers and sisters, since we have confidence to enter the Most Holy Place by the blood of Jesus. . . . Let us hold unswervingly to the hope we profess, for he who promised is faithful. And let us consider how we may spur one another on toward love and good deeds, *not giving up meeting together, as some are in the habit of doing,* but encouraging one another—and all the more as you see the Day approaching. (Heb 10:19, 23–25)

The way in which the exhortation not to give up meeting together is framed in this passage says something about the purpose and nature of such meetings. Note first

2. See also Acts 2:38, which associates baptism with forgiveness: "Repent and be baptized, every one of you, in the name of Jesus Christ for the forgiveness of your sins. And you will receive the gift of the Holy Spirit."

3. BDAG defines the Greek *baptisma* here in the metaphorical sense of "an extraordinary experience akin to an initiatory purification rite, *a plunge* . . . a metaphor of martyrdom Mk 10:38f" (165).

4. Closing charge for service of adult baptism, "The Ministration of Publick Baptism to Such as are of Riper Years, and Able to Answer for Themselves." Emphasis added.

of all who is being addressed: "Therefore, *brothers and sisters.*" As we saw in chapter nine, being siblings in the family of God is a major focus of a biblical theology of personal identity. It is in fact one of the best answers to the question, "Who are we?" The readers of Hebrews are urged to meet to encourage and love each other as those who share the deep bond of being adopted as God's children.

The passage also gives us some clues as to the character of such meetings, which once again relate to our identity as the people of God. Along with meeting for the purpose of mutual care and support, Christians meet to remember two things in particular: "the blood of Jesus" (Heb 10:19) and "the Day approaching" (10:25). We meet to be reminded of the gospel, our shared memory of Christ's death for us, and our defining destiny with him. Attending family gatherings helps us to "hold unswervingly to the hope we profess" (10:23). Church attendance confirms and strengthens our identity as those known by God as his children.

As it turns out, the constituent elements of church services likewise remind us of who we are in relation to God. These elements include Bible reading and preaching from the Bible, prayer, singing, saying the creed, and taking communion. The following sections examine these in turn to show the way in which each one reminds us of our true identity.

Read and Hear the Bible

Why should we read the Bible? Why listen to sermons where the Bible is preached? The best way to relate to the Bible is to allow it to shape our faith, life, worship, and service. This includes everything from private prayers to political engagement. The Bible can be a subversive and unsettling text, as well as comforting and reassuring. At root, it seeks to transform all our relationships, not only with God, but also with families, enemies and friends, and society as a whole. In addition, the Bible transforms our relationship with ourselves. A good reason to read the Bible is for self-knowledge.

Although the Bible is a collection of historical documents addressed to God's people at different stages of salvation history, *the Bible was also written for you and to you.* Jesus prays in John 17:20 not for his disciples alone but "also for those who will believe in me through their message." Paul writes not only to "the church of God in Corinth," but to them "together with all those everywhere who call on the name of our Lord Jesus Christ" (1 Cor 1:2). And John addresses "those who keep God's commands and hold fast their testimony about Jesus" (Rev 12:17).[5] While it is a mistake to ignore the Bible's historical context, it is equally wrong to forget that Scripture was written "also for us" (Rom 4:24; see also 1 Cor 9:10).

---

5. Brian S. Rosner, "Biblical Theology," in *New Dictionary of Biblical Theology*, ed. T. D. Alexander and B. S. Rosner (Downers Grove, IL: InterVarsity Press, 2000), 5.

The Bible knows the human condition. Its many genres include instructions for every age group, condition, and circumstance, including young and old, happy and sad, rich and poor. It knows us inside out and from every angle, including body, soul, spirit, mind, and heart. It addresses our desires and yearnings, our frustrations and sorrows. And given that it was written in ancient times, its insights into modern human behavior are uncanny. The Bible, we might say, has "high emotional intelligence." Paul, for example, tells fathers not to exasperate their children; those undertaking deeds of mercy are to do so with cheerfulness; those showing hospitality are not to grumble; those in dispute are not to judge or despise each other, and so on.[6] As John Dickson observes, "this book knows us."[7]

"The word of God is alive and active. Sharper than any double-edged sword, it penetrates even to dividing soul and spirit, joints and marrow; it judges the thoughts and attitudes of the heart."

Hebrews 4:12[8]

Furthermore, *the Bible tells the human story.* From our creation as God's offspring in the garden, through our ruinous rebellion, to God's determination to set things right, the human story, "warts and all," is the main plot of the Bible's larger narrative. And the history of Israel as God's chosen people, from the covenant promises to Abraham, the Law to Moses, the conquest, and kingship to the exile and return, is the backstory of every believer's narrative identity. The same history is the heritage of belivers in Christ, both Jews and gentiles. Paul writes to the Christians in Corinth concerning "our ancestors" (1 Cor 10:1), referring to the history of the nation Israel. Matthew opens the New Testament with a genealogy that demonstrates the continuity of "Jesus the Messiah, the son of David, the son of Abraham" (Matt 1:1) with the story of Israel. And with the coming of Christ, the second Adam and the climax of biblical prophecy, the human story takes a long-awaited and decisive turn.

In addition, *the Bible tells us who we are and also who we aren't.* From cover to cover, God tells his people who they are: made in the image of God (Gen 1:26–27); a chosen people, a royal priesthood (1 Peter 2:9); wonderfully made (Ps 139:14), the apple of God's eye (Zech 2:8); the light of the world, the salt of the earth, a city on a hill (Matt 5:13–14); the temple of the Holy Spirit (1 Cor 3:16; 6:19), the body of Christ (1 Cor 12:27); a new creation (2 Cor 5:17); a child of God (Gal 3:26), known by God (Gal 4:6–7).

Equally, God reminds his people that they are not among those who do not know God, who are darkened in their understanding, separated from the life of God, children of wrath and disobedience.[9] If with Adam we were banished as rebellious children and experience death before death, in Scripture we hear God say to all of

6. Examples could easily be multiplied from other parts of the Bible. See especially the timeless wisdom of Proverbs.

7. John Dickson, *A Doubter's Guide to the Bible: Inside History's Bestseller for Believers and Skeptics* (Grand Rapids: Zondervan, 2014), 201.

8. Note the way in which the Word of God is said to pierce several aspects of our persona: soul, spirit, body (joints and marrow), and heart.

9. See Eph 4:17–18.

those who believe in Jesus Christ, both males and females, what he said to Jesus Christ at his baptism: "You are my beloved son, in whom I am well pleased" (Matt 3:17; Mark 1:11; Luke 3:22).

Even if the Bible's teaching about humanity "is implicit and derivative, not explicit and foundational,"[10] almost every page contributes to self-knowledge. It provides satisfying answers to three of life's most fundamental questions: What is a human being? Who am I? Who are we? Reading the Bible is like looking in a mirror: it reminds you who you are.[11]

As well as reading the Bible's larger narrative to learn the backstory of your life, in great gulps if you like, there are many small morsels to chew on that speak directly to the question of personal identity. Consider the following examples that have occupied much of our attention in this book:

- "You are not your own" (1 Cor 6:19b).
- "Your life is hidden with Christ in God" (Col 3:3).
- "Christ ... is your life" (Col 3:4a).
- "Now I know in part; then I shall know fully, even as I am fully known" (1 Cor 13:12b).
- "Formerly, when you did not know God, you were slaves . . . now that you know God—or rather are known by God" (Gal 4:8–9).
- "Do not rejoice that the spirits submit to you, but rejoice that your names are written in heaven" (Luke 10:20).

Pray to Your Heavenly Father

No one finds praying easy. In Romans, Paul is realistic about the difficulty of prayer and spells out why praying is so difficult:

> In the same way, the Spirit helps us in our weakness. We do not know what we ought to pray for, but the Spirit himself intercedes for us through wordless groans. And he who searches our hearts knows the mind of the Spirit, because the Spirit intercedes for God's people in accordance with the will of God. (Rom 8:26–27)

In order to pray effectively, we need God's help not only to overcome our weakness, but also our ignorance: "We do not know what we ought to pray for" (v. 26). And God facilitates our prayers not only through helping us in our weakness but also by knowing our heart (v. 27); that is, our deepest emotions, thoughts, and desires. In Matthew 6:8, Jesus makes the same point just before giving a model prayer to his disciples: "Your Father knows what you need before you ask him." Being known by God makes prayer possible.

Just as prayer is possible because we are known by God, so also our experience of being known by God is facilitated by prayer. The Lord's Prayer demonstrates the role prayer plays in recalling and rehearsing key aspects of our identity. We do not simply pray to receive good gifts from God. The act of prayer reminds us who we are in relation to God:

10. Kevin Vanhoozer, "Human Being, Individual and Social," in *The Cambridge Companion to Christian Doctrine*, ed. Colin E. Gunton (Cambridge: Cambridge University Press, 1997), 159.

11. See Jas 1:23–24.

Our Father in heaven,
hallowed be your name,
your kingdom come,
your will be done,
  on earth as it is in heaven.
Give us today our daily bread.
And forgive us our debts,
  as we also have forgiven our debtors.
And lead us not into temptation,
  but deliver us from the evil one. (Matt 6:9–13)

Praying the Lord's Prayer is an exercise in knowing ourselves as we are known by God. It reminds us *to whom we belong, what we are a part of, what we need, and where we are headed.*

We pray to "Our Father in heaven," and we belong to him. Praying to God as our Father brings to mind the sonship of Adam, Israel, and David and our own adoption as God's children. It also reminds us of Jesus's intimate and familial approach to God. As we saw in chapter nine, the Sermon on the Mount (Matthew 5–7), at the center of which stands the Lord's Prayer, connects God as the Father of Jesus and God as the Father of Jesus's disciples. Fifteen times, Jesus speaks of "your Father" or "our Father" before he refers at the end of the sermon to "my Father who is in heaven" (Matt 7:21). Here he teaches us to pray, "Our Father in heaven." Fundamentally in Matthew, Jesus is the Son of God. And when we pray to our heavenly Father, we share in his identity as God's children and identify ourselves as part of his family.

"In prayer we rightly seek the joy which the presence of the Spirit brings, the knowledge of the Father and the Son. Yet the highest goal of prayer is not to claim the Lord as our inheritance, *but to be claimed by him as his own.*"

Ed Clowney[12]

"Prayer is the only entryway into genuine self-knowledge."

Timothy Keller[13]

The first petition of the Lord's Prayer, "your kingdom come" (Matt 6:9), reminds us of the central theme of Jesus's proclamation. To pray for God's kingdom to come means to pledge allegiance to the rule of the one true God and to embrace the agenda of that rule as set out in the rest of the Sermon on the Mount. It is also to locate your life in the narrative of God's unfolding plan.

Likewise, to pray "your will be done, on earth as it is in heaven" (6:10) is to pray for the integration of earth and heaven through that kingdom, with its many implications for love and justice that God's reign brings. It is to live now in the light

12. Edmund P. Clowney, "Prayer," in *New Dictionary of Biblical Theology* (Downers Grove, IL: InterVarsity Press, 2000), 691. Emphasis added.

13. Timothy Keller, *Prayer: Experiencing Awe and Intimacy with God* (London: Hodder and Stoughton, 2014), 18.

of your defining destiny. Implicitly, it is a renunciation of both self-assertion and the desire to build your own kingdom.

To ask God to "give us today our daily bread" (Matt 6:11) is an admission that our lives are in God's hands and that he knows how to give good gifts to his children. It is no accident that the next topic in the Sermon on the Mount that Jesus addresses concerns money and greed. Praying the Lord's Prayer reminds us that our lives do not consist of food and clothes (6:25) and that we worship God and not money (6:24).

"The church that prays the Lord's Prayer claims the status of the eschatological people of God. In so praying, it locates itself between Calvary, Easter, and Pentecost, on the one hand, and the great consummation, on the other hand. *The Lord's Prayer is thus a marker, a reminder, to the church of who it is and why.*"

N. T. Wright[14]

The petition to "forgive us our debts, as we also have forgiven our debtors" (Matt 6:12) brings both comfort and a challenge. It reminds us of our status as forgiven sinners, forever grateful that "the Son of Man has authority on earth to forgive sins" (Matt 9:6). We are not those who are too proud to admit our wrongdoing. On the other hand, the inner connection between being forgiven and forgiving others goes to the heart of our character. As Jesus taught in the parable of the unmerciful servant (Matt 18:21–35), we are to forgive from the heart and "seventy-seven times" if necessary.

"The Lord's Prayer marks out Jesus's followers as a distinct group not simply because Jesus gave it to them, but because it encapsulates his own mission and vocation."

N. T. Wright[15]

Finally, the request "lead us not into temptation [Greek *peirasmos*], but deliver us from the evil one" (Matt 6:13) reminds us of our inherent weakness and vulnerability and the extent of our need for God. As John Nolland suggests, it is a request "to be spared times of great pressure, times which would prove very trying. . . . [and] reflects a sense of one's own frailty and limitation."[16] To be delivered from the evil one is a reminder of Jesus's own temptation, and of Adam and Eve's disastrous transgression. As Craig Keener notes, "testing with a view to bringing people to succumb was the business of the 'evil one' (6:13b), a characteristic Matthean title for the devil."[17]

This final petition is another reminder that the Lord's Prayer is an invitation to share the priorities and pattern of life of Jesus: "In giving this prayer, Jesus is inviting his followers to share his own struggles and to experience the same spirituality that sustained him."[18] As Jesus says to his disciples at the Last Supper, "You are those who have stood by me in my trials [Greek *en tois peirasmois mou*]" (Luke 22:28). In short, the Lord's Prayer reminds us that our identity is found in Christ.

14. N. T. Wright, "The Lord's Prayer as a Paradigm of Christian Prayer," in *Into God's Presence: Prayer in the New Testament*, ed. R. L. Longenecker (Grand Rapids: Eerdmans, 2001), 148, emphasis added.

15. Ibid., 150.

16. John Nolland, *The Gospel of Matthew: A Commentary on the Greek Text*, NIGTC (Grand Rapids: Eerdmans, 2005), 292.

17. Craig S. Keener, *The Gospel of Matthew: A Socio-Rhetorical Commentary* (Grand Rapids: Eerdmans, 2009), 223. See also Matt 5:37; 13:19, 38.

18. Wright, "The Lord's Prayer as a Paradigm of Christian Prayer," 138.

Sing the Faith

Singing in the Bible serves many purposes. There are songs of praise and thanksgiving, of joy and celebration, of victory and deliverance, and also of sadness and mourning. One thing is clear: believers in Christ are singers. Being filled with the message of Christ and the Spirit of God leads us to "teach and admonish one another with all wisdom through psalms, hymns, and songs from the Spirit, *singing to God* with gratitude in your hearts" (Col 3:16; see also Eph 5:18–19).

One of the main functions of singing is to reinforce our identity as people who belong to God. Consider two of the most famous songs in the Bible. The first is the Song of Moses and the Israelites in Exodus 15, sung to the Lord after the exodus deliverance: "I will sing to the Lord, for he is highly exalted. Both horse and driver he has hurled into the sea" (15:1). Along with celebrating the incomparability of God—"Who among the gods is like you, Lord?" (15:11)—and his victory over his adversaries, those who sing the song identify themselves as those redeemed and loved by God (15:13) and as God's people purchased by him (15:16).

Similarly in the new song of the four living creatures and the twenty-four elders in Revelation 5, praise directed to the worthiness of the Lamb spills over into a recognition and celebration of the identity of God's people:

> You are worthy to take the scroll
>   and to open its seals,
> because you were slain,
>   and with your blood you purchased for God
>   persons from every tribe and language and people and nation.
> You have made them to be a kingdom and priests to serve our God,
>   and they will reign on the earth. (Rev 5:9–10)

Singing simultaneously offers praise to God and reinforces the identity of God's people. In this new song, we are those whom God has redeemed, gathered from the ends of the earth, a kingdom of priests defined by our common destiny of reigning with Christ on earth.

The idea that singing is connected to identity is not unique to the Bible. In his book *The Singing Thing*, John L. Bell argues that songs have always been the means whereby people created or celebrated their identity. Many such songs are distinctive to particular cultural or sub-cultural groups:[19]

> The study of ethno-musicology has charted how different parts of the world have indigenous scales in which their peculiar melodies are written. Indeed, in parts of China there are specific combinations of sounds which are believed

19. See chapter three.

to have moral quality, as they signify good and evil. Some of these scales and some tunes from other cultures may be awkward for us to sing. In short, the singing of songs can be a tribal activity.[20]

National anthems and songs are obvious examples of the way in which singing creates and reinforces identity. Nothing prompts Americans to reflect on and own their national identity more than singing "The Star-Spangled Banner." The songs of sporting teams are also powerful expressions of group identity that sharply differentiate one group from another. Think of a Welsh crowd at a rugby international competition or Liverpool football supporters singing "You Never Walk Alone." Singing stirs the emotions and engages the whole person.

When it comes to Christians singing, Mike Raiter and Rob Smith go even further and argue that "singing creates a world":

> The songs we sing as Christians remind us of the different reality of which we are a part. They remind us of the truths of the gospel and therefore, implicitly, expose and undermine the lies of Satan and the world. And *these songs which we sing together reinforce our identity.* When Christians of different backgrounds come together, there are certain songs that immediately we all participate in and give us a sense of a common identity and heritage.[21]

Singing is one means by which we inhabit our destiny as God's people. We confirm that we belong to a different world. In this sense, singing can be a deeply subversive activity, asserting that our ultimate allegiance lies outside of the dominant narrative identities of our day.

> "Vaclav Havel, a playwright who was also the president of the Czech Republic, was asked how the revolution to overthrow communism in the Czech Republic was bloodless and yet had experienced real staying power. He simply replied, 'We had our parallel society. And in that parallel society, we wrote our plays and *sang our songs* and read our poems, until we knew the truth so well that we could go out into the streets of Prague and say, "We don't believe your lies anymore!" And communism had to fall. *The songs created a parallel society which gave people a vision for their future.* It's been said that, "You can make all the laws you want. Let me have a nation's music and I will rule that nation's hearts."'"
>
> *Mike Raiter and Rob Smith*[22]

Say the Creed

The use of succinct statements to encapsulate what we believe has a long pedigree in the Bible:

> The OT depicts the people of God confessing truths about Him and then offering their allegiance to him. Deuteronomy 6:4–25 calls for Israel to confess the truth about God (His oneness) and salvation (deliverance from pharaoh's armies), and then to offer allegiance to Him in terms of personal devotion (love

20. Mike Raiter and Rob Smith, *Singing the Faith.* Forthcoming book, emphases added.

21. Ibid., emphasis added.

22. Ibid., emphasis added.

> Him with all your heart, v. 5), passing on the heritage of God's message (teach [the commands] diligently to your children, v. 7), be always remembering God's word (vv. 8–10), telling the story of their deliverance to the next generation (vv. 20–25). This passage has for centuries served a confession used regularly in Jewish homes.[23]

The New Testament witnesses to the use of the words "Jesus is Lord" as an early confession of allegiance to the risen Christ (Rom 10:9; 1 Cor 12:3; Phil 2:11). And although scholars debate their significance, there are several other examples of statements in the New Testament that summarize early Christian belief, including Philippians 2:5–11; Colossians 1:15–20; 1 Timothy 3:16; Hebrews 1:1–3; 1 Peter 3:18–22; 1 John 4:2; and 2 John 7. Following these biblical precedents, many churches include reciting a creed as an affirmation of faith in their regular services.

Why do churches say a creed? There are many reasons: to teach doctrine, to underscore our links with Christians of all ages and across denominations, to worship God, and to combat heresy. A neglected purpose is to affirm our identity as the people of God. As Michael Bird puts it,

> The creeds remind us who we are as Christians and that we are part of God's plan to gather his people around himself and to bring all of his children into his new creation.[24]

In affirming that we are part of the story of God, Christians at the same time deny that we are part of another story. As N. T. Wright notes, when we recite a creed we affirm that

> we are renewed as *this people*, the people who live within *this* great story, the people who are identified precisely as people-of-this-story, rather than as people of one of the many other stories that claim for attention all around.[25]

Matt Chandler makes the same point with reference to the Apostles' Creed, arguably the best-known and most widely used creed in our day:

> When the early church recited [the Apostles' Creed], it was simultaneously their greatest act of rebellion and their greatest act of allegiance. When the church gathered and they stood . . . they rejected the popular narratives of their day, whatever their day was.
>
> So in Rome they rejected that Caesar was lord. They rejected the narrative

23. Chad Brand with Norman Stan, "Confessions and Credos," in *Holman Illustrated Bible Dictionary*, ed. C. Brand, C. Draper, A. England (Nashville: Holman, 2003), 328.

24. Michael F. Bird, *What Christians Ought to Believe: An Introduction to Christian Doctrine through the Apostles' Creed* (Grand Rapids: Zondervan, 2016), 40.

25. N. T. Wright, "Reading Paul, Thinking Scripture," in *Scripture's Doctrine and Theology's Bible: How the New Testament Shapes Christian Dogmatics*, ed. M. Bockmuehl and A. J. Torrance (Grand Rapids: Baker, 2008), 64, emphases original.

> of the first century and said, "No, no, no. I reject that. I believe that Jesus is Lord." . . . They said, "We don't believe the story our culture is telling."
>
> That story has some similarities, but it has changed throughout human history. In our day, by reciting [the Apostles' Creed], if we believe, we're saying, "We reject the narrative of materialism. We reject that stuff will satisfy our souls." We're saying, "We reject the notion that what I need to be physically satisfied is more and more and more partners. I reject that there's not *a* way but everybody has their own." We just fundamentally reject that narrative. Our narrative is that we believe in the God of the Bible.
>
> When the church recites this creed, distilled, pulled from, wrung out of the Word of God, we're saying, "We reject the modern narrative. We believe the historic narrative, the narrative that God has come into the world to save sinners, that Jesus Christ has died for our sins, and we believe and trust that he has made known to us the path of life."[26]

When we say the Apostles' Creed, we repudiate the creeds of alternative visions of what it means to be a human being in our day.

The Apostles' Creed

I believe in God, the Father almighty,
Creator of heaven and earth.
I believe in Jesus Christ, God's only Son, our Lord,
who was conceived by the Holy Spirit,
born of the Virgin Mary,
suffered under Pontius Pilate,
was crucified, died, and was buried;
he descended into hell.
On the third day he rose again;
he ascended into heaven,
he is seated at the right hand of the Father,
and he will come to judge the living and the dead.
I believe in the Holy Spirit,
the holy catholic Church,
the communion of saints,
the forgiveness of sins,
the resurrection of the body,
and the life everlasting. Amen.[27]

26. Matt Chandler, "The Apostles Creed: I Believe In," sermon, August 22, 2015, www.thevillagechurch.net/resources/sermons/detail/i-believe-in/.

27. *A Prayer Book for Australia* (Sydney: Broughton, 1999), 12.

Take Communion

The Lord's Supper, like baptism, raises a number of questions that divide churches. In what sense is Jesus present in the elements of bread and wine? What do communicants gain in partaking of those elements? How often should it take place; who may partake; and who should lead? Our specific interest in communion at this point concerns its meaning in connection with our identity as God's people.

"The meaning of the Eucharist is ultimately anchored in a story, in fact, *the story*. It is a snapshot of the grand narrative about God, creation, the fall, Israel, the exile, the Messiah, the church, and the consummation. The bread and the wine tell a story about God, redemption, Jesus, and salvation."

Michael F. Bird[28]

Communion is an identity-forming and confirming emblem of the gospel. In taking communion, believers are prompted: (1) to *look back* to a shared memory; (2) to *look around* at their brothers and sisters in the family of God; and (3) to *look forward* to their defining destiny. The Lord's Supper includes many of the features of personal identity that this biblical theology has explored.

Looking back is the most obvious purpose of the meal. The famous words of institution that Paul records in 1 Corinthians 11 make this clear in Jesus's call to "do this in remembrance of me":

> The Lord Jesus, on the night he was betrayed, took bread, and when he had given thanks, he broke it and said, "This is my body, which is for you; *do this in remembrance of me*." In the same way, after supper he took the cup, saying, "This cup is the new covenant in my blood; do this, whenever you drink it, *in remembrance of me*." (1 Cor 11:23–25)

In remembering Christ, and in particular his death on the cross, we recall his suffering and shame. But in eating and drinking the bread and wine, we also remember as those who have a personal stake in his sacrifice. As Jesus stated in connection with the wine, "This is my blood of the covenant, which is poured out for many for the forgiveness of sins" (Matt 26:28). We remember his death as what changes us from people under God's wrath into his forgiven people.

In *looking around*, we acknowledge our identity as part of the reconciled family of God. When John Calvin discusses the Lord's Supper in the *Institutes of the Christian Religion*, he opens by referring to our identity as children of God:

> *God has received us, once for all, into his family, to hold us not only as servants but as sons*. . . . [God provides for us] a spiritual banquet, wherein Christ attests himself to be the life-giving bread, upon which our souls feed unto true and

28. Michael F. Bird, *Evangelical Theology: A Biblical and Systematic Introduction* (Grand Rapids: Zondervan, 2013), 777–78, emphasis original.

> blessed immortality, . . . [for] Christ is the only food of our soul, and therefore *our Heavenly Father* invites us to Christ.[29]

Paul's warnings in 1 Corinthians 11 relates to this very point:

> So then, whoever eats the bread or drinks the cup of the Lord in an unworthy manner will be guilty of sinning against the body and blood of the Lord. *Everyone ought to examine themselves* before they eat of the bread and drink from the cup. For those who eat and drink without discerning the body of Christ eat and drink judgment on themselves. . . .
>
> So then, *my brothers and sisters*, when you gather to eat, *you should all eat together*. Anyone who is hungry should eat something at home, so that when you meet together it may not result in judgment. (1 Cor 11:27–29, 33–34)

The passage in question contains two imperatives: "everyone ought to examine themselves" (v. 28) and "you should all eat together" (v. 33). Both relate to maintaining harmony and expressing love in the family meal. Note how Paul addresses believers as "my brothers and sisters" in verse 33. "Self-examination" is not so much a matter of confessing sins to God, which the passage takes for granted, as it concerns being reconciled to each other. The requirement to discern the body of Christ (v. 29) is a call to concord in the church: "If anyone eats of the bread and drinks of the cup without recognizing their relationship with the body of the Lord will eat and drink judgment to themselves."[30]

Finally, taking communion requires *looking ahead* to our defining destiny with Christ. With reference to the cup, Jesus promises: "I tell you, I will not drink from this fruit of the vine from now on until that day when I drink it new *with you* in my Father's kingdom" (Matt 26:29). Similarly, Paul teaches that, "Whenever you eat this bread and drink this cup, you proclaim the Lord's death *until he comes*" (1 Cor 11:26). We take communion in the joyous prospect of reunion with Christ and in anticipation of the final messianic banquet: "Blessed are those who are invited to the wedding supper of the Lamb!" (Rev 19:9).

If baptism dramatizes our initiation into Christ's body and our identification with him, communion is the second

The *Kenyan Anglican Communion Liturgy* points to our identity as God's children. It includes the prayer: "*Thank you Father*, for forgiveness; we come to your table *as your children*, not presuming but assured, not trusting ourselves but your word; we hunger and thirst for righteousness, and ask for our hearts to be satisfied with the Body and Blood of your son, Jesus Christ the righteous. Amen."

The liturgy closes with words that point to our shared memory of dying with Christ and our defining destiny of rising with him: "Christ has died, Christ is risen, Christ will come again. *We are brothers and sisters through his blood. We have died together, we will rise together, and we will live together.*"[31]

29. John Calvin, *The Institutes of the Christian Religion*, ed. John T. McNeill, trans. Ford Lewis Battles, Library of Christian Classics (London: SCM, 1961), 4.17.1, emphases added.

30. Paul Ellingworth and Howard Hatton, *A Handbook on Paul's First Letter to the Corinthians* (New York: United Bible Societies, 1995), 267, quoting a translation of the French Common Language Bible.

31. "A Kenyan Liturgy," globalanglican, https://globalanglican.wordpress.com/a-kenyan-liturgy/. Emphases added.

act in the drama of salvation, or more accurately a rehearsal for the final act. Its performance reminds us that we are no mere spectators when it comes to the death, resurrection, and final destiny of God's Son. In eating his flesh and drinking his blood, we declare that Christ is our life (Col 3:4). And we reserve our seats for the banquet to end all banquets!

Live the Gospel

The final thing to do to know yourself as you are known by God concerns everyday life. It is the hardest and requires the most effort: to live in a manner "worthy of the gospel of Christ" (Phil 1:27; see also Eph 4:1).

Along with being saved by the cross of Christ, we are also to live the story of the cross in our daily lives. In the words of Jesus, those who wish to follow him must "take up their cross daily" (Luke 9:23). We are to live cruciform lives, putting self-interest to death and serving others in costly love. Having a share in Christ's resurrection in the future entails serving and suffering with Christ in the present:

> I want to know Christ—yes, to know the power of his resurrection and participation in his sufferings, becoming like him in his death, and so, somehow, attaining to the resurrection from the dead. (Phil 3:10–11)

In fact, suffering with Christ confirms our identity as God's children and reminds us that we live as those who are being conformed to the image of God's Son:

> Now if we are children, then we are heirs—heirs of God and co-heirs with Christ, if indeed we share in his sufferings in order that we may also share in his glory. (Rom 8:17)

Living lives worthy of the gospel means living according to the pattern of Christ's life and thereby reminding ourselves that our true identity is found in him.[32]

Summary

If you want to know yourself as you are known by God:

1. Get baptized to signify your past joining to Christ, your present journeying with Christ, and your future joy because of Christ—baptism reminds us that Christ is our life.
2. Go to church to confirm and strengthen your identity as a member of God's family.

32. On Christ's death and resurrection supplying the narrative for our lives, see chapter ten. For more on how this impacts our everyday conduct and gives direction for living, see chapter fourteen.

3. Read the Bible and hear the Bible preached, not only to know God but also to know yourself.
4. Pray, not only to seek God's help and to acknowledge him in grateful praise, but also to remember to whom you belong, what you are a part of, what you need, and where you are headed.
5. Sing the faith to confirm your identity as someone who belongs to God and is known by him.
6. Say the Creed to affirm your place and part in the story of God and not some other story.
7. Take communion to remember not only Jesus Christ, but also yourself in union with him.
8. Live in a manner worthy of the gospel in order to be true to yourself.

REMEMBERING WHO YOU ARE

Who are you? The Bible acknowledges the legitimacy of the traditional markers of personal identity. Your race, ethnicity, nationality, culture, gender, sexuality, family of origin, physical and mental capacities, age, relationships, occupation, possessions, religion, character, and personality are all important dimensions of your identity. But none of them is all important. Instead, if you trust in Christ, you have a secret identity. You are not self-made but know yourself in being known by someone else: You are known intimately and personally by God as his adopted child. This identity recalls the status of the first human beings who were made in the image of God, and it is modeled on Jesus Christ, the true Son of God, being known and loved by his Father. In fact, you are known and loved by God in him.

As well as the gift of being known by God as his child, God provides the means for you to know yourself as you are known by him. These means include baptism, the church, the Bible, prayer, singing, a creed, taking communion, and living the gospel. All but the last one are undertaken regularly in the weekly gatherings of Christians around the world. They involve your whole person, engaging you visually, socially, physically, verbally, and aurally. They engage your body, mind, heart, soul, spirit, and inner person. Together they tell a story that matters into which your life fits, the amazing story of the Creator God who lovingly redeemed the broken world through his beloved Son and adopted us into his family. They recall the defining memory of your life, the death and resurrection of Jesus Christ, and hold out the hope of sharing his destiny at his return. Together they call you to perform your signature move in daily life, sacrificial love in imitation of him. When you avail yourself of these means, you will remember not only who God is but also who you are. And you will receive the eternal significance, needed humility, soothing comfort, and clear direction that being known by God so richly supplies.

RELEVANT QUESTIONS

1. Many of the regular activities or disciplines of the Christian life help confirm your true identity. Which of these (saying a creed, church attendance, reading the Bible, prayer) could you participate in more fully in order to know yourself as you are known by God?
2. The Bible can be a subversive and unsettling text as well as comforting and reassuring. Has the Bible "spoken" to you deeply recently? In what way?
3. How can prayer, and in particular the Lord's Prayer, help to locate your life in the narrative of God's unfolding plan?
4. This book's big idea is that the Bible's most comprehensive answer to the question of personal identity is that rather than knowing ourselves, believers in Christ are known by God as his children. How do you think this approach to personal identity might make a difference to you?

SCRIPTURE INDEX

Mark

Luke

John

Acts

Romans

1 Corinthians

2 Corinthians

Galatians

SUBJECT INDEX

AUTHOR INDEX